1991

CONSEQUENCES OF THEORY

Selected Papers from the English Institute
New Series

Consequences of Theory

Selected Papers from the English Institute, 1987–88

New Series, no. 14

Edited by Jonathan Arac and Barbara Johnson

THE JOHNS HOPKINS UNIVERSITY PRESS
BALTIMORE AND LONDON

The Johns Hopkins University Press, 701 West 40th Street,
Baltimore, Maryland 21211
The Johns Hopkins Press Ltd., London

The paper used in this book meets the minimum requirements of American
National Standard for Information Sciences—Permanence of Paper for
Printed Library Materials, ANSI Z39.48-1984.

Library of Congress Cataloging-in-Publication Data

Consequences of theory / edited by Jonathan Arac and Barbara Johnson.
        p. cm. — (Selected papers from the English Institute ;
    1987–88, new ser., no. 14)
    Includes bibliographical references.
    ISBN 0-8018-4044-9. — ISBN 0-8018-4045-7 (pbk.)
    1. Literature—History and criticism—Theory, etc.   2. Literature—
Philosophy.   I. Arac, Jonathan, 1945- . II. Johnson, Barbara,
1947- . III. Series: Selected papers from the English Institute :
new ser., no. 14.
PN51.C623   1991
809—dc20   90-32670
                                                                   CIP

801.95
A 658

Contents

142, 268

Introduction

"It's nothing," declared the doctor. "He's working too hard. He'll be back on his feet in a week."

"He'll get better? Are you sure?" asked Louise, looking distraught.

"He'll get better."

In the other room, Rateau was looking at the canvas, completely blank, in the middle of which Jonah had merely written, in tiny letters, a word that was decipherable, but it was impossible to tell whether it said *solitaire* or *solidaire*.

—Albert Camus, "Jonah"

"Is Friday learning to write?" asked Foe.

"He is writing after a fashion," I said. "He is writing the letter *o*."

"It's a beginning," said Foe. "Tomorrow you must teach him *a*."

—J. M. Coetzee, *Foe*

Figaro: My Lord and Gentlemen! Hem! There is in this case either fraud, error, malice, or mischievous intention, for the words of the acknowledgement are, I promise to repay the said Marcelina-Jane-Maria-Angelica-Mustachio, the said sum of two thousand piasters *or* to marry her, which is very different.

Doctor: I affirm it is AND.

Figaro: I affirm it is OR.

Doublefee: . . . *and—or—and—or—or,* the word is blotted.

—Beaumarchais, *The Marriage of Figaro*

 No one can deny that something called *theory* has made a difference in the institutional and intellectual shape of literary studies over the past twenty years. Indeed, as W. J. T. Mitchell points out in his introduction to a volume called *Against Theory*,[1] "Theory has, for a variety of reasons, become one of the 'glamour' fields in academic literary study" (1–2). While the day of Theory (in its monolithic, hegemonic form) may be passing (when a book entitled *The Future of Literary Theory* appears,[2] you know it is time to stop investing in theory futures), the impact of theory not only on literary studies but also on many other disciplines—indeed, on the notion of disciplinarity itself—has been tremendous. The passing of theory may in itself be a consequence of theory.

When Jonathan Arac designed and introduced the first English Institute panel entitled "Some Consequences of Theory," he jokingly alluded to the name of a television game show to claim that, since theory has taught us the groundlessness of truth, what we must have instead are consequences. The papers collected here (drawn from Arac's panel and from one I organized a year later) amply bear out the truth of his assertion. In an effort to map some of the routes taken by theory in a variety of disciplines, we have assembled essays by three literary critics, three philosophers, a historian, and a legal scholar.

Lest one take this list to imply that literary theory has become some sort of masterplot introduced, with devastating/revivifying consequences, *into* other disciplines from a point of origin in literary studies, it is important to note, as does literary critic Bruce Robbins in the first essay in this volume, that "theory emanated largely *from* other disciplines" (emphasis mine). Yet Robbins goes on to state that even within those other disciplines "it was in a profound sense *literary* theory: Foucault, Derrida, Lacan, and Lyotard all made frequent and self-conscious use of the putatively undisciplined and nondiscursive imagination of literary texts in their alliance against the certainties of their own discourses and disciplines." As Robbins suggests, literature is that which, within every discipline, offers resistance to the very process of discipline formation—which means that the transformation of literature *itself* into a discipline can hardly be taken for granted as a starting point. Robbins self-ironically suggests as much by beginning his essay "Once upon a time . . . " Taking off from narratives of the professionalization of literary studies, Robbins goes on to investigate the role of professionals in the process of social change. By analyzing the institutional role of academic literary theorists, Robbins breaks down the barrier between the academy and the purported "real world" and takes the hypothetical debate about "the politics of theory" to the level of "the territory we already occupy."

In "Theory, Pragmatisms, and Politics," philosopher and theologian Cornel West extends the interimplications of politics and theory still further. "To be against theory *per se* is to be against inquiry into human posits regarding the institutional and individual causes of alterable forms of human misery and human suffering." Yet, at the same time, "uncritical allegiance to Grand Theories can blind one from seeing and examining kinds of human oppression." Working within a conception of pragmatism as a practical kind of epistemic antifoundationalism that is nevertheless *not* antitheoretical, West describes the role of the intellectual as "critical organic catalyst." In order to intervene effectively to change prevailing structures of domination, the intellectual must work both within the academy and within political organizations out- side the academy. Contrasting the notion of "vocation" to the notion of "career," West outlines three vocational models of intellectual work: the analysis of power plays within the disciplinization process; the use of disciplinary expertise to intervene in public policy; and the institu- tionalization of legitimate space for oppositional agendas within the academy. West's emphasis on the importance of emergent theoretical projects (feminist, Afro-American, gay) suggests something that Bruce Robbins also points out: that the current stories of the profession's decline may be only the story of a diminished white male *share* in the consequences of theory.

Philosopher Nancy Fraser picks up on the gender implications of models of intellectual work in her analysis of Richard Rorty's hesita- tions between romanticism and pragmatism, singularity and solidar- ity. Is genius always elitist and potentially fascistic? Does community imply consensus? How does solidarity deal with conflict? Can the col- lectivity do without the anomalous? Doesn't the attempt to separate the pragmatic and the romantic into separate spheres simply duplicate the public/private split that has ensured the disempowerment of women? In the course of her canny analysis of the political implica- tions of Rorty's three versions of the *solitaire/solidaire* relation, Fraser moves from an opening set of imperatives ("Consider ... Think ...

Now contrast . . . ") to a concluding set of imperatives ("Begin with . . .
Then, add . . . Next, add . . . Stir . . . Combine"). This passage from command to recipe may very well act out some of the problems of *address*
which underlie the articulation between singularity and solidarity.

The next three essays take up, in various ways, the challenge posed
by history to theory and by theory to history. In "Tolerable Falsehoods," philosopher Anthony Appiah looks at the opposition between
structural determinism and individual agency in social theory, particularly in the work of the new historicists. However compelling the
notion of structural causality or the dialectic of subversion and containment may be, Appiah suggests, they imply two conditions that are
never in fact met: that social structures are without internal contradictions, and that hegemony can be complete. Although debates about
structure and agency tend to revolve around the question of which is
to be master, Appiah sees them as neither opposed nor simply interdependent but rather as located in different theoretical practices and as
competing "not for causal space but for *narrative* space." No matter
how sophisticated our theories of structural determination, Appiah
argues, we cannot, within a capitalist society, overcome the fact that
humanistic individualism remains as "the call of our everyday
affections," the default directory of common sense. "There is much to
be said," he writes, "for the noncoherence of our different theoretical
practices," each "challenging each other not for the one truth but for
our time, our interest, our passion."

In "History as Gesture, or the Scandal of History," historian Lynn
Hunt analyzes several exemplary encounters between history and theory (the de Man and Heidegger affairs, on the one hand; and the
debates over work by David Abraham, Natalie Davis, and Robert Darnton, on the other). The articulation between the two, she suggests, is
structured like scandal. Antifoundationalist theory is as scandalous to
traditional historians as de Man's past is to literary critics. "In literature
and philosophy as disciplines," she writes, "theory is contaminated by
history; in history as a discipline, history is contaminated by theory."
This leads her to a cautionary note concerning the major contemporary effort to work out a *synthesis* of theory and history: the work of

the new historicists. In seeking to relate different modes of cultural production as "signifying practices," to see history and literature as *continuous* with each other, Hunt suggests, new historicists are in danger of
reducing history (and, by extension, theory and literature) to *gesture*, of
smoothing out their disruptive and destabilizing force as *scandal*. The
relation between de Man's past and deconstruction, for example, is not
a matter of mere "circulation of energy."

Mentioned in these last two essays, the work of Stephen Greenblatt
would appear to be central to contemporary reflections on the relations among history, literature, and theory. In "Toward a Sociology of
Literary Knowledge: Greenblatt, Colonialism, and the New Historicism," literary critic Donald Pease focuses extensively on Greenblatt's
intellectual itinerary, particularly on his changing interpretation of
Prospero's statement about Caliban: "this thing of darkness I / Acknowledge mine." At issue is the status of colonialism in Greenblatt's practice. In an early essay entitled "Learning to Curse," Pease argues, Greenblatt sees this quotation as a sign of Prospero's (and, by extension,
Shakespeare's) ambivalence toward colonialism. Later, however, Greenblatt shifts to a more encompassing and theatricalized interpretation of
Renaissance structures of power, such that all subversion is recontained
within the dominant interpretive and political paradigms. Prospero's
statement now expresses merely his absorption of Caliban's otherness.
This shift in Greenblatt's reading is enabled by a series of homologies:
between colonial archives and Shakespeare's plays, between the colonist and the dramatist. What Pease attempts to demonstrate is that new
historicism, while it may be emancipatory with respect to "old" historicism, functions nevertheless *like* colonialism within the field of Renaissance studies, absorbing and containing all possible space for otherness.
Pease contrasts Greenblatt's use of theatricality with Frantz Fanon's:
for Greenblatt, theater is that through which hegemony wins; for
Fanon in *Black Skin, White Masks,* theater is that through which hegemony can be resisted. Throughout the essay, Pease cautions against the
conflation of intellectual and cultural structures with "plain old colonial subjection."

It is perhaps no accident that the two literary texts to which sustained attention is paid in this volume (in the essay by Pease and in the essay that follows) are Shakespeare's *The Tempest* and J. M. Coetzee's *Foe:* two important sites for the contemporary rewriting of the colonialist project. In "Theory in the Margin: Coetzee's *Foe* Reading Defoe's *Crusoe/Roxana*," Gayatri Chakravorty Spivak notes the current centrality of philosophical and political margins in literary theory and criticism and asks what happens to the guardianship of the margins as *resistance* when they become too easily mainstreamed and commodified. Whether as the complacent undecidability of aporia or as the repressive tolerance of pluralism, the current interest in margins risks either domesticating or romanticizing the heterogeneity of the wholly other. Spivak pursues the question of the margin in *Foe,* the rewriting of a British classic by a white male South African, narrated in the voice of Susan Barton, a white female European castaway shipwrecked into the homosocial world of Crusoe and Friday. It is the story of a narrative in search of an author: Susan Barton attempts, with uncertain success, to get her story "fathered" by a writer named Mr. Foe. Two stories here are represented as missing: the story of Susan Barton's missing daughter (she refuses to acknowledge the daughter who returns as her own) and the story of Friday's missing tongue (which remains wholly irretrievable). Cautioning against the dream of an alliance politics based on overdetermination, Spivak suggests that "the book may be gesturing toward the impossibility of restoring the history of Empire and recovering the lost text of mothering *in the same register of language*" (emphasis Spivak's). In the end, "Theory is a bit like Mr. Foe. It is always off the mark, yet it is what we undo. Without it, nothing but the wished-for inarticulation of the natural body: 'a slow stream, without breath, without interruption,' betrayed by the spacing of the words that wish it."

In the concluding essay, "And We Are Not Married: A Journal of Musings upon Legal Language and the Ideology of Style," law professor Patricia Williams meditates precisely upon the complex relations between bodies and articulations. She shows how the ideology of neutrality upon which post–civil rights guidelines are supposed to be based actually obscures the racism such guidelines are designed to combat. Documenting the successive moments of erasure to which one of her articles was subjected in a law review, she writes that "what was most interesting to me in this experience was how the blind application of principles of neutrality, through the device of omission, acted either to make me look crazy or to make the reader participate in the mental habits of cultural bias." In the course of the essay, she narrates the double-binds faced by three different black women—the author herself, Tawana Brawley, and Judge Maxine Thomas—as they find themselves "articulated" by the extraordinary representation machine of the American legal and cultural system. By the end of the essay, Williams has demonstrated in a multitude of ways both the impossibility and the inevitability of the dream of peeling off the skin of constructedness.

In light of the essays collected here, it would seem reductive and somehow beside the point to assert, as does Stanley Fish in an essay entitled "Consequences," that "theory's day is dying; the hour is late; and the only thing left for a theorist to do is to say so, which is what I have been saying here, and, I think, not a moment too soon."[3] Fish himself may have decided to switch from playing Truth or Consequences to playing Beat the Clock, but that may be merely one of the hazards of Duke. It seems to me, rather, that an ongoing struggle with "theory—our friend Foe" is the only possible response to the noncoherence of practices (Appiah), the incommensurability of narrative registers (Spivak), or the trauma or dream of uncanny returns—the return of the young Paul de Man, of the first Martin Guerre, of Susan Barton's daughter, and perhaps of Tawana Brawley and of Friday's missing tongue. Theory, as Spivak asserts, is always off the mark, but without it we would have nothing to (un)do.

BARBARA JOHNSON
Harvard University

NOTES

1. W. J. T. Mitchell, *Against Theory: Literary Studies and the New Pragmatism* (Chicago: University of Chicago Press, 1985).

2. Ralph Cohen, ed., *The Future of Literary Theory* (New York: Routledge and Kegan, 1989).

3. These are the concluding lines of "Consequences," which is included in Mitchell, *Against Theory*, p. 128. The essay glosses Fish's earlier response to the question of whether his view of theory had any consequences: "None whatsoever."

CONSEQUENCES OF THEORY

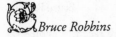 *Bruce Robbins*

Oppositional Professionals

THEORY AND THE NARRATIVES OF
PROFESSIONALIZATION

Once upon a time, literary criticism told itself the story of its professional rise. In classic midcentury works like *Literary Criticism: A Short History* (1957) by Wimsatt and Brooks, René Wellek's multi-volume *History of Modern Criticism* (begun in 1955), and, less obviously, in M. H. Abrams's *The Mirror and the Lamp* (1953) and Hazard Adams's anthology *Critical Theory Since Plato* (1971), a common narrative takes shape. Whatever criticism's distant ancestors, its immediate antecedents include the sloppy moralism, strident didacticism, belle-lettristic impressionism, and pedantic philology of a few gentlemen-amateurs. This amateurism is in the process of being overthrown (or dialectically canceled, preserved, and raised to a higher level) by the methodological rigor and seriousness of the hard-working new critics, operating upon a tougher, tighter version of their subject matter. Excising "literature" from history and refashioning it as a formal, self-sufficient object, the new critics and the historians who consolidated their gains gave it an autonomy that could guarantee the proud self-reliance of the new profession. This triumphant happy ending was then identified with the final professionalization of literary studies. Only the peculiarity of "literature" thus defined could keep most critics from seeing that, sociologically speaking, the history of literary criticism in its received versions was indeed a narrative of professionalization.[1]

Lately sociologists have been criticizing the very concept of professionalization for assuming the evolution of an identical subject through fixed stages.[2] But literary critics did not need to be told that the new criticism was not the *telos* of criticism's evolutionary narrative. The problems of that narrative of professionalization have become generally visible, since the 1960s, because of the ascendancy of "literary theory."

The stories we have been telling ourselves more recently, which set out (less teleologically?) from theory's real or apparent rupture in the history and practice of criticism, express a similar ambivalence, however, as to whether or not literary criticism *is* a profession. To many critics and champions alike, theory has seemed a radical departure both from the professional status quo and from professionalism as such. The period following the Johns Hopkins conference of 1966, "The Languages of Criticism and the Sciences of Man," when theory made its start in the United States, also witnessed the general crisis of American professionalism which has been labeled the "revolt of the client." Across the whole spectrum of professions from law and medicine to engineering, social work, and university teaching, agitation on behalf of "relevance" and "responsiveness" engaged both clients and professionals themselves, who probed into the theoretical grounds as well the practical effects of professional expertise and authority. It seems plausible that literary theory, coming in the same years, was our version of the general phenomenon. While some of our clients—especially women and minority students—were voicing their dissatisfactions with the professional status quo, literary theory was working in unison. Its undermining of authorial intention, historical reference, and textual coherence compromised the claim to objectivity in interpretation and with it the sanction of the professional interpreter. It became unclear, as theory's antagonists complained, what if anything could now count as our unique critical expertise. And if nothing could, then could criticism still claim to *be* a profession?

Many of theory's allies, especially those based in other disciplines, were only too happy to agree. For them, the fact that literary criticism had graciously made a home for theory, while other fields resisted it, suggested that criticism transcends the vulgar, positivistic, or tyrannical logic of the other disciplines or of disciplinarity as such. Although theory emanated largely from other disciplines, it was in a profound sense *literary* theory: Foucault, Derrida, Lacan, and Lyotard all made frequent and self-conscious use of the putatively undisciplined and nondiscursive imagination of literary texts in their alliance against the certainties of their own discourses and disciplines.[3] *Professional* concern with *literature* thus seemed close to a contradiction in terms. In *Consequences of Pragmatism* (1982), Richard Rorty argued that criticism has taken over philosophy's place at the apex of the humanities precisely because in the last decades philosophy has professionalized while criticism has theorized. Criticism owes its success to having achieved, through its embrace of theory, a unique *un*professionalism—or perhaps to having maintained that unprofessionalism by enjoying from the outset a "knowledge base," literature, defined by its refusal to convey knowledge.[4]

Did criticism deprofessionalize just now, because of theory, or was it *always* unprofessional, thanks to the special nature of literature itself? Without necessarily approving either term of Rorty's equivocation, one can see in it one reason why theory's celebration of the literary at the expense of the professional remains an issue. Not only are critics legitimately unsure whether they want to surrender "unprofessional" as a term of abuse, let alone surrender the benefits of professional status, they may also suspect that these expressions of extra- and antidisciplinary friendship thrust them back into an all too familiar isolation, the isolation of aesthetic inconsequentiality. In *Tombeau de l'Intellectuel* (1984), Jean-François Lyotard posits that the free-floating, oppositional intellectual is dead, along with the free-floating universals to which the intellectual appealed. Yet James Joyce, he says, remains oppositional, as do those who teach him. For Lyotard, literature's irreducible particularity thus becomes the last valid universal.[5] As a position specifically *about literature,* this is not much different from the celebration of "culture" by Matthew Arnold. Once again the custodians of literary tradition find themselves in permanent opposition, uniquely free amid everyone else's philistinism and barbarity—and at the same time uniquely weightless and ineffective in a world of weighty institutions.

For better or worse, our new common sense insists on the contrary that we are historically, institutionally, and professionally situated. The embarrassment of being reminded by theory of a flatteringly heroic self-conception that we have only recently learned to do without may be a small price to pay for the influence over other disciplines that theory-inspired criticism has been exerting and that may be thus far—to judge from other papers in this volume—theory's most inspiring consequence. Still, the anomaly remains: criticism as a profession (the one profession) that embraces theory's antiprofessionalism. For some of us, it is an urgent one. If we accept some version of the narrative that professionals (defined by their competence) have replaced intellectuals (defined as oppositional by virtue of stepping outside their competence), then what becomes of our critical, transgressive, oppositional functions? As Raymond Williams showed in the professional creation myth entitled *Culture and Society*, the specific line that runs from the romantics through Matthew Arnold and into professional literary criticism has largely defined itself in oppositional terms. If we think of criticism as a profession among others, thus acknowledging the social determination of our activities, how far does this determination extend? What specific determinations are brought to bear upon criticism, and what openings for oppositionality are left or created for it by the professional status it enjoys, or at any rate cannot repudiate?

These questions seem to me worth pursuing because the words "oppositional" and "professional" are not antithetical. In arguing this case, I will not talk concretely about actual or potential critical activities, but only about their conditions of possibility. In order to believe that what we do is meaningful, as our persistence in it suggests we do believe, some effort to understand how oppositional work is conceivable within a professional framework seems helpful, and that is what I will undertake. Incidentally, I am happy to provide evidence that the so-called academic left, to which I belong, does not exempt itself from its own analyses: we do not claim an inexplicable immunity to the determinations we analytically discover everywhere else, but are willing to try to account for the fact of our own existence.

The 1987 market success of Allan Bloom's *The Closing of the American Mind*, on the right, and of Russell Jacoby's *The Last Intellectuals*, on the left, suggests that the general or reading public has been eager to buy the story of professionalization as the tragic or at any rate debilitating result of the fall or withdrawal of formerly public-spirited writers and intellectuals from (the double-articulation is emphatic) the public itself. As Jacoby writes: "Younger intellectuals are occupied and preoccupied by the demands of university careers. As professional life thrives, public culture grows poorer and older."[6] To enter the academy or the professions, for this narrative, is to forsake both the public and, by the same token, oppositionality. One oblique but provocative argument against the opposition of "public" and "professional" emerges, however, from the fact that this same narrative shows up both outside and inside the academy. Judging from existing histories of literary criticism, critics seem ready enough to see criticism as having sunk into professionalism—perhaps too ready. Like Rorty's disapproving narrative of philosophy (rather than his respectful account of criticism), criticism's own creation myths are often slightly contemptuous stories of professionalization as decline and fall. According to David Bromwich's version, for instance, theory represents professionalization's most advanced and sterile stage. The once genuinely subversive literary and political avant-garde, Bromwich says, "has taken up residence in the academy," and in becoming "identified with literary study in the universities" (35), it has lost any pretension to political significance. "The consequential debates in our culture," Bromwich adds, "have always taken place somewhere else" (36).[7]

Two detailed examples specific to literary criticism, one from outside and one from inside the academy, are John Gross's *The Rise and Fall of the Man of Letters* (1969) and Terry Eagleton's *The Function of Criticism: From 'The Spectator' to Poststructuralism* (1984).[8] Both subscribe, with differences that are surprisingly slight, given the magnitude of the political gulf between them, to the professional myth: we have fallen into lamentable specialization from a formerly higher, more public, and more adversarial estate. Both of them oppose an oppositional public "before," conveniently located elsewhere, to a complicitous professional "after," right before our eyes. But both in Eagleton and in Gross, there is a curious inability to make this "decline" narrative stick. In his "Epilogue," Gross announces the sad fall of the man of letters into professionalization—triviality, specialization, false originality, and so on (290)—as both already having occurred and as imminent, hence not quite complete. Although the critic "may take a certain pride in being the last amateur in a world of professionals" (287), the reality is that "Most English literary critics and scholars are already academics by profession, and in the nature of things the proportion is going to grow" (292). But reading backward from the present (when, after Thatcher's cuts, it no longer seems so inevitable that the academy will offer critics ever expanding shelter), one sees that professionalization has in fact always already occurred. "By the 1920s, a mood of sombre professionalism had set in, best exemplified by the founding of the Review of English Studies in 1925. The academic *apparatchiks* were in full command" (189). Professionalism has also already triumphed in the 1960s and finally, at the very beginning of the book, in the eighteenth century. On the very first page, Gross finds in Goldsmith "the professional critic" already arisen.

The same multiplication of falls structures Eagleton's narrative. By the twentieth century, Eagleton says, a "socially marginal professionalism" (69) has resulted from "the founding of English as a university 'discipline.'" "The academicization of criticism provided it with an institutional basis and professional structure; but by the same token it signalled its final sequestration from the public realm" (65). In fact, the book describes a *series* of sequestrations from the public realm. Within the fall from the exemplary public sphere of Addison and Steele into the narrow professional specialization of our century, each chapter represents another fall from another Golden Age: from Samuel Johnson, then from the Victorian man of letters, and then from Leavis and *Scrutiny*. This cyclical subnarrative permits Eagleton to praise each of the figures he discusses—praise being an apparently indispensable component of our professional rhetoric, thanks to the assumption of an always already wise cultural heritage that it is our residual function to transmit—and to praise them for a public responsibility that the overarching narrative would otherwise deny them. But there are other reasons for believing that praiseworthy public responsibility is distributed more generously than that master narrative suggests. The *repetition* of these sequestrations from the public realm indicates that criticism successfully withdrew from the public realm neither in the first act nor, more importantly, in the last. In fact, the point at which English criticism supposedly touches bottom, its entrance into the university—that is, the moment of *Scrutiny*—is also, in Eagleton's own account, the moment of the strongest critique of professionalism and the strongest assertion of public responsibility. Public responsibility, it would seem, belongs within rather than outside professionalism.

The moral of these stories is that there *is* no clear opposition between the public and the professional. The narratives go up as well as down because their principle of buoyancy, the public, inheres in their very substance and thus cannot be jettisoned. This principle also suggests why public-spirited Marxists like Eagleton do not necessarily sink to the nethermost depths of their profession, as Eagleton's account would lead one to predict, why Eagleton himself could write a Marxist introduction to theory viewed by most of the profession as required reading—one of theory's more devious political consequences—and, most important if also most paradoxical, why academics, like readers outside the academy, should be so supportive of books that bemoan their falling away from the public. Negotiating and renegotiating relations with the public are not extrinsic to academic work.

It is a short step from the public to the oppositional. Barbara and John Ehrenreich point out, in their essay on the "Professional–Managerial Class," that while most professionals may not be leftists, a great many American leftists have been professionals.[9] You do not have to buy the idea of professionals as a potentially revolutionary "new class" (an idea that I for one do not buy at all) in order to feel that this coexistence says as much about the professions as about the leftists. After all, the pronounced if minoritarian tendency of professions to attract, produce, and value political progressives can be explained entirely without idealism. Most service professions have come into existence within the past hundred years. In order to do so, they had to convince the state, which controls licensing, that there was a problem that they (and only they) could properly treat. No problem, no profession. In this basic sense, service professions feed off the social miseries they are called in to remedy. Social conscience is not only in their interest, but in many cases their *sine qua non*.

According to Christopher Lasch or to the essayists in *The Culture of Consumption* (1983), this point would have to be made with pointed cynicism.[10] But if we cannot assume that the self-interests of the new deliverers of professional service are identical to the interests of those who receive their services, must we really assume, on the contrary, that their interests are opposed? Consider one narrative by which literary criticism itself creates a demand for its services. Society has fallen from the great civilizations of the past into a commercial wasteland, we declare; this cultural decline makes our conservation of the cultural heritage necessary and makes the value of that heritage indisputable. Like other "therapeutic" professions, literary criticism deploys narratives like this one to convince people that they're sick so they will come to it for a cure. One can dispute both the diagnosis and the remedy. But neither criticism's self-interest nor its homology with consumer capitalism, which is also committed to the definition of new needs, says anything one way or the other about the value of the need addressed.

John Ehrenreich makes just this point in his history of the professionalization of social work, *The Altruistic Imagination* (1985). If the task of "mitigat[ing] the worst features of industrial capitalism . . . also corresponded to the psychological, occupational, and social needs of the newly emerging class of professionals and managers, it is neither coincidental nor damning. During the Progressive Era, in the context of working-class unrest, the moral vision of the young professionals, their occupational needs, and the desperate need of the poor for social amelioration and reform more or less coincided with, and could be incorporated into, the needs of the capitalists for political-economic rationalization" (42).[11] Just because you are looking for trouble does not mean there is not trouble there to be found—and it may mean that you will have the chance to do something about it. Professionalization is not a zero-sum game in which every gain is someone's loss. There are of course instances of professional independence won specifically by reducing nonprofessionals to dependence. Taylorite scientific management and the suppression of midwives by physicians, for example, demonstrate how some monopolies of expertise are achieved only by expropriating knowledge that already exists. It is true, as Sherry Gorelick shows, that public education (which enabled teachers to profession-alize) was attractive to capitalists because it "substitut[ed] publicly taught skill for union-controlled apprenticeship." But it is also true that "Workers *demanded* compulsory schooling" (my italics—204).[12] Their demand was constitutive of the profession, and it remains oper-ative within the profession as we have it.

A number of recent historians have insisted, in this vein, that the pro-fessions are inexplicable if one does not factor in public demand and public opinion. The guiding principle of their research, according to Gerald Geison, is "that the public (or the laity) also plays a crucial role in the success of professional market strategies" and that historians must therefore "take account of the demand for professional services as well as the willingness of the public (or at least their elected represen-tatives) to grant special status and privileges to specific occupational groups."[13] For those groups, this means that—as Magali Larson writes—"Persuasion tends to be typically directed to the outside—that is, to the relevant elites, the potential public or publics, and the political author-ities" (xii). For "[p]rofessional indifference may be broken from the out-side" (188). Administrators too can evoke the public welfare, and "privileges can always be lost." With regard to knowledge bases that are excessively esoteric, Larson finds it "doubtful . . . that specialities whose functions are not really understood by any significant sector of the public" can survive as professions (231).[14]

Historically, failure to professionalize often depended on the inabil-ity to mobilize public support, in the form of state licensing or market demand. Success, for example, in the case of lawyers discussed by Stephen Botein, depended as much on "the 'claim' . . . to be oriented toward the public good" as on the "'claim' to 'esoteric knowledge.'"[15] Jan Goldstein gives the example of French medicine in the early nine-teenth century. Again, it was the intervention of the state rather than their own expertise that won doctors their professional monopoly: "In terms of the therapies they offered, 'official' accredited medical practi-tioners were . . . virtually indistinguishable from their competitors, the mass of unaccredited healers whom they typically called 'charla-tans'" (184). Doctors obtained the state's support partly by promoting the concept of "moral contagion," which linked their efforts to government policy against other sorts of disturbance.[16]

What I have been offering is empirical evidence of the real historical power of persuasion. This evidence suggests that professions are not, in George Bernard Shaw's phrase, conspiracies against the laity. If the laity, in the form of state and/or market, is not a *party* to the conspiracy, if the conspiracy is not leaked, then it cannot achieve its desired effects. Professions are not hermetically sealed, but porous. To associate professional language with jargon incomprehensible to outsiders is thus a serious historical error. Address to outsiders, according to these histories, is indispensable to professional speech.

A good illustration is Thomas Haskell's book *The Emergence of Professional Social Science* (1977). Haskell articulates an older narrative that professions still often tell about themselves. On his account the replacement of the amateur by the professional in social science was required by the specialization of expertise, which was required in turn by the facts themselves: the increasing complexity of modern society. What Haskell calls "the interdependence of society" requires long years of specialized, esoteric study on the part of professionals who want to master it and, on the part of nonprofessionals who cannot master it, contributes to "an erosion of confidence that made men receptive to claims of social science expertise" (47). But "interdependence" is not simply a descriptive term for "the facts" on which professionalization is ostensibly founded. It is also a prescriptive term that sets an ideal for the new professional community. In a figurative doubling, Haskell also speaks of *professional* interdependence, the cooperation and reciprocal accountability of an "ongoing, disciplined community of inquiry," as a socially desirable alternative to the selfish individualism of amateurs and, by extension, of the capitalist marketplace. Throughout the book, he thus insinuates that to accept interdependence is a *moral* imperative, both for professionals and for a public unconvinced about the authority of expert professional advice. Only this insinuation can explain why professionalization should belong, in Haskell's phrase, to a "movement to establish or reestablish authority in intellectual *and moral* matters" (vi—my emphasis). In sounding this note, Haskell is himself making a rhetorical appeal to the public, on behalf of professional social science, for which he can find no place in his account of how the profession was established.[17]

In the current field of professional metanarratives, there are two active contenders to replace Haskell's self-congratulatory narrative of professionalization founded on expertise. The first is the counternarrative of *de*professionalization, exemplified by C. Wright Mills's remark that "Bureaucratic institutions invade all professions" (115).[18] Its end point is not the achievement of professional autonomy, but the loss of that autonomy. The narrative of deprofessionalization is certainly pertinent today, when even doctors and lawyers find their privileges threatened by bureaucracies and corporations and when literature departments in pursuit of excellence are increasingly urged by their administrations (though not by the Modern Language Association) to hire part-time, non–tenure track staff. It also has the virtue of mobilizing otherwise divergent political energies behind a popular and viable line of defense. At the same time, it undercuts its own mobilization by making surrender seem inevitable, while passing over in silence the *complicity* between professions and bureaucracies, the continuing role of "outside" power and persuasion in constituting professions. The foundational force of expertise goes unchallenged, for in this narrative as in the other, it is expertise that confers and legitimates autonomy. Thus professions remain collective surrogates for the heroic individual, defending an autonomy that never existed.

As a descent from the (unquestioned) authority of expertise, the new narrative of deprofessionalization mirrors the earlier, self-congratulatory story of professional ascent to that authority. The second new professional metanarrative, which is associated with theory itself, bears the same inverse relation to the earlier account of "decline into professionalism." The latter looks upon the Fall from public concern into professionalization, and despairs. Theory's narrative retains the "decline" plot but reverses the moral emphasis. It *welcomes* this unprecedented separation from public concerns—if theory does not often recognize this narrative *as* a narrative, it is precisely because, for theory, narrative is closely associated with "legitimation" before the public—and exhorts intellectuals to sever their remaining ties. Like other illicit claims to the authority of other universals, recourse to the public has never been anything but a self-aggrandizing illusion, it says. Local isolation, at a safe distance from the public, is a fate for which both we and they should be grateful.

This poststructuralist narrative of retreat into the local can be illustrated by the recent work of Stanley Fish and Paul Bové. Bové launches a powerful political assault on the profession; Fish, who more than anyone else has set the terms of the debate, takes "antiprofessionalism" like Bové's as his target. But both argue that if only intellectuals would stop claiming to be socially responsible and instead cultivate their own gardens (either by doing what they always already know how to do, for Fish, or by giving up all pretension to understand, represent, or lead anyone else, for Bové), everything would be fine. What I want to suggest—something that could also be argued about Lyotard's *The Postmodern Condition,* which follows much the same narrative—is that the rhetoric of both indulges in precisely that activity of public legitimation that both outlaw, thus showing that professional discourse, even when it self-consciously refuses any appeal to the public, seems obliged to make such an appeal.

Fish's essay "Anti-Professionalism" (1985/86) explicitly addresses the subject of my title, the existence of opposition within professions. Opposition, Fish argues, is central to professionalism. "Far from being a stance taken at the margins or the periphery, anti-professionalism is the very center of the professional ethos, constituting by the very vigor of its opposition the true form of that which it opposes" (106). In brief, the argument is that professions work by denying that they *are* professions. The professional wants to believe in his or her own merit, which requires freedom. But since self and merit are in fact constructed and determined by the profession (this is the strong, foundational sense of the term), you have to attack the profession in order to assert your own freedom *vis-à-vis* the profession. And in so doing, you are asserting the ideology of professionalism: freedom, merit, etc. The thrust of the argument is to take any merit away from opposition; in being oppositional, Fish says, you are just following the profession's orders.[19]

I will not go into the means by which this argument is enforced—most notably, an unacknowledged slide toward the self and away from considerations of justice, the general welfare, and the interests of clients, considerations that might seem to account for antiprofessionalism better. Fish's point is precisely that these considerations are external and irrelevant. Constituting itself by attacking itself, the profession becomes invulnerable to attack from outside. Indeed, it has trouble recognizing that there *is* an outside. Fish has since conceded that professions must after all send up a smokescreen of legitimacy talk in order to pacify nonmembers. But the concession does not change the thrust of the argument, which is to deny any articulation between opposition inside the profession and outside.

This argument is another version of Fish's notorious argument "against theory." In both cases, Fish argues *for* the inviolable independence of professional skill from any authoritative public scrutiny—public scrutiny being one of the better explanations of what theory is. Fish combines the two arguments in a recent article in the *Yale Law Journal* called "Dennis Martinez and the Uses of Theory."[20] Dennis Martinez, then a pitcher for the Baltimore Orioles, figures as an illustration of the futility of coaching. All his coach can tell him about pitching is what he already knows, namely, "Throw strikes and keep 'em off the bases." The point of all this is that theory is like coaching (a redundant if not offensive advising of those who can by those who can't), and professional practice is like pitching: something that every professional always already knows how to do—hence the proper indifference of the profession to any public advice or accountability. Among the several vulnerabilities of this argument—for example, the appeal by a supposed antifoundationalist to professional skill or expertise as an unquestioned and unquestionable foundation—what seems most pertinent is the rhetorical return of the repressed public. According to Fish, professions are monads, entirely distinct unto themselves, hence unassailable by outside critique. As in the stirring conclusion to the "Dennis Martinez" essay: theorists, Fish says, like philosophers, "want us to believe that the only good king is a philosopher-king, and that the only good judge is a philosopher-judge, and that the only good baseball player is a philosopher-baseball player. Well, I don't know about you, but I hope that my kings, if I should ever have any, are good at being kings, and that my judges are good at being judges, and that the players on my team throw strikes and keep 'em off the bases."

What is so extraordinary about this celebration of tautological, self-enclosed specialization is that by the very act of talking baseball, Fish steps out of the enclosure. It is exactly the point at which his professional audience is *not* specialized or self-enclosed, the point at which professionals overlap with some version of the general public, to which Fish the rhetorician specializes in appealing.

Although his case for the professions is essentially antidemocratic (note that his king, if he ever has one, will not be taking advice), and although the probable gender and demographics of his hypothetical reader, the baseball fan in all of us, make for interesting speculation, it remains true that Fish makes, and it appears must make, a public, mass cultural, even democratic appeal. Such it seems are the dictates of competent professional discourse.

Unlike Fish, Paul Bové agrees in his book *Intellectuals in Power* (1986) that opposition within the profession *does* involve rhetorical appeal to the public.[21] The problem, in his opinion, is that our best and brightest appeal to the public all too successfully. Figures like Edward Said, he says, offer an attack on "narrow professionalism" which seems "politically radical" but is actually "conservative," for it does "more to sustain the professional institution's structure and affiliations than to subvert or challenge them" (298). It does this, exactly as I have just finished arguing, by adopting a moral language aimed implicitly at those *outside* the profession. The "influential work" of "leading intellectuals" like Said "represents and, in part, legitimates the profession in the eyes of the state and the public" (110). This is true even of our most agonistic self-images, as restless controversialists and embattled critics of the status quo, proving our combativeness in jousts with other intellectuals. Agonism hides but also supports competition "for social power and authority" (222); it is efficacious. Our agony is our efficacy.

Bové's condemnation of "leading intellectuals" who set themselves up as defenders of such universals as truth, justice, and "the people" is particularly violent with regard to "arrogant imaginings and affirmations of other people's struggles." It is particularly interesting, therefore, that he cannot seem to make his own eloquent critique of such intellectuals without doing the same thing. By a sort of inverse populism, the proposition that we should never speak for or to the people, just let them speak for themselves, becomes the claim that "I speak for the people better than you do." On the last page of the book, Bové offers a concluding tableau of professional malevolence: "Forceps in the hands of male medical experts." The figure works as well as it does because it is rhetoric of just the moral, legitimating sort Bové has been attacking. Having broken down the false unity of "the people" into various local fragments and factions, in order to stop intellectuals from borrowing its authority, Bové now borrows that authority himself, reshaping his factions and fragments back into the singleness of a body that can be vulnerable, victimized, allegorized. It is a *female* body, moreover—again the part offered for the whole—with moral credit thus accruing to the male speaker for his championing of the Other. The Other as Mother: for all its Foucaultian trappings, the move to motherhood belongs with politicians kissing babies. (If you add Bové's use of motherhood to Stanley Fish's references to baseball, the only thing missing from this poststructuralist populism is apple pie.) At a moment when Bové concedes that his argument "might seem amoral or immoral"—he has just listed "the temptations to build a better world" among those that specific intellectuals have to renounce—it is not hard to see why he needs so widespread and popular an appeal. What *is* hard to see is why the principle of such rhetoric, articulating linkages to feminism and other political movements and publics, should not be embraced as a legitimately professional mode of oppositional discourse.

Absolute dedisciplining remains beyond the horizon of actuality, and a call for it is likely to do nothing more than reinforce existing professional isolationism (hence the partial symmetry between the narratives of Bové and Fish). But if theory's isolationist narratives cannot appreciate how the outside is always already inscribed inside the profession, then what sort of narrative can? What sort of provisional narrative closure will guide attention to the profession's real and potential public openness? What narrative can better locate the theoretical renaissance itself and its consequences for the profession?

Richard Rorty's story of criticism's victory over philosophy provides one suggestion. Rorty is clearly wrong in exempting criticism from the general professionalization. To critics, at least, it seems obvious that literary theory was not after all the ultimate challenge to professionalism, but a power play in which certain professional values and structures were traded in for others. But Rorty is right to insist that theory has effected a realignment among disciplines, and in so doing he exposes the place of the public in theory's new professionalism. Whether or not one accepts the simplicity of a narrative in which criticism wins out over other disciplines, criticism's influence over the disciplines is undeniable. Criticism has exerted that influence by exporting its highly developed qualifications of interpretive authority to fields like law and anthropology, whose interpretive procedures and authority had remained largely unqualified. In other words, qualifications that within criticism itself seemed to sap professional authority were in fact extending it—as long as one understands that professionalism in any one discipline is inseparable from, and indeed defined by, the relations *among* disciplines. The foundation of professional authority is not unchanging control over one's own exclusive expertise, but rather an ever shifting relation to other, competing disciplines and professions. From this perspective, theory represents a questioning of criticism's professional "knowledge base," but it also, simultaneously, expands that base. (The fact that there is nothing shockingly unprofessional about comparing professionalization narratives from various disciplines, as I have been doing, is a sign of that expansion.) Criticism loosens its grip over its own territory in order to seize *more* territory, thus indulging its (higher) professional self-interest.

This does not mean, however, that it is either publicly inconsequential or reducible to mean-spirited territoriality. If Rorty is unjustified in concluding, on the contrary, that success in interdisciplinary competition is *necessarily* in the public interest—his model here is Adam Smith's invisible hand—his idea that the constellation of disciplines at a given moment will both reflect and help constitute the social order of that moment and that a shift in the first will therefore constitute a shift in the second deserves to be rescued from his free-market assumptions, for this idea also rescues the concept of the public from the realm of ideal constructs and historical elsewheres to which our narratives so often relegate it. In order to touch the public, on this reading, one would not have to reach *down*, as to a base or foundation. Lateral movement on the same plane, as for example between disciplines, would already be movement within the public domain.[22] This is precisely what happened, I would argue, when literary theory spread a militant, interpretive antiauthoritarianism to disciplines whose authority visibly matters, such as the law.

Another way to state this, without pressing so hard on interdisciplinary competition, would be to say that rather than a decline of the public, we have seen a *transformation* of the public, a redistribution of those qualities we associate with "publicness": openness to observation or scrutiny and, as a corollary, openness to change by human agency.[23] Taking an instance from the 1960s, where the supposed decline is so often located, one thing 60s feminism was all about was the opening up of the formerly private domain of the family to outside scrutiny and to possible change. The fact that you do not get that opening without capitalism for its own reasons putting women on the job market and without bureaucratic or professional services substituting for familial (often female) services does not mean that what has occurred is a regrettable "invasion" of the family. For women, entering the market has been a move *into* the public sphere. (It helps to be reminded that the Greek word *agora* meant both "market" and "public forum.") In the same way, the fact that professions like lawyers, doctors, social workers, and academics have acquired recognized jurisdictions over what had been seen as private domains (childcare, health, sex, and so on) does not mean only that the state has delegated its repressive authority to professionals, but also that a new site of possibility and contestation has been formed, a new instance of publicness, and one that is closer to hand.

The "decline" narrative makes the same mistake with the universities. The moment of the Fall in that narrative is precisely the moment (again, the 1960s) when previously privatized groups were for the first time gaining significant access to the public forum of the university. It may be that what the system wanted or needed was to reproduce a new, better-trained work force. But there was also a push from below, and the result was not a diminishment of "publicness" but rather (as new groups pushed their way into decision-making positions) a diminished white, male *share* in public discourse—which may be what much of the fuss is really about. "Where male critics may well feel themselves both belated and diminished," Sandra Gilbert declares in answer to Gerald Graff, "where they may fear, indeed, that they have fallen from a lost and glamorous wholeness into the grimy holes of academic bureaucracy, their female peers see themselves as just beginning to enter intellectual culture and, more specifically, academic society."[24]

It is tempting to rest the case for a qualifiedly progressive reading of the professional-theoretical phenomena of the last two decades on the exemplary authority of feminism. Although an appeal to a feminist constituency would be an example of the rhetoric of professional legitimacy which this essay has been at pains to define and defend, however, there are also reasons for making such gestures only sparingly and with great care. One reason is the real and sustained abuse of such appeals, which writers like Paul Bové have rightly cautioned against. Another is suggested by the voices of the younger feminist generation itself, which cannot celebrate earlier feminist accomplishments without ambivalence about the structures, hierarchies, burdens, and absences it is now inheriting. Any complacency now would be a betrayal of the immense, unsatisfied oppositional energies that continue to emerge. A third and final reason is also the reason I cannot be satisfied with a more intuitive explanation for the existence of oppositional professionals: the argument that every professional is always also something else—a feminist or potential draftee or churchgoer or union member—and that this second, overlapping identity may produce imperatives inconsistent with professional business as usual. In both arguments, what is indulged is the tendency to believe that all moral and political imperatives arise and all public consequences are felt "somewhere else." Opposition originates elsewhere. The universality of this displacement—I am sure you could find the same explanatory regress in any trade union, church, or law court—argues that at some place people have to stop and say, "Here." This is what I have tried to initiate and encourage, in an abstract and preparatory way, for literary criticism. If the result is lacking in final uplift, it may be that we have had too much uplift, both in and about the ends of our professional writing, and that what we need now is fewer ascents to a sublimely distant and abstract oppositionality and more explorations of the territory we already occupy, where we will rediscover the oppositional as a familiar though still vigorous and surprising presence.

NOTES

1. For a more detailed discussion see my "The History of Literary Theory: Starting Over," *Poetics Today* 9, no. 4 (1989): 767–81.

2. See for example Andrew Abbott, *The System of Professions* (Chicago: University of Chicago Press, 1988).

3. For a critique of literariness in Foucault, see John Rajchman, *Michel Foucault and the Freedom of Philosophy* (New York: Columbia University Press, 1985).

4. Richard Rorty, *Consequences of Pragmatism: Essays 1972–1980* (Minneapolis: University of Minnesota Press, 1982).

5. Jean-François Lyotard, *Tombeau de l'Intellectuel* (Paris: Galilée, 1984).

6. Russell Jacoby, *The Last Intellectuals* (New York: Basic Books, 1987). This narrative is discussed at greater length in the Introduction to Bruce Robbins, ed., *The Grounding of Intellectuals: Politics, Aesthetics, and Academics* (Minnesota: University of Minnesota Press, 1990).

7. David Bromwich, "Literary Radicalism in America," *Dissent* 32 (1985). A refreshingly alternative history appears in Gerald Graff, *Professing Literature* (Chicago: University of Chicago Press, 1987).

8. John Gross, *The Rise and Fall of the Man of Letters* (New York: Macmillan, 1969); Terry Eagleton, *The Function of Criticism: From 'The Spectator' to Poststructuralism* (London: Verso, 1984). These two paragraphs draw on my "Profes-

sionalism and Politics: Toward Productively Divided Loyalties," *Profession 85* (1985): 1–9.

9. Barbara and John Ehrenreich, "The Professional-Managerial Class," in *Between Labor and Capital,* ed. Pat Walker (Boston: South End Press, 1979). On radicalism in the professions, see also Edwin T. Layton, Jr., *The Revolt of the Engineers: Social Responsibility and the American Engineering Profession* (Cleveland: Case Western Reserve University Press, 1971); Ronald Gross and Paul Ostermann, eds., *The New Professionals* (New York: Simon and Schuster, 1972); Joel Gerstl and Glenn Jacobs, eds., *Professions for the People: The Politics of Skill* (New York: Schenkman, 1976).

10. Christopher Lasch, *Haven in a Heartless World* (New York: Basic Books, 1977); Richard Wightman Fox and T. J. Jackson Lears, eds., *The Culture of Consumption* (New York: Pantheon, 1983).

11. John Ehrenreich, *The Altruistic Imagination* (Ithaca: Cornell University Press, 1985). For another view of social work that does not assume an opposition between the professionalism and social reform, see Rick Spano, *The Rank-and-File Movement in Social Work* (Washington, D.C.: University Press of America, 1982).

12. On Taylorism, see Harry Braverman, *Labor and Monopoly Capital* (New York: Monthly Review Press, 1974); Sherry Gorelick, "Class Relations and the Development of the Teaching Profession," in *Class and Social Development: A New Theory of the Middle Class,* ed. Dale Johnson (Beverly Hills, Calif.: Sage, 1982).

13. Gerald L. Geison, ed., *Professions and Professional Ideologies in America* (Chapel Hill: University of North Carolina Press, 1983), 7.

14. Magali Sarfatti Larson, *The Rise of Professionalism: A Sociological Analysis* (Berkeley and Los Angeles: University of California Press, 1977).

15. Stephen Botein, "'What We Shall Meet Afterwards in Heaven': Judgeship as a Symbol for Modern American Lawyers," in Geison, *Professions,* 121.

16. Jan Goldstein, "Moral Contagion: A Professional Ideology of Medicine and Psychiatry in Eighteenth- and Nineteenth-Century France," in *Professions and the French State, 1700–1900,* ed. Gerald L. Geison (Philadelphia: University of Pennsylvania Press, 1984), 181–222.

17. Thomas Haskell, *The Emergence of Professional Social Science* (Urbana: University of Illinois Press, 1977).

18. C. Wright Mills, *White Collar* (New York: Oxford University Press, 1953).

19. Donald Pease's argument about Stephen Greenblatt in this volume offers an interesting parallel.

20. Stanley Fish, "Anti-Professionalism," *New Literary History* 17, no. 1 (Autumn 1985); "Dennis Martinez and the Uses of Theory," *Yale Law Journal* 96 (1987): 1771. An additional point about the category of rhetoric: Fish says that antiprofessionalism is another instance in the long war of philosophy against rhetoric. Here as elsewhere he takes the side of rhetoric. However, when the subject of rhetoric comes up again, he stops to insist that he is not falling into a dichotomy of praise and blame. The remark is of a piece with Fish's most characteristic gesture: the paradox that his own argument, like theory in general, has "no consequences." Praise and blame involve, precisely, taking sides and having consequences. The traditional goal of rhetoric was of course persuasion: winning a verdict of guilty or innocent, seeing a course of action adopted or defeated, having a decisive effect upon one's hearers—what Paul de Man called, with audible displeasure, "actual action upon others." In recognizing its dependence on an audience, rhetoric cannot avoid being kinetic and consequential. All of this is what Fish denies when he affirms that his own words have not after all been for or against anything. In the very act of championing rhetoric, he himself takes a position outside it; but in championing rhetoric, he also champions the principles of public consequence and constituency which his argument otherwise denies.

21. Paul Bové, *Intellectuals in Power: A Genealogy of Critical Humanism* (New York: Columbia University Press, 1986).

22. On the advantages of seeking the political via a lateral rather than a downward movement, see Jonathan Arac, *Critical Genealogies: Historical Situations for Postmodern Literary Studies* (New York: Columbia University Press, 1987), 264–65.

23. The growing literature on *glasnost* should be pertinent to this issue. For a brilliant summary of the developing critique and elaboration of Habermas's "public sphere" concept by Oskar Negt and Alexander Kluge, see Fredric Jameson, "On Negt and Kluge," *October* 46 (Fall 1988).

24. Gerald Graff, "Feminist Criticism in the University: An Interview with Sandra M. Gilbert," in *Criticism in the University*, ed. Gerald Graff and Reginald Gibbons (Evanston, Ill.: Northwestern University Press, 1985), 112.

Cornel West

Theory, Pragmatisms, and Politics

Pragmatism has emerged within contemporary literary criticism in relation to two fundamental issues: the role of theory and the vocation of the humanistic intellectual. The most influential pragmatic literary critics such as Stanley Fish and Frank Lentricchia are masterful mappers; that is, they clearly situate and sort out various positions in the current debate and give some idea of what is at stake. Masterful mappers in the pragmatic grain such as Richard Rorty's illuminating narratives about modern philosophy are demythologizers. To demythologize is to render contingent and provisional what is widely considered to be necessary and permanent. Yet to demythologize is not to demystify. To demystify—the primary mode of critical theory—is to lay bare the complex ways in which meaning is produced and mobilized for the maintenance of relations of domination.[1]

Demythologization is a *mapping* activity that reconstructs and redescribes forms of signification for the purpose of situating them in the dynamic flow of social practices. Demystification is a *theoretical* activity that attempts to give explanations that account for the role and function of specific social practices. Both activities presuppose and promote profound historical consciousness—that is, awareness of the fragile and fragmented character of social practices—but demythologization leaves open the crucial issues of the role of theory and the vocation of the humanistic intellectual. In sharp contrast, demystification gives theory a prominent role and the intellectual a political task. Needless to say, sophisticated demystifiers neither consider theory as an attempt "to stand outside practice in order to govern practice from without"[2] nor view the political task of intellectuals to be the mere articulation of a theoretical enterprise. The former assumes a rather naïve conception of theory, and the latter presupposes that theory is inherently oppositional and emancipatory. Rather, appropriate forms of demystification subsume the pragmatic lessons of demythologization, preserve a crucial role for theory as a social practice, and highlight how modes of interpretation "serve to sustain social relations which are asymmetrical with regard to the organization of power."[3]

In a renowned essay, Arthur O. Lovejoy examined the difficulty of defining the often used yet slippery rubric "romanticism."[4] In a less well-known paper, Lovejoy put forward thirteen different varieties of "pragmatism."[5] I suggest that we map the versions of pragmatism on the current scene in reference to three major axes: namely, the levels of philosophy, theory, and politics. The philosophical level highlights various perspectives regarding epistemological foundations and ontological commitments; the theoretical level, attitudes toward the possibility for or role of theory; and the political level, the vocation of the humanistic intellectual.

All pragmatists are epistemic antifoundationalists, though not all epistemic antifoundationalists are pragmatists. To be an epistemic antifoundationalist is simply to agree with the now familiar claims that "all interpretation is value laden," "there are no unmediated facts," "there is no such thing as a neutral observation language," etc. One may unpack these assertions in various ways, with the help of Hegel, Nietzsche, Derrida, Quine, Davidson, Goodman, Wittgenstein, or Rorty, but it means that one gives up on the notion that epistemic justification terminates in something other than social practice.

Yet not all pragmatists are ontological antirealists. To be a realist is principally to be worried about the bottomless pit of relativism. Therefore philosophical restraints and regulations are set in place to ward off an "anything goes" ontological position. Conservative pragmatists such as Charles Sanders Peirce and Hilary Putnam (in his present incarnation) put forward limiting processes and procedures to ensure that some notion of scientific objectivity (grounded in social practices) is preserved. For Peirce, this means conceiving truth as whatever results in the long run reached by the unending community of inquirers who deploy a reliable method based on deduction, induction, and, to some degree, inference to the best explanation. Putnam builds on Peirce by affirming the need for constraints yet allowing for the proliferation of methods of inquiry and styles of reasoning. Therefore Putnam pro-

motes two limiting processes: the long-term results of a dominant style
of reasoning among inquirers who pull from accumulated modes of
thinking and the long-term results of the facts produced by this dominant style of reasoning yielded by evolving kinds of thinking.[6] In this
sense, conservative pragmatists like Peirce and Putnam are "regulative
realists" in that "reality" is what inquirers agree on owing to rational
canons that regulate and restrain inquirers.

Moderate pragmatists such as John Dewey and William James are
not worried about relativism. They are minimalist realists in order to
shun the position of idealism but remain more concerned with the plurality of versions of "reality." Like Peirce and Putnam, they put a pre-
mium on restraints and regulations yet do so not with the intention of
privileging scientific objectivity but rather with the aim of noting how
different forms of rational deliberation achieve their respective goals.
In this way, the notion of scientific objectivity is not rejected; it simply
becomes a self-complimenting term for a particular community who
excel at explaining and predicting experience. The notions of inquiry
and experimentation remain crucial but only insofar as they promote
self-critical and self-correcting enterprises in the varieties of human
activities, be they in sciences, arts, or everyday life.

Avant-garde pragmatists such as Richard Rorty not only jettison
anxieties about relativism but also adopt a thoroughgoing antirealism.
Rorty's concern here is not to ensure that restraints and regulations are
in place, as they always already are, but to explode these restraints and
regulations for the edifying purpose of creating new vocabularies of
self-description and self-creation. For Rorty, these transgressions—
Kuhnian paradigm-shifts—consist of new and novel moves in the ongoing conversation of intellectuals.

For most literary critics, these philosophical differences within the
pragmatist camp are mere intramural affairs with little relevance. This
is so because once one adopts the epistemic antifoundationalist position, the issue of ontological realism or antirealism primarily concerns
whether the language of physicists actually refers or not; that is, the terrain is confined to the philosophy of science. Yet this philosophical
debate does pertain indirectly to literary critics in that the status, role,

and function of restraints and regulations relate to the fundamental issues of objectivity and relativism in literary hermeneutics.

The obsessive concern with theory in literary criticism has much to do with the status, role, and function of restraints and regulations in literary interpretation after a rather widespread agreement on epistemic antifoundationalism. The unsettling impact on literary studies of Derrida, de Man, Foucault, Said, Jameson, Showalter, Baker, and others is not that relativism reigns, as old-style humanists tend to put it, but rather that disagreement reigns as to what the appropriate restraints and regulations for ascertaining the meanings of texts ought to be after epistemic antifoundationalism is accepted. To put it another way, the debate over the consequences of theory emerged not as a means of settling upon the right restraints and regulations outside of practice in a foundationalist manner, as Steven Knapp and Walter Benn Michaels misleadingly view it, but rather as a way of rendering explicit the discursive space or conversational activity now made legitimate owing to widespread acceptance of epistemic antifoundationalism. This hegemony of epistemic antifoundationalism in the literary academy has pushed critics in the direction of historicism and skepticism.

At the level of theory, there are moderate pragmatists such as Knapp and Benn Michaels who are against theory because they see the theoretical enterprise as a cover for new forms of epistemic foundationalism—as attempts to "occupy a position outside practice."[7] Unfortunately, they view theory as *grand theory* and consider practice as close reading in search of agential-inscribed intentions and thereby truncate the debate on the consequences of theory.

On the other hand, there are proponents of grand theory such as Fredric Jameson who associate pragmatism with this antitheory stance, who deny that grand theorists must locate theory outside social practice and who insist that historicist forms of demystification are preferable to limited historicist forms of demythologization. For Jameson, only grand theory of a certain sort can provide the adequate explanatory model for detecting the role and function of literary meanings in relation to larger developments and happenings in society and history.

Between these two positions lurk ultratheorists like Frank Len-

tricchia, Paul Bové, and Jonathan Arac who acknowledge the indis-
pensability of theory, especially the insights of Marxists and feminists,
yet who also shun the option of grand theory. Following exemplary
ultratheorists—Michel Foucault and Edward Said—who move skill-
fully between theory and politics, Lentricchia, Bové, and Arac stand at
the crossroads of history and rhetoric, at the intersection of the operations of institutional powers and the operations of linguistic figures
and tropes.

All pragmatists are against grand theory, but not all pragmatists need
be against theory. Lentricchia, who describes himself loosely as a "dialectical rhetorician" drawing from pragmatism,[8] must be challenged
when he asserts that

> to be a pragmatist is in a sense to have no theory—and having a position
> requires having a theory. The liberating, critical move of pragmatism
> against the "antecedent" is compromised by its inability—built into the posi-
> tion of pragmatism as such—to say clearly what it wants for the future.
> Though not practice for its own sake, pragmatism cannot say what practice
> should be aimed at without ceasing to be pragmatism, without violating its
> reverence for experimental method.[9]

This critique, echoing that of Randolph Bourne more than half a century ago, holds only for certain crude versions of pragmatism which
have not adequately confronted the ideological and political issue concerning the vocation of humanistic intellectuals.

This issue of vocation is a political and ideological one even though
it surfaces in our time as a discourse about professionalism.

The term *vocation* is rather unpopular these days in academic circles
principally owing to the predominance of words like *profession* and
career. Yet I suggest that recent historical investigations into the rise of
professionalism and sociological inquiries into the content and character of careerism require that we rethink, revise, and retain a notion of
vocation. Such a notion must not presuppose that we have an unmediated access to truth nor assume that we must preserve a pristine tradition free of ideological contamination. Rather we live at a particular
historical moment in which a serious interrogation regarding "voca-

tions" of intellectuals and academicians in American society can contribute to *a more enabling and empowering sense of the moral and political dimensions of our functioning in the present-day academy.* To take seriously one's vocation as an intellectual is to justify in moral and political terms why one pursues a rather privileged life of the mind in a world that seems to require forms of more direct and urgent action.

Allan Bloom's bestseller, *The Closing of the American Mind*—a nostalgic and, for some, seductive depiction of the decline and decay of the highbrow, classical humanist tradition—and Russell Jacoby's provocative book, *The Last Intellectuals*—a premature requiem for left public intellectuals—are both emblematic symptoms of the crisis in vocation of contemporary intellectuals. The professionalization, specialization, and bureaucratization of academic knowledge-forms has become a kind of *deus ex machina* in discussions about the crises of purpose among the humanistic intelligentsia. Yet even these noteworthy developments along with others such as the intensified commodification of intellectuals themselves and the reification of intellectual conversation fail to capture crucial features of the lived experience of many intellectuals in the academy. If we take Bloom, Jacoby, and others at their word, the lives of many academic intellectuals are characterized by *demoralization, marginalization,* and *irrelevance.*

Demoralization results from a variety of reasons, but the primary ones consist of what Roberto Unger has called the "Downbeat Alexandrian Cynicism" of the American academy, in which the obsession with status often overshadows the preoccupation with substance, and the naked operations of power are usually masked behind a thin veil of civility. Needless to say, demoralization takes different forms among the tenured faculty than among the untenured ones, with the former often fearful of becoming mere deadwood and the latter usually mindful of being too creative (adventurous). It is important to keep in mind that most serious intellectuals today become academics by default; that is, they simply cannot pursue the life of the mind anywhere but in the academy and maintain upper-middle-class life-styles that provide leisure time. Self-invested, hedonistic indulgence in precious moments of reading, lecturing, writing, and conversing indeed occurs alongside the demoralization of many academic intellectuals. Yet few intellectuals would justify their activity on sheer hedonistic grounds. Most would candidly acknowledge the pleasure of their intellectual work yet cast the justification of this work on a higher moral and political ground. And it is precisely this ground that seems to be slipping away.

For example, the increasing marginalization of humanistic studies in the academy primarily due to the popularity of business schools and computer studies is depriving many intellectuals of their "higher" moral and political reasons for remaining in the academy, for they can no longer claim that they train the best and the brightest undergraduates in order to preserve the best that has been thought and known in the world, or hold to what Richard Rorty has called the "Cynical Prudential Strategy" of academic humanists which says to American society: "You let us have your gifted children for our universities, where we will estrange them from you and keep the best ones for ourselves. In return, we will send the second-best back to keep you supplied with technology, entertainment, and soothing presidential lies."[10]

In the past few decades, it is clear that most of the "best ones" have not gone into the humanities or politics but rather into the private sphere of quick money making, be it in business, legal, or medical enterprises. This has resulted not simply in a relative brain drain in humanistic studies but also in a sense that humanistic intellectuals are missing out on where the "real action" is. This situation is compounded by ideological dynamics; that is, those students most attracted to humanistic studies tend to be those of a slightly more left-liberal bent, in part due to a revulsion from a boring life of money making and rat racing. As a result, many students and faculty (especially younger faculty) find themselves rather adverse to a pecuniary oriented life-style on moral and ideological grounds yet compelled to spell out to themselves and others the *political relevance* of their academic life-styles; and yet the sense persists that what they are doing is, in large part, irrelevant. I shall put forward my response to this situation in the form of an examination of the three major vocational models of intellectual work. I will highlight the blindness and insights, strengths and weaknesses of these models. Then I shall suggest that a more acceptable model may be on the horizon.

Before specifying what these models are, I think it instructive to mention briefly the most influential and celebrated literary theorist of our time, the late Paul de Man. In fact, his little book, *The Resistance to Theory* (1986), is an appropriate starting place for considering the complex relation of the vocational and the theoretical. Furthermore, to render invisible his enormous presence and challenge in our discussion, especially given the recent revelations of his youthful anti-Semitic writings, is to impoverish the discussion. It is always sad to discover that one of the most engaging minds of one's time succumbed years ago to one of the most pernicious prejudices of our century. Yet it only reminds us that even the finest of intellects must breathe the polluted air of any *Zeitgeist*. And few escape some degree of moral asphyxiation. To use this profound moral lapse to downplay de Man's later insights is sophomoric, just as to overlook it in the name of these insights is idolatrous.

I am interested here in de Man's sense of vocation as an intellectual. I would go as far as to suggest that what separated de Man as a literary theorist from his contemporaries—besides his prodigious talent, intense discipline, and cautious scholarship—was his dogged single-mindedness regarding his conception of himself as an intellectual. To put it boldly, de Man seemed never to waver in viewing himself as a philological scholar, as one dedicated and devoted to a critical discourse that examines the rhetorical devices of language. For de Man, the vocation of the literary intellectual was to stay attuned to the multifarious operations of tropes in language, especially literary language, which are in no way reducible to religious, moral, political, or ideological quests for wholeness and harmony. His aim was to push to the limits by means of high-powered rigor and precision the inherent inability to control meaning even as we inescapably quest for it. His kind of philological scholarship revealed the various ways in which "simultaneous asymmetry" is shot through the semantic operations of language.

De Man's viewpoint is not a simple relativism in which epistemic restraints and regulations are nonexistent, but is rather a tortuous rendering of how such restraints and regulations ineluctably fail to contain transgressions. His perspective is not a form of idealism in that it is grounded in the material practices of language using decentered subjects, that is, human bodies who try to generate meanings by way of speech and texts. It is rather a version of linguistic materialism which focuses narrowly on select conditions under which meaning is both produced and undone.

For de Man, theory is an integral part of one's vocation as an intellectual. He paradoxically argued that theory is inescapable yet unable to sustain itself as theory owing to its self-undermining character—a character that yields more theory only to be resisted by means of more theory. This theoretical resistance to theory could not but be shot through with ideology, a focus de Man was deepening before his death.

De Man's formulations may be persuasive or unpersuasive. My aim here is neither to explicate them nor defend them, but rather to note how a clear sense of one's vocation shapes a project—one that seizes the imagination of a generation of critics. The loss of Paul de Man, his authorizing and legitimizing intellectual presence, intensified the crisis of vocation among humanistic intellectuals. Some simply abandoned his challenge. Others tried to follow but found the going too tough. Many slavishly jumped from one bandwagon to the other, often dictated by market forces and personal inertia with little sense of how positions enrich or impoverish the sense of what we are about, who we are, and why we do what we do. It strikes me that much of the attraction to Foucault and Said is due to the fact that they grapple with vocational questions as part and parcel of their critical practice. In addition, much of the hoopla about the new pragmatism and new historicism—even as we leave most of the formidable challenges of de Man unmet—has to do with the hunger for vocational purpose in the profession.

In the current and rather confused discussion about vocation and intellectual work, three major models loom large. First, there is the *oppositional professional intellectual* model that claims that we must do political work where we are in the academy. This model encompasses liberals who call for cultivating critical sensibilities; Marxists such as Jim Merod, who promote a revolutionary trade union of oppositional critics; and leftists such as Paul Bové, who envision an unceasing attack on the reigning "regimes of truth" with no humanist illusions about "truth" or "revolution." Second, there is the *professional political intel-lectual* model that encourages academicians to intervene into the pub-lic conversation of the nation regarding some of the most controversial issues as citizens who bring their professional status and expertise to bear in a political manner. The outstanding exemplar of this model is Edward Said, although people such as Catharine MacKinnon and Wil-liam Julius Wilson also come to mind. The last model is that of the *oppositional intellectual groupings within the academy* which seek to create, sustain, and expand intellectual subcultures inside the univer-sity networks, usually with little success at gaining visibility and potency in the larger culture and society. The pertinent figures here would be Fredric Jameson, Elaine Showalter, and Henry Louis Gates, Jr., namely leading Marxist, feminist, and Afro-American critics who remain thoroughly inscribed in the academy and have successfully col-onized legitimate space for their oppositional agendas. Analogues can be found in the critical legal studies movement in law schools and the liberation theology subgroups in seminaries.[11]

Each of these models is regulated by a dominant theoretical orienta-tion. The guiding spirit behind the first model is that of the late Michel Foucault. It is, I conjecture, the most attractive model for young aspir-ing oppositional humanistic intellectuals, although it may fade quickly in the coming years. To put it crudely, Foucault admonishes intellectuals to scrutinize the specific local contexts in which they work and highlight the complex operations of power which produce and perpetuate the kind of styles and standards, curriculum and com-mittees, the proliferation of jargon, and the relative absence of comic high spirits in the academy. Foucault holds that different societies pre-serve and reproduce themselves in part by encouraging intellectuals to be unmindful of how they are socialized and acculturated into prevail-ing "regimes of truth"; that is, intellectuals often remain uncritical of the very culture of critical discourse they inhabit and thereby fail to inquire into why they usually remain within the parameters of what is considered "legitimate," "tactful," "civil" discourse. Furthermore, Fou-cault suggests that this failure leads intellectuals often to overlook the ways in which these mainstream (or malestream) discourses construct identities and constitute forms of subjectivity that devalue and degrade, harm and harass those who are viewed as other, alien, marginal, and abnormal owing to these discourses.

The basic insight of this model is that it rightly understands the academy to be an important terrain for political and ideological contestation; and because it grasps the degree to which knowledges are forms of power in societies, this model correctly views battles over the kind of knowledge produced in the academy as forms of political practice. The major shortcoming of this model is that it feeds on an excessive pessimism regarding the capacity of oppositional intellectuals to break out of the local academic context and make links with nonacademic groups and organizations. This viewpoint is echoed in Jim Merod's noteworthy text, *The Political Responsibility of the Critic:* "Right now and for the imaginable future we have no intellectual, professional, or political base for alliances between radical theorists and dispossessed people . . . It seems, therefore, that the concrete political means to build an intellectual coalition of professional and nonprofessional groups are not available."[12]

Yet the overriding theoretical perspective of the second model, that of Edward Said, calls this excessive pessimism into question. Motivated by the historical voluntarism of Vico, the antidogmatic sense of engagement of R. P. Blackmur, and the subversive worldliness of Antonio Gramsci, Said stands now as the towering figure among left humanistic intellectuals. Said creatively appropriates Gramsci's notions of hegemony and elaboration in light of his own ideas of filiation and affiliation. For Said, intellectuals are always already implicated in incessant battles in their own local academic contexts. Yet these contexts themselves are part of a larger process of mobilizing and manufacturing a dynamic "consent" of subaltern peoples to their subordination by means of the exercise of moral, cultural, and political leadership. Following Gramsci, Said acknowledges that neither force nor coercion is principally responsible for the widespread depoliticization and effective subordination of the populace. Instead, the particular ways of life and ways of struggle, values, and sensibilities, moods and manners, structures of seeings and structures of feelings promoted by schools, churches, radio, television, and films primarily account for the level of political and moral consciousness in our country. And intellectuals of various sorts—teachers, preachers, journalists, artists, professors—play a partisan role in this never ceasing struggle.

This model is instructive in that it leads academic intellectuals outside the academy and into the more popular magazines and mass media; and for Said, it has led to the White House (meeting with George Schultz) due to the unprecedented heroic resistance of Palestinians on the West Bank and Gaza strip against the inhumane treatments and pernicious policies of the conservative Israeli government. Such public interventions by academic intellectuals (especially that of left intellectuals) broaden the political possibilities for present day intellectual work. The recent example of Yale's Paul Kennedy (*The Rise and Fall of the Great Powers: Economic Change and Military Conflict from 1500 to 2000*) is worth noting in this regard.

The major shortcomings of this model are first that the public intervention of select intellectual celebrities gives even more authority and legitimacy to their academic professions owing to the status of the expert and second that the scope of the public intervention is usually rather narrow, that is, confined to one issue with little chance of making connections to other issues. In this way, the very way in which one is a political intellectual promotes academic respectability, careerist individualism, and a highly confined terrain of political maneuvering.

The last model—of oppositional intellectual groupings within the academy constituting vital subcultures for space and resources— accents the crucial issues of *community* and *camaraderie* in left intellectual work. Unlike conservative intellectuals who have access to well-funded think tanks, foundations, and institutes, progressive academics must gather within the liberal universities and colleges and thereby adjust their agendas to the powers that be for survival and sustenance. The grand contribution of the Frederic Jamesons, Elaine Showalters, and Henry Louis Gates, Jrs. has been to bombard the academy with texts, students, and programs that ride the tide of intellectual interest in—and political struggle influenced by—Marxism, feminism, and Afro-American studies. This model surely signifies the academization of Marxism, feminism, and black studies, with the concomitant problems this entails. Yet it also constitutes noteworthy efforts of left community building among academics in relatively anti-Marxist, patriarchal, and racist environments, in regard to the academy and the larger American culture and society.

Yet the major challenges of this model, namely the spilling over of Marxist, feminist, and black studies into working-class, women's, and black communities, remain unmet; and without significant social motion, momentum, and ultimately movements, this situation will remain relatively the same. The crucial questions facing progressive humanistic intellectuals are how to help generate the conditions and circumstances of such social motion, momentum, and movements that move society in more democratic and free directions. How to bring more power and pressure to bear on the status quos so as to enhance the life chances of the jobless and homeless, landless and luckless, empower degraded and devalued working people, and increase the quality of life for all?

I suggest that these challenging queries can be answered through a conception of the intellectual as a critical organic catalyst. This conception requires that the intellectual function inside the academy principally in order to survive and stay attuned to the most sophisticated reflections about the past, present, and future destinies of the relevant cultures, economies, and states of our time. This conception also entails that the intellectual be grounded outside the academy: in progressive political organizations and cultural institutions of the most likely agents of social change in America, for example, those of black and brown people, organized workers, women, lesbians, and gays. This model pushes academic intellectuals beyond contestation within the academy—be it the important struggles over standards and curriculum or institutionalizing oppositional subcultures—and links this contestation with political activity in grass roots organizations, pre-party formations, or progressive associations intent on bringing together potential agents of social change. In this sense, to be an engaged progressive intellectual is to be a critical organic catalyst whose vocation is to fuse the best of the life of the mind from within the academy with the best of the organized forces for greater democracy and freedom from outside the academy. This model is neither a panacea for the crisis of vocation of humanistic intellectuals nor a solution to the relation of academics to grass roots organizing. Rather it is a candid admission that this may be simply the best one can do in the present situation, a situation that can change in the near future depending in part on what some intellectuals do.

This primacy of the vocational has much to do with pragmatism in that pragmatism began and prospered due in part to a new conception of the vocation of the humanistic intellectual in America at the turn of the century. Although initiated by that reclusive genius, Charles Sanders Peirce, pragmatism served as a beacon for intellectuals under the leadership of William James and John Dewey. Similar to the attraction to Marxism among serious European thinkers at the time (and Third World intellectuals in our time), pragmatism gave many American intellectuals a sense of political purpose and moral orientation. At its worst, it became a mere ideological cloak for corporate liberalism and managerial social engineering which served the long-term interests of American capital; at its best, it survived as a form of cultural critique and social reform at the service of expanding the scope of democratic process and broadening the arena of individual self-development here and abroad. The story of the rise and fall of American pragmatism is a fascinating one—one that I try to tell elsewhere.[13] Yet the resurgence of pragmatism in our time will be even more impoverished and impotent if the vocational questions are jettisoned.

My own kind of pragmatism—what I call prophetic pragmatism—is closely akin to the philosophy of praxis put forward by Antonio Gramsci. The major difference is that my attitude toward Marxism as a grand theory is heuristic rather than dogmatic.[14] Furthermore, my focus on the theoretical development in emerging forms of oppositional thought—feminist theory, antiracist theory, gay and lesbian theory—leads me to posit or look for not an overarching synthesis but rather an articulated assemblage of analytical outlooks to further more morally principled and politically effective forms of action to ameliorate the plight of the wretched of the earth.

On the philosophical level, this means adopting the moderate pragmatic views of John Dewey. Epistemic antifoundationalism and minimalist ontological realism (in its pluralist version) proceed from taking seriously the impact of modern historical and rhetorical consciousness on truth and knowledge. "Anything goes" relativism and disenabling forms of skepticism fall by the wayside, serving only as noteworthy reminders to avoid dogmatic traps and to accept intellectual humility rather than as substantive philosophical positions.

On the level of theory, to be against theory *per se* is to be against inquiry into heuristic posits regarding the institutional and individual causes of alterable forms of human misery and human suffering, just as uncritical allegiance to grand theories can blind one from seeing and examining kinds of human oppression. Therefore I adopt strategic attitudes toward the use and deployment of theory, a position more charitable toward grand theory than are the ultratheorists and more suspicious of grand theory than are the grand theorists themselves.

Lastly, at the level of politics and ideology, I envision the intellectual as a critical organic catalyst, one who brings the most subtle and sophisticated analytical tools to bear to explain and illuminate how structures of domination and effects of individual choices in language and in nondiscursive institutions operate. The social location of this activity is the space wherein everyday affairs of ordinary people intersect with possible political mobilization and existential empowerment, for example, in churches, schools, trade unions, and movements. The moral aim and political goal of such intellectual activity are the creation of greater individual freedom in culture and broader democracy in the economy and society. In this sense, the consequences of my own intervention into the debate over the consequences of theory are understood as being explicitly though not exclusively political.

NOTES

1. John B. Thompson, *Studies in the Theory of Ideology* (Berkeley and Los Angeles: University of California Press, 1984), 5ff.

2. Steven Knapp and Walter Benn Michaels, "Against Theory," *Critical Inquiry* 8, no. 4 (1982): 742.

3. John B. Thompson, *Studies in the Theory of Ideology*, 6.

4. Arthur O. Lovejoy, "On the Discrimination of Romanticisms," *Essays in the History of Ideas* (Baltimore: Johns Hopkins University Press, 1948), 228–53.

5. Arthur O. Lovejoy, "The Thirteen Pragmatisms," *The Thirteen Pragmatisms and Other Essays* (Baltimore: Johns Hopkins University Press, 1963), 1–29.

6. Hilary Putnam, *Reason, Truth and History* (Cambridge: Cambridge University Press, 1981), 103–26, 174–200. For a brief interpretation of Putnam that chimes with mine, see Ian Hacking, *Representing and Intervening: Introductory Topics in the Philosophy of Natural Science* (Cambridge: Cambridge University Press, 1983), 60.

7. Steven Knapp and Walter Benn Michaels, "A Reply to Richard Rorty: What is Pragmatism?" *Critical Inquiry* 11, no. 3 (1985): 470.

8. Frank Lentricchia, *Criticism and Social Change* (Chicago: University of Chicago Press, 1983), 34.

9. Ibid., 4.

10. Richard Rorty, Review of Allan Bloom's *The Closing of the American Mind*, *The New Republic*, 4 April 1988.

11. See Cornel West, "Third Annual Brendan Brown Lecture: Reassessing The Critical Legal Studies Movement," *Loyola Law Review* 24, no. 2 (1988): 265–75; idem, "Critical Legal Studies and a Liberal Critic," *The Yale Law Journal* 97, no. 5 (1988): 757–71; idem, "On Christian Intellectuals" and "The Crisis in Theological Education," *Prophetic Fragments* (Grand Rapids, Mich.: Eerdmans, 1988), 273–80.

12. Jim Merod, *The Political Responsibility of the Critic* (Ithaca: Cornell University Press, 1988), 191, 261.

13. Cornel West, *The American Evasion of Philosophy: A Genealogy of Pragmatism* (Madison: University of Wisconsin Press, 1989).

14. For an elaboration of the differences between Gramsci's subtle version of historical materialism and my own genealogical materialism, see Cornel

West, "Race and Social Theory: Towards a Genealogical Materialist Analysis," in *The Year Left 2*, ed. Mike Davis, Manning Marable, Fred Pfeil, and Michael Sprinker (London: Verso Books, 1987), 74–90. For further explication of this conception of the intellectual, see idem, "The Dilemma of the Black Intellectual," *Cultural Critique*, no. 1 (Fall 1985): 109–24.

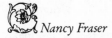 *Nancy Fraser*

Solidarity or Singularity?

RICHARD RORTY BETWEEN ROMANTICISM AND
TECHNOCRACY

> Nothing can serve as a criticism of a final vocabulary save another
> such vocabulary; there is no answer to a redescription save a re-re-
> description.
> —Richard Rorty, "Private Irony and Liberal Hope"

Consider a somewhat cartoonish characterization of the romantic impulse. Think of this impulse as the valorization of individual
invention understood as self-fashioning. A romantic impulse of this
sort would lionize the figure of the extraordinary individual who does
not simply play out but rather rewrites the cultural script his socio-
historical milieu has prepared for him. It would represent this individual as a genius or "strong poet," irrespective of the field of his
inventiveness. Science, politics, whatever—from the standpoint of the
romantic impulse, every arena of invention would be a branch of literature in an extended sense, just as every significant act would be an aesthetic act and every making a self-making. Here, novelty would be
valued for its own sake; it would be the sheer difference between what
is merely found or inherited, on the one hand, and what is made or
dreamed up *ex nihilo*, on the other, which would confer value and
importance. Insofar as the romantic impulse figures such difference
making as the work of extraordinary individuals; insofar as it treats
them and their work as the source of all significant historical change;
insofar as it views history largely as the succession of such geniuses; it
becomes aestheticizing, individualist, and elitist. It is, in short, the
impulse to father oneself, to be *causa sui*, to separate from one's community. Thus, the masculine pronoun is appropriate.[1]

Now contrast this cartoon version of the romantic impulse with
an equally cartoonish characterization of the pragmatic impulse. Take

the latter to consist in an impatience with differences that do not make a difference. Take it as a distaste for baroque invention and for useless epicycles, for whatever does not get to the point. Thus, the pragmatic impulse would be goal directed and purposive; it would care less for originality than for results. Problems solved, needs satisfied, well-being assured, these would be its emblems of value. For the romantic's metaphorics of poetry and play, it would substitute a metaphorics of production and work. It would scorn gears that engage no mechanism, tools that serve no useful purpose, Rube Goldberg contraptions that do no real work. Indeed, from the standpoint of this impulse, words would be tools and culture an outsized toolkit, to be unceremoniously cast off in the event of obsolescence or rust. The pragmatic impulse, then, would be bright and busy. It would prefer the civic mindedness of the problem-solving reformer to the narcissism of the self-fashioning poet. Its hero would be the fellow who gets the job done and makes himself useful to his society, not the one who is always preening and strutting his stuff. Moreover, the pragmatic impulse would see history as a succession of social problems posed and social problems solved, a succession that is in fact a progression. Crediting progress to the account of common sense, technical competence, and public spiritedness, its ethos would be reformist and optimistic, its politics liberal and technocratic.

If these cartoonlike characterizations do not do justice to the complexities of the romantic and pragmatic traditions, I trust that they nonetheless mark out two recognizable strands in the recent writings of Richard Rorty. These writings, in my view, are the site of a struggle between just such a romantic impulse and pragmatic impulse. Moreover, it is a struggle that neither impulse seems able decisively to win. Sometimes one, sometimes the other gains a temporary advantage here or there. But the overall outcome is stalemate.

It is symptomatic of Rorty's inability to resolve this contest that he oscillates among three different views of the relationship between romanticism and pragmatism, poetry and politics. These in turn carry three different conceptions of the social role and political function of intellectuals. The first position I call the *invisible hand* conception. It is the view that romanticism and pragmatism are "natural partners." Here the "strong poet" and the "utopian reform politician" are simply two slightly different variants of the same species. Their respective activities are complementary if not strictly identical, providing grist for the same liberal democratic mill.

The second position I call the *sublimity or decency?* conception. It is the view that romanticism and pragmatism are antithetical to one another, that one has to choose between the sublime "cruelty" of the strong poet and the beautiful "kindness" of the political reformer. This view emphasizes the dark side of romanticism, its tendency to aestheticize politics and, so, to turn antidemocratic.

Evidently, the *invisible hand* conception and the *sublimity or decency?* conception are converses of one another. Thus, each can be read as a critique of the other. Rorty's third position, which I call the *partition* position, represents a compromise. If romanticism and pragmatism are not exactly natural partners, but if, at the same time, one is not willing to abandon either one of them, then perhaps they can learn how to live with one another. Thus, Rorty has recently outlined the terms of a truce between them, a truce that allots each its own separate sphere of influence. The romantic impulse will have free rein in what will henceforth be "the private sector," but it will not be permitted any political pretensions. Pragmatism, on the other hand, will have exclusive rights to "the public sector," but it will be barred from entertaining any notions of radical change which could challenge the "private" cultural hegemony of romanticism.

An ingenious compromise, to be sure. Yet compromises based on partition are notoriously unstable. They tend not truly to resolve but only temporarily to palliate the basic source of conflict. Sooner or later, in one form or another, that conflict will out.

THE SORELIAN TEMPTATION

Consider the role the romantic impulse plays in Rorty's thought. Recall his insistence on the difference between vocabularies and propo-

sitions. It is precisely the tendency to confound them, to treat vocabularies as if they could be warranted like propositions, that is for him the
cardinal sin of traditional philosophy. In Rorty's view, vocabulary
choice is always underdetermined. There are no non–question-begging
arguments, no reasons not already couched in some vocabulary, which
could establish once and for all that one had the *right* vocabulary. To pre-
tend otherwise is to seek the metaphysical comfort of a God's-eye view.

Now consider, too, how much hinges on vocabulary shifts, in
Rorty's view. The mere redistribution of truth values across a set of
propositions formulated in some taken-for-granted vocabulary is a pal-
try thing compared with a change in vocabulary. With vocabulary
shifts, urgent questions suddenly lose their point, established practices
are drastically modified, entire constellations of culture dissolve to
make room for new, heretofore unimaginable ones. Thus, vocabulary
shifts are for Rorty the motor of history, the chief vehicles of intellectual and moral progress.

Consider, finally, exactly how it is, according to Rorty, that vocabulary shifts occur. A vocabulary shift is the literalization of a new metaphor, the application across the board of somebody's new way of
speaking, the adoption by an entire community of some poet's idio-
syncrasy. It follows that poets, in the extended sense, are "the unacknowledged legislators of the social world."[2] It is their chance words,
coming like bolts from outside logical space, that determine the shape
of subsequent culture and society.

The romantic impulse in Rorty is the impulse that thrills to the sublimity of metaphor, the headiness of "abnormal discourse." When he is
under its sway, Rorty figures the culture hero as the poet, allowing the
latter to outrank not only the priest and the philosopher but even the
pragmatist's traditional heroes, the scientist and the reform politician.
In general, then, it is Rorty's romantic impulse that dictates his "utopian ideal" of "an aestheticized culture," a culture with no other goal
than to create "ever more various, multi-colored artifacts," no other purpose than "to make life easier for poets and revolutionaries."[3]

The romantic impulse is fairly strong in Rorty; but it is not an
impulse with which he is entirely comfortable.

And for good reason. Consider what a politics that gave free rein to the romantic impulse would look like. Recall the individualist, elitist, and aestheticist character of that impulse, its deification of the strong poet, its fetishization of creation *ex nihilo.* It takes only the squint of eye to see here the vision of a Georges Sorel: a "sociology" that classifies humanity into leaders and masses; a "theory of action" whereby the former mold the latter by means of a sheer triumph of the will; a "philosophy of history" as an empty canvas awaiting the unfettered designs of the poet leader.[4]

I take it that something like this Sorelian nightmare is what disturbs the sleep of Richard Rorty. For a long time now, he has been at pains to show that his own romantic streak does not lead down this road, that his own "utopian vision" of an "aestheticized culture" is liberal and democratic rather than Sorelian and potentially fascistic.

THE INVISIBLE HAND; OR, BETTER LIVING THROUGH CHEMISTRY AND POETRY

One way in which Rorty has sought to exorcize the Sorelian demon is by providing a positive political defense of his version of romanticism. Thus, he has tried to portray the romantic dimension of his thought as compatible with, indeed even as fostering, the apparently opposing pragmatic dimension. More strongly, he has tried to show that the two dimensions are "natural partners," that the fit between them is extremely tight and that the strong poet is the democrat personified.

The chief strategy here is to link poetizing with community mindedness, romantic making with social identification. Thus, Rorty argues that, in giving up Kantian buttresses for liberal views, one goes from "objectivity" to "solidarity," for to cease pinning our hopes on such God substitutes as reason, human nature and the moral law is to start pinning them on one another.[5]

Likewise, Rorty claims that the aesthetic stance and the moral stance are not antithetical to one another. On the contrary, they are not even distinct, for in adopting the aesthetic attitude, we dedeify or disenchant the world, thereby promoting tolerance, liberalism, and instrumental reason.[6] The refusal to mortgage culture making to ahistorical authorities liberates us for experimentalism in politics, for that simultaneously utopian and down-to-earth sort of "social engineering" that is the very soul of moral progress.

Moreover, claims Rorty, to treat the strong poet as one's hero and role model is "to adopt an identity which suits one for citizenship in an ideally liberal state." For there is a fairly tight fit, supposedly, between the freedom of intellectuals and "the diminution of cruelty." We only see practices of earlier ages as cruel and unjust because we have learned how to redescribe them, and we have only done that by virtue of vocabulary shifts owing to the metaphors of poets. Thus, contrary to initial appearances, it is not really elitist to "treat democratic societies as existing for the sake of intellectuals."[7] On the contrary, only by making society safe for poets can we ensure that language keeps changing, and only by ensuring that language keeps changing can we prevent the normalization of current practices that might later look cruel and unjust. Thus, to make society safe for poets is to help make it safe for everyone.

Finally, claims Rorty, a culture organized for the sake of poetry and play would foster decency and kindness. It would diminish or equalize the liability to a specifically human form of suffering, namely, the humiliation that comes from being redescribed in someone else's terms while one's own vocabulary is peremptorily dismissed. The best safeguard against this sort of cruelty is an awareness of other people's vocabularies. Such an awareness in turn is best acquired by reading lots of books. Thus, a culture that fosters a cosmopolitan literary intelligentsia will promote the greatest happiness of the greatest number.[8]

In short, Rorty claims that cultural innovation and social justice go together. They are united in the liberationist metaphorics of liberal societies, where history is figured as a succession of emancipations: serfs from lords, slaves from plantation owners, colonies from empires, labor from the unlimited power of capital. Since both are dominated by these images of opening up, romanticism in the arts goes with democracy in politics.

In all these arguments, what is really at stake is the accusation of elitism. Rorty seeks to rebut the charge that a romantic politics must elevate liberty over equality, sacrificing the greatest happiness of the greatest number on the altar of the strong poet. His general approach is to invoke a version of the old trickle-down argument: liberty in the arts fosters equality in society; what's good for poets is good for workers, peasants, and the hard-core unemployed.

Here, then, is the Rorty who has sought a seamless joining of romanticism and pragmatism. Adopting an invisible hand strategy, he has tried to show that aesthetic play and liberal reformist politics are but two sides of the same coin, that what promotes one will also promote the other; that we can have better living through the marriage of chemistry and poetry.

These arguments do not represent Rorty at his most persuasive. On the contrary, they tend to raise far more questions than they answer. For example, is to say goodbye to objectivity really to say hello to solidarity? Surely, there is no relation of logical entailment between anti-essentialism and loyalty to one's society. Nor is there even any contingent psychological or historical connection, if modern Western societies are considered any measure. Moreover, why assume a quasi-Durkheimian view according to which society is integrated by way of a single monolithic and all-encompassing solidarity? Why not assume rather a quasi-Marxian view according to which modern capitalist societies contain a plurality of overlapping and competing solidarities?

Next, is it really the case that societies that produce the best literature are also the most egalitarian? Do poets' interests and workers' interests really coincide so perfectly? And what about women's interests, given that, Rorty's use of the feminine pronoun notwithstanding, his poets are always figured as sons seeking to displace their cultural fathers? Moreover, does poetizing really dovetail so neatly with social engineering? How does the down-to-earth, results-oriented character of the latter square with the extravagant playfulness of the former? For that matter, why is social engineering the preferred conception of political practice? And why is equality cast in terms of kindness and decency? Why is it made to hinge on a virtue of the literary intelligentsia, on the latter's supposed inclination to forebear humiliating others? Why is equality not instead considered in terms of equal participation in poetizing, culture making, and politics?

SUBLIMITY OR DECENCY? OR, THE DARK SIDE OF ROMANTICISM

As usual, no one states the case against the invisible hand "solution" better than Rorty himself. Recently, he has acknowledged that there is a dark side of romanticism, a side he now designates as *ironism*. By *ironism*, Rorty means the modernist literary intellectual's project of fashioning the best possible self by continual redescription. Identifying himself as such an ironist, Rorty wonders whether it really is possible to combine "the pleasures of redescription" with sensitivity to "the sufferings of those being redescribed." He fears that the ironist demand for maximum cultural freedom may indeed be elitist, compatible with indifference to the sufferings of nonpoets. Ironism, he concedes, is by definition reactive, requiring a nonironist public culture from which to be alienated. Thus, even in a postmetaphysical culture, ironism cannot be the generalized attitude of the entire social collectivity. It can only be the attitude of one stratum of society, a literary intelligentsia or cultural elite. Moreover, there is no denying that ironism can be cruel. It delights in redescribing others instead of taking them in their own terms. There is no question but that this is often humiliating, as when a child's favorite possessions are set next to those of a richer child and thereby made to seem tacky. To make matters worse, the ironist cannot claim that, in redescribing others, he is uncovering their true selves and interests, thereby empowering them and setting them free. Only the metaphysically minded politician can promise that. It follows that, even were the ironist to profess support for liberal politics, he could not be very "dynamic" or "progressive."[9]

Considerations like these lead Rorty to a dramatic reversal of his earlier view. Now he no longer assumes that to substitute making for finding is to serve one's community, that to abandon objectivity is necessarily to promote solidarity. On the contrary, what they really do is express the traditional vanguardist contempt for their fellow human beings. Heideggerians, deconstructionists, neo-Marxists, Foucaultians, and assorted New Leftists—these are not differences that make a difference. All are potential Sorelians who confuse the ironist intellectual's special yen for the sublime with society's general need for the merely beautiful.[10]

It is in this vein that Rorty has recently taken care explicitly to distinguish the pragmatic and the romantic conceptions of philosophy. He argues that romanticism and pragmatism represent two distinct reactions against metaphysics and that they ought not to be conflated with one another. Granted, both reject the traditional view of *philosophy as science,* as the search, that is, for a permanent neutral matrix for inquiry. However, whereas romanticism wants to replace this with a view of *philosophy as metaphor,* pragmatism prefers to substitute the view of *philosophy as politics.* It follows that the two approaches differ sharply in their views of the ideal person: on the metaphor view, this must be the poet; whereas on the political view, it is the social worker and the engineer. Granted, both perspectives are holistic; both distinguish abnormal discourse from normal discourse, the invention of a new metaphor from its literalization or social application. But they part ways over the value of turning live metaphors into dead metaphors by disseminating them in the service of society. For the romantic, this sort of applied poetry is the vilest hack work, whereas for the pragmatist it is exactly what the best metaphors are made for. It follows that the two views entail very different social attitudes. On the romantic view, the social world exists for the sake of the poet. On the pragmatic view, on the other hand, the poet exists for the sake of the social world.[11]

In this rather more complicated scenario, then, there are not one but two alternatives to objectivity. Only one of these leads to solidarity and democracy, while the other leads to vanguardism if not to fascism.

Here Rorty frames the issue as romanticism *versus* pragmatism. He treats the two impulses as antithetical to one another, and he forces a choice. Romanticism or pragmatism? Sublimity or decency? Strong poetry or dead metaphors? Self-fashioning or social responsibility? One cannot have it both ways.

Or can one?

THE PARTITION POSITION

In his most recent essays, Rorty refuses to choose between sublimity and decency, romanticism and pragmatism. He has instead contrived a new formulation aimed at letting him have it both ways: he will split the difference between romanticism and pragmatism along a divide between private and public life.

The idea is that two things that cannot be fused into one may nonetheless coexist side by side, if clear and sharp boundaries are drawn between them. Now, sublimity cannot be fused with decency, nor strong poetry with social responsibility. But if each were allotted its own separate sphere and barred from interfering with the other, then they might just make passably good neighbors.

This, then, is the strategy of Rorty's partition position: to bifurcate the map of culture down the middle. On one side will be public life, the preserve of pragmatism, the sphere in which utility and solidarity predominate. On the other side will be private life, the preserve of romanticism, the sphere of self-discovery, sublimity, and irony. In the public sphere, one's duty to one's community takes precedence; social hope, decency, and the greatest happiness of the greatest number are the order of the day. In the private sphere, by contrast, the reigning cause is one's duty to oneself; here, one may disaffiliate from the community, attend to the fashioning of one's self and, so, deal with one's aloneness.[12]

Thus, Rorty wishes to preserve both ecstasy and utility, "the urge to think the Unthinkable" and "enthusiasm for the French Revolution"[13] — but only by strictly isolating them from one another. Indeed, he now claims that it is the desire to overcome the implacable split between public and private life that is at the root of many theoretical and political difficulties. This desire, it turns out, is common to metaphysics and

its ironist critique, to Marxism and to various non-Marxist forms of radical politics. It is what led even the later Heidegger astray, causing him
to confound what was actually his private need to get free of some
local, personal authority figures named Plato, Aristotle, and Kant with
the destiny of the West.[14]

Rorty claims that there is a lesson to be learned from the difficulties
of all these opponents of liberalism: When irony goes public, it gets
into trouble. Thus, ironist theory has to stay private if it is to stay
sane.[15]

It turns out, happily, that there is a way to neutralize the nonliberal
political implications of radical thought. It is to deny that radical
thought has any political implications. So, Heidegger was simply mistaken in imagining his work had any public relevance. Ditto for all
those would-be leftists who aim to make political hay of deconstruction, postmodernism, Foucaultianism, and neo-Marxism. In fact, the
sole use of ironist theory is a private one: to bolster the self-image and
aid the self-fashioning of the literary intelligentsia.

Clearly, the partition position entails a revised view of the social role
and political function of intellectuals. The strong poet as heretofore
conceived must be domesticated, cut down to size, and made fit for private life. He must become the Aesthete,[16] a figure denuded of public
ambition and turned inward. Thus, the intellectual will be king in the
castle of his own self-fashioning, but he will no longer legislate for the
social world. Strictly speaking, indeed, the intellectual will have no
social role or political function.

It is a measure of the domesticated status of Rorty's aesthete that he
may only pursue sublimity on his "own time, and within the limits set
by *On Liberty*."[17] He may think ironic thoughts involving cruel redescriptions within the privacy of his own narcissistic sphere, but he
must not act on them in ways that might cause pain or humiliation to
others. This means that the aesthete must have a bifurcated final vocabulary, a vocabulary split into a public sector and a private sector. The
private sector of the aesthete's final vocabulary will be large and luxu-
riant, containing all manner of colorful and potentially cruel terms for
redescribing others. The public sector of his vocabulary, on the other

hand, will be smaller, consisting in a few flexible terms like *kindness* and *decency* which express his commitment to the politics of liberalism.[18]

The partition position represents a new and extremely interesting development in Rorty's thinking. It is his most sophisticated effort to date to take seriously the problem of reconciling romanticism and pragmatism. And yet this position is seriously flawed. It stands or falls with the possibility of drawing a sharp boundary between public and private life. But is this really possible? Is it really possible to distinguish redescriptions that affect actions with consequences for others from those that either do not affect actions at all or that affect only actions with no consequences for others?[19] Surely, many cultural developments that occur at some remove from processes officially designated as political are nonetheless public. And official political public spheres are by no means impermeable to developments in cultural public spheres since cultural processes help shape social identities which in turn affect political affiliations. Moreover, the social movements of the last hundred or so years have taught us to see the power-laden and therefore political character of interactions that classical liberalism considered private. Workers' movements, for example, especially as clarified by Marxist theory, have taught us that the economic is political. Likewise, women's movements, as illuminated by feminist theory, have taught us that the domestic and the personal are political. Finally a whole range of New Left social movements, as illuminated by Gramscian, Foucaultian and, yes, even by Althusserian theory, have taught us that the cultural, the medical, the educational—everything that Hannah Arendt called *the social*, as distinct from the private and the public—that all this, too, is political.[20] Yet Rorty's partition position requires us to bury these insights, to turn our backs on the last hundred years of social history. It requires us, in addition, to privatize theory. Feminists, especially, will want to resist this last requirement, lest we see our theory go the way of our housework.

ABNORMAL DISCOURSE RECONSIDERED

None of Rorty's three positions represents a satisfactory resolution of the tension between pragmatism and romanticism. The invisible hand position fails because to say goodbye to objectivity is not necessarily to say hello to a single, unitary solidarity; and because what's good for poets is not necessarily good for workers, peasants, and the hardcore unemployed. The sublimity–or–decency position fails because not all radical theorizing is elitist, antidemocratic, and opposed to collective concerns and political life. Finally, the partition position fails because final vocabularies do not neatly divide into public and private sectors; nor do actions neatly divide into public or private.

If none of the three proffered solutions is adequate, then it may be worth reconsidering the terms of the original dilemma. We might take a closer look at the categories and assumptions that inform Rorty's thinking about culture and politics.

Begin with the key distinction in Rorty's framework: the contrast between normal discourse and abnormal discourse. In fact, Rorty oscillates between two views of abnormal discourse. The first view is the one developed in *Philosophy and the Mirror of Nature,* and it is derived from the work of Thomas Kuhn. It is the simple negation of the discourse of normal science, that is, of discourse in which interlocutors share a sense of what counts as a problem or question, as a well-formed or serious hypothesis, and as a good reason or argument. Abnormal discourse, then, is discourse in which such matters are up for grabs. It involves a plurality of differentiatible if not incommensurable voices, and it consists in an exchange among them which is lively if somewhat disorderly. Call this the *polylogical conception* of abnormal discourse.

Now contrast the polylogical conception with another conception of abnormal discourse which is also found in Rorty: a *monological conception.* The monological view is the romantic individualist view in which abnormal discourse is the prerogative of the strong poet and the ironist theorist. It is a discourse that consists in a solitary voice crying out into the night against an utterly undifferentiated background. The only conceivable response to this voice is uncomprehending rejection or identificatory imitation. There is no room for a reply that could qualify as a different voice. There is no room for interaction.

Clearly, these two different conceptions of abnormal discourse correspond to the two different impulses I identified earlier. The monological view develops under the spur of Rorty's romantic impulse, whereas the polylogical view is fed by his pragmatic impulse. In addition, the monological view maps onto Rorty's notions of radical theory-cum-strong poetry and privacy, whereas the polylogical view maps onto his notions of practice, politics, and publicity.

At one level, this mapping makes good sense. It seems that Rorty is perfectly right to want a polylogical politics instead of a monological politics, indeed, to reject a monological politics as an oxymoron. However, at another level, there is something profoundly disturbing here. It is the sharply dichotomous character of the resulting map of culture, the abstract and unmediated opposition between poetry and politics, theory and practice, individual and community.

Consider the impact of the monological conception of abnormal discourse on the various regions of Rorty's map of social space. The monological conception, we have seen, is individualistic, elitist, and antisocial. Moreover, it is associated by Rorty with radical theorizing, which is itself treated as a species of poetizing. As a result, radical theorizing assumes individualistic connotations, becoming the very antithesis of collective action and political practice. Radical theory, in other words, gets inflected as a sphere apart from collective life, a sphere of privacy and of individual self-fashioning. It becomes aestheticized, narcissized, and bourgeoisified, a preserve in which strivings for transcendence are quarantined, rendered safe because rendered sterile.

Now, this privatized, narcissistic conception of radical theory has two important social consequences. First, there can be no legitimate cultural politics, no genuinely political struggle for cultural hegemony; there can only be Oedipal revolts of genius sons against genius fathers. Second, there can be no politically relevant radical theory, no link between theory and political practice; there can only be apolitical ironist theory and atheoretical reformist practice. Thus, both culture and theory get depoliticized.

The privatization of radical theory takes its toll, too, on the shape of the political. In Rorty's hands, politics assumes an overly communitarian and solidary character, as if in reaction against the extreme egotism and individualism of his conception of theory. Thus, we can supposedly go straight from objectivity to solidarity, from the metaphysical comfort of traditional philosophy to the communitarian comfort of a single "we." Here, Rorty homogenizes social space, assuming, tendentiously, that there are no deep social cleavages capable of generating conflicting solidarities and opposing "we's." It follows from this assumed absence of fundamental social antagonisms that politics is a matter of everyone pulling together to solve a common set of problems. Thus, social engineering can replace political struggle. Disconnected tinkerings with a succession of allegedly discrete social problems can replace transformation of the basic institutional structure. And the expert social problem solver and top-down reformer can replace the organized social movement of people collectively articulating their own interests and aspirations, as the political agent gets typified by the social worker or the engineer instead of by, say, the members of the National Welfare Rights Organization or of the Clamshell Alliance. Moreover, with no deep rifts or pervasive axes of domination, practice can float entirely free of theory. If there are no mechanisms of subordination inscribed in the basic institutional framework of society, then *a fortiori* there can be no need to theorize them. Thus, politics can be detheoreticized.

Clearly, this cultural map presupposed a substantive political diagnosis, one with which I shall later take issue. But is also possesses a noteworthy formal feature: Rorty's conceptions of politics and of theory are obverses of one another. If theory is hyperindividualized and depoliticized, then politics is hypercommunalized and detheoreticized. As theory becomes pure *poesis*, then politics approaches pure *techne*. Moreover, as theory is made the preserve of pure transcendence, then politics is banalized, emptied of radicalism and of desire. Finally, as theory becomes the production *ex nihilo* of new metaphors, then politics must be merely their literalization; it must be application only, never invention.

It is paradoxical that such a dichotomous picture should be the upshot of a body of thought that aimed to soften received dichotomies like theory *versus* practice, aesthetic *versus* moral, science *versus* literature. It is also paradoxical that what was supposed to be a political polylogue comes increasingly to resemble a monologue.

Consider that Rorty makes nonliberal, oppositional discourses nonpolitical by definition. Such discourses are associated by him with romanticism, the quest for the uncharted. They are made the prerogative of free-floating intellectuals who are bored with widely disseminated vocabularies and who crave the new and the interesting. Radical discourses, then, are inflected as a turning away from the concerns of collective life. Thus, Rorty casts the motive for oppositional discourse as aesthetic and apolitical. He casts the subject of such discourses as the lone, alienated, heroic individual. And he casts the object or topic of radical discourses as something other than the needs and problems of the social collectivity.

With radical discourses thus aestheticized and individualized— indeed Oedipalized and masculinized—political discourse, in turn, is implicitly deradicalized. Political discourse in fact is restricted by Rorty to those who speak the language of bourgeois liberalism. Whoever departs from that vocabulary simply lacks any sense of solidarity. Likewise, it turns out that the adherents of bourgeois liberalism have a monopoly on talk about community needs and social problems. Whoever eschews the liberal idiom must be talking about something else—about, say, individual salvation.

Thus, in Rorty's recent essays social solidarity and nonliberal discourses are seen as antithetical to one another. Discourse rooted in solidarity and oriented to collective concerns is restricted to liberal problem solving. Nonliberal discourse, on the other hand, is reduced to aestheticism, apoliticism, and romantic individualism.

Clearly, this way of mapping the discursive terrain effects some significant exclusions. There is no place in Rorty's framework for *political* motivations for the invention of new idioms, no place for idioms invented to overcome the enforced silencing or muting of disadvantaged social groups. Similarly, there is no place for *collective* subjects of nonliberal discourses, hence, no place for radical discourse communities that contest dominant discourses. Finally, there is no place for *nonliberal* intepretations of social needs and collective concerns, hence, no place for, say, socialist-feminist politics. In sum, there is no place in Rorty's framework for genuinely radical political discourses rooted in *oppositional* solidarities.

Thus, Rorty ends up supposing there is only one legitimate political vocabulary, thereby betraying his own professed commitment to a polylogical politics. This, too, is a paradoxical result for a thought that seemed always to insist on the decisive importance of vocabulary choice for the framing of issues.

In any case and whatever his intentions, by dichotomizing private and public, singular individual and homogeneous community, Rorty cuts out the ground for the possibility of democratic radical politics.

How can we build this possibility back into the picture? How can we retrieve a version of pragmatism which is compatible with radical democracy, polylogical abnormal political discourse and socialist-feminist politics?

RECIPE FOR A DEMOCRATIC-SOCIALIST-FEMINIST PRAGMATISM

Rorty has recently summarized the aim of his latest round of essays: "to separate . . . 'postmodernism' from political radicalism[,] polemics against 'the metaphysics of presence' from polemics against 'bourgeois ideology', criticisms of Englightenment rationalism and universalism from criticisms of liberal, reformist, political thought."[21]

In contrast, I would like to summarize *my* aim in the present essay: to separate pragmatism from cold war liberalism, polemics against traditional foundationalist philosophy from polemics against social theory, criticisms of romantic Sorelian politics from criticisms of radical democratic-socialist-feminist politics.

Let me conclude by sketching very roughly how such a separation can be effected. Since the point is to show that one can indeed put asunder what Rorty hath joined together, my sketch will be a recipe for an alternative combination, a democratic-socialist-feminist pragmatism.[22]

Begin with the sort of zero-degree pragmatism that is compatible with a wide variety of substantive political views, with socialist feminism as well as bourgeois liberalism. This pragmatism is simply anti-essentialism with respect to traditional philosophical concepts like truth and reason, human nature and morality.[23] It implies an appreciation of the historical and socially constructed character of such categories and of the practices they get their sense from, thereby suggesting at least the abstract possibility of social change. This sort of zero-degree pragmatism is a useful, though hardly all-sufficing, ingredient of socialist feminism.

Then, add the kind of zero-degree holism that combines easily with radical democratic politics. This holism is simply the sense of the difference between the frame of a social practice and a move within it. It implies an appreciation of the way background institutions and habits prestructure the foreground possibilities available to individuals in social life. This zero-degree holism does not necessarily lead to conservative politics. On the contrary, it is a necessary ingredient for any politics that aspires to radical social transformation as opposed to simple amelioration.

Next, add a keen sense of the decisive importance of language in political life. Mix with the pragmatism and the holism until you get a distinction between making a political claim in a taken-for-granted vocabulary and switching to a different vocabulary. This distinction clears a space for those far-reaching redescriptions of social life at the heart of every new political vision, from bourgeois liberalism to Marxism to contemporary feminism. This distinction also allows for contestatory interactions among competing political vocabularies. It thus makes conceivable the sort of robust, polylogical abnormal discourse that is essential to radical democratic politics in a multicultural society.

Next, add a view of contemporary societies as neither hyperindividualized nor hypercommunitarian. This view should allow for social divisions capable of generating multiple, competing solidarities and multiple, competing political vocabularies. It should allow also for inequality and for power. Thus, it should distinguish dominant from subordinated solidarities, hegemonic from counterhegemonic vocabularies. This view of society should be mixed with the preceding ingredients to get a keen sense of social contestation.

Contestation, in turn, should be broadly conceived to include struggle over cultural meanings and social identities as well as over more narrowly traditional political stakes like electoral office and legislation. It should encompass struggles for cultural hegemony, the power to construct authoritative definitions of social situations and legitimate interpretations of social needs. This broad sense of contestation allows for a politics of culture that cuts across traditional divisions between public and private life. It allows also for the possibility of radical democratic social movements: broad, informally organized, collective formations wherein politics and poetry form an unbroken continuum as struggles for social justice shade into the unleashing of creativity.

Next, add a view of social change as neither determined by an autonomous logic of history nor as simply contingent and utterly inexplicable. Consider the agents of historical change to be social movements rather than extraordinary individuals. Avoid a rigid, dichotomous opposition between playing the game in the same old way and starting completely from scratch; between boring, stable, frozen normality and the sudden, novel bolt from the blue. Avoid, also, a dichotomy between sheer invention and mere application, between the heretofore undreamt of and its routinization. Instead, see these extremes as mediated in the social practice of social movements. See such practice as spanning the gulf between the old and the new, as application that is always at the same time invention. This allows for the possibility of a radical politics that is not Sorelian, not the expression of the elitist and masculinist will to the wholly other. It allows for the possibility of a radical democratic politics in which immanent critique and transfigurative desire mingle with one another.

Next, add the view that, multiplicity and contestation notwithstanding, contemporary societies are organized around a basic institutional framework. Of course, any precise characterization of the structure of this framework will suppose contestable political commitments and a contestable political vocabulary. Nonetheless, suppose that among the candidates for core elements of this framework are ingredients like the following: an organization of social production for private profit rather than for human need; a gender-based division of social labor that separates privatized childrearing from recognized and remunerated work; gender- and race-segmented paid labor markets that generate a marginalized underclass; a system of nation-states that engage in crisis management in the form of segmented social welfare concessions and subsidized war production.

Now, add to this the possibility that the basic institutional framework of society could be unjust, that it could work to the systematic detriment of some social groups and to the systematic profit of others. Stir with the preceding ingredients to get a sense of the possible political uses of a critical social theory. Consider, for example, the utility of a theory that could specify links among apparently discrete social problems via the basic institutional structure, thereby showing "how things, in the broadest sense, hang together, in the broadest sense."[24] or consider the utility of a social theory able to distinguish system-conforming reforms that perpetuate injustices, on the one hand, from radical and empowering social changes, on the other hand.

Next, add some distinctions among different kinds of theories. Distinguish, for example, traditional, ahistorical foundationalist theories, as in epistemology or moral philosophy, from the ironist pragmatic metatheories that provide their critique. Then, distinguish both of these from a third kind of theory, to wit, first-order, substantive social theory that is nonfoundational, fallibilistic, and historically specific. Now, use these distinctions to avoid throwing out the baby of critical social theory with the bathwater of traditional philosophy. Use them, also, to avoid conflating social theory with Heideggerian bathos, private irony or Oedipal hijinks. Instead, use these distinctions to make room for politically relevant radical social theory and thus for theoretically informed radical democratic politics.

Then, add a non-Leninist, nonvanguardist conception of the role of intellectuals in radical leftwing democratic politics. Think of such intellectuals first and foremost as members of social groups and as participants in social movements. Think of them, in other words, as occupying specifiable locations in social space rather than as freefloating individuals who are beyond ideology. Think of them, in addition, as having acquired as a result of the social division of labor some politically useful occupational skills: for example, the ability to show how the welfare system institutionalizes the feminization of poverty or how a poem orientalizes its subject. Think of them as potentially capable of utilizing these skills both in specialized institutions like universities and in the various larger cultural and political public spheres. Think of them, thus, as participants on several fronts in struggles for cultural hegemony. Think of them, also, alas, as mightily subject to delusions of grandeur and as needing to remain in close contact with their political comrades who are not intellectuals by profession in order to remain sane, level headed, and honest.

Combine all these ingredients with a nonindividualist, nonelitist, nonmasculinist utopian vision. Articulate this utopian vision in terms of relations among human beings instead of in terms of individuals considered as separate monads. Imagine new relations of work and play, citizenship and parenthood, friendship and love. Then, consider what sort of institutional framework would be needed to foster such relations. Situate these relations in the institutional framework of a classless, multicultural society without racism, sexism, or heterosexism, an international society of decentralized, democratic, self-managing collectivities.

Combine all the above ingredients and season to taste with social hope. Garnish with just the right mix of pessimism of the intellect and optimism of the will.

NOTES

This essay is reprinted from Nancy Fraser, *Unruly Practices: Power, Discourse, and Gender in Contemporary Social Theory* (Minneapolis: University of Minnesota Press, 1989). Copyright ©1989 by the Regents of the University of Minnesota. Reproduced courtesy of the University of Minnesota Press. I am grateful to Jonathan Arac for suggesting this title as well as for the invitation that provided the occasion for writing this essay. I benefited from helpful discussions with Jonathan Arac, Sandra Bartky, Jerry Graff, Carol Kay, Tom McCarthy, Linda Nicholson, Joe Rouse, Michael Williams, and Judy Wittner and from stimulating questions from members of the audience at the English Institute, Harvard University, August 1987. Richard Rorty generously provided copies of unpublished drafts of several essays cited here.

Epigraph: Richard Rorty, "Private Irony and Liberal Hope" in *Contingency, Irony, and Solidarity* (Cambridge: Cambridge University Press, 1989), 80.

1. It is worth recalling that one of Rorty's heroes is Harold Bloom, especially the Bloom of *The Anxiety of Influence.* My own view of the masculinist character of Rorty's romantic impulse has been influenced by the feminist critique of Bloom by Sandra M. Gilbert and Susan Gubar in *The Madwoman in the Attic: The Woman Writer and the Nineteenth-Century Literary Imagination* (New Haven: Yale University Press, 1979).

2. This is Rorty echoing Shelley. "Philosophy as Science, as Metaphor and as Politics," in *The Institution of Philosophy: A Discipline in Crisis?* ed. Avner Cohen and Marcelo Descal (La Salle, Ill.: Open Court Publishing Co., 1989), 17, 21.

3. "The Contingency of Community," *London Review of Books,* 24 July 1986, 11, 13. A revised version of this essay appears under the title "The Contingency of a Liberal Community" in Rorty, *Contingency, Irony, and Solidarity.*

4. The choice of Sorel as the personification of this possibility is mine, not Rorty's. He tends rather to represent it with Lenin. In my view, Lenin is far less appropriate here than Sorel. The "sociology," "theory of action" and "philosophy of history" I have sketched bear little resemblance to Lenin's and much to Sorel's. Moreover, Sorel's much greater ambiguity in terms of standard notions of right and left better captures the flavor of the sort of political romanticism I am trying to characterize here. Finally, Rorty's choice of Lenin as the personification of romanticism run amok is an anti-Marxist political gesture that I do not wish to repeat. In general, Rorty shows no awareness of the tradition of Western Marxism nor of attempts within Marxism to find alternatives to vanguardist conceptions of the relation between theory and practice.

5. "Solidarity or Objectivity?" in *Post-Analytic Philosophy,* ed. John Rajchman and Cornel West (New York: Columbia University Press, 1985), 3–19.

6. "The Priority of Democracy to Philosophy," in *The Virginia Statute for Religious Freedom*, ed. Merrill Peterson and Robert Vaughn (Cambridge: Cambridge University Press, 1988), 272–73. See also "From Logic to Language to Play," *Proceedings and Addresses of the American Philosophical Association* 59 no. 2 (1986): 747–53.

7. "The Contingency of Community," 14.

8. "Private Irony and Liberal Hope," 89, 94–95.

9. Ibid., 87–91.

10. "Habermas and Lyotard on Postmodernity," in *Habermas and Modernity*, ed. Richard J. Bernstein (Cambridge: Polity Press, 1985); Richard Rorty, "Method, Social Science and Social Hope," *Consequences of Pragmatism: Essays 1972–1980* (Minneapolis: University of Minnesota Press, 1982); "Thugs and Theorists: A Reply to Bernstein," *Political Theory* 15, no. 4 (1987): 564–80.

11. "Philosophy as Science, as Metaphor and as Politics," 13, 21.

12. "The Priority of Democracy to Philosophy," 263, 270–71.

13. "Habermas and Lyotard on Postmodernity," 175.

14. "Self-Creation and Affiliation: Proust, Nietzsche, and Heidegger," in Rorty, *Contingency, Irony, and Solidarity*, 100, 110, 114, 118–21.

15. "Self-Creation and Affiliation," 120.

16. I am grateful to Michael Williams for the suggestion that Rorty's view of the intellectual here is that of the Aesthete.

17. "Posties," *London Review of Books*, 3 September 1987, 11.

18. "Private Irony and Liberal Hope," 92–93.

19. This problem is posed but by no means resolved in Mill's *On Liberty.*

20. To insist on the power-laden and therefore political character of these matters is not necessarily to authorize unlimited state intervention. One can favor, instead, the use of nongovernmental counterpowers like social movements and democratic political associations. This is the view of many feminists, including myself, with respect to pornography: pornography that is harmful to women in a diffuse rather than a direct way is better opposed via boycotts, pickets, counterpropaganda, and consciousness raising than by state censorship.

21. "Thugs and Theorists," 564.

22. The recipe form has a number of advantages, not least of which is a certain gender resonance. In choosing this genre, I am taking seriously Rorty's

implicit assimilation of theorizing to housework. For me, however, this means deprivatizing housework rather than privatizing theory. It also suggests a non-technocratic and more genuinely pragmatic view of the relation between theory and practice, since cooks are expected to vary recipes in accordance with trial and error, inspiration, and the conjunctural state of the larder. Finally, the recipe form has the advantage of positing the outcome as a concoction rather than as a system or synthesis. It thus avoids those hyperbolic forms of theoretical totalization of which the democratic left has rightly grown suspicious.

23. "Pragmatism, Relativism and Irrationalism," in *Consequences of Pragmatism*, 162.

24. This is one of Rorty's favorite positive characterizations of philosophy. He attributes the characterization to Wilfred Sellars.

Anthony Appiah

Tolerable Falsehoods

AGENCY AND THE INTERESTS OF THEORY

Wittgenstein is widely regarded as having argued for a variety of relativism: more precisely, for the view that questions of truth and rationality can be assessed only from within what he called a "form of life." Thus Peter Winch argues—with explicit debt to Wittgenstein—in a famous paper, "Understanding Primitive Religion," that Evans-Pritchard was wrong to claim that the witchcraft beliefs of the Azande were "not in accord with objective reality" because the notion of according or failing to accord with an objective reality is one that we cannot apply to whole conceptual frameworks, whole languages. For, Winch says, "Reality is not what gives language sense. What is real and unreal shows itself in the sense that language has."[1] This characteristically Wittgensteinian apothegm—characteristic, that is, of Wittgensteinians, if not of Wittgenstein—is (characteristically) not as transparent as we might like. But we may take from Winch's discussion the idea that, for the Wittgensteinians, questions of truth and rationality must always arise within a form of life; and, since a form of life is the way in which a certain community "goes on," we may see them as claiming that it is only from within the practices of a certain community—against a background in which these practices are taken as given—that we can ask the questions "Is this so?" and "Is that reasonable?".

It follows also that the practice of reflecting on practices (which we can call "theory" or "philosophy," depending on the context) itself must occur within a given framework, against the background of the givens of a certain community; and, since every practice can be judged only by its own standards, we are left with the conclusion that Wittgenstein expressed in the formula: "Philosophy leaves everything as it is."

I trust that you will by now have gathered that I am not really talking about Wittgenstein or even, insofar as they are philosophers by profession, of Wittgensteinians: the resonances with a certain other way of going on—one that also speaks of the communities only within which interpretation is possible—and that claims, also, that philosophy (which it usually calls "theory") has no consequences, "leaves everything as it is," are clear enough. I mention Wittgenstein only because, from my own institutional position as a professor of philosophy, his is the label under which these questions first addressed themselves to me, and because, having so placed the issues, there is, for me, a familiar sequence of moves which surrounds both the claim that theory is consequenceless and the view of interpretation which undergirds it. I proceed, then, with a certain understanding of the Wittgensteinian arguments for the inconsequentiality of theory; I also have conjectures, which I have no space to discuss here, about what made them attractive.

Writing six years ago, Franco Moretti observed that "in the rather frenetic world of literary criticism, theoretical speculation enjoys the same symbolic status as cocaine: one *has* to try it."[2] Today, on the issue of theory, a new vanguard seems to take as its motto: Just say no. I suppose I should begin in this spirit then, by confiscating some paraphernalia; and it is to that main business that Wittgenstein will come to be relevant. But the paraphernalia I wish to confiscate are precisely not the instruments of what the new pragmatists have called "theory"; and by the end, let me warn you, even Wittgenstein will have disappeared from view and we shall be left in the looming shadow of Marx.

I want to start, then, by identifying in the project of the recent versions of historicist criticism problems that only reflection on theory—on the nature of interpretation—can uncover and correct. Such an offense will be not only more interesting than a mere defense of theory but also, in the end, as I hope, more instructive. What I want to argue is that theoretical reflection is necessary not least because the project that, for example, Walter Benn Michaels, advocate of a Wittgensteinian form of "pragmatism," is engaged in—the project that flies under the banner of a reconstituted historicism—is one that shares with much current theory—notably both discourse theory and poststructuralism—a problem in the presuppositions of its account of structure and agency.

That there are thought to be problems here will hardly be news to anyone who has been following the conversations that surround the practice of theory, but my object will be to try to relocate our understanding of the issues. As you will see, my sense is that the problem is with our setting up of the problem. My sentiments about the current debate are those of the unhelpful peasant—in England it is always an Irishman—who is supposed to have answered the visiting tourist's question, "How would you get to Dublin?" with the thoughtful response: "I would not start from here."

Still, it will be as well to start by saying where I think "here" is. The "problem of agency" in the kind of cultural analysis that Michaels wishes to make possible is conceived of as a problem of its relation to the general structuring of the social world within which agency occurs. That Michaels (for whom, of course, there are no theoretical problems) considers it at least a practical problem—a problem that arises in critical practice—is clear in the introduction to *The Gold Standard and the Logic of Naturalism.* Here he is revising his own earlier account of *Sister Carrie,* an account that represented the novel as an "unequivocal endorsement" of "the unrestrained capitalism of the late nineteenth and early twentieth centuries."

> Almost as soon as that essay was published, however, I began to feel unhappy with this aspect of its argument . . . What exactly did it mean to think of Dreiser as approving (or disapproving) consumer culture? Although transcending your origins to evaluate them has been the opening move in cultural criticism at least since Jeremiah, it is surely a mistake to take this move at face value: not so much because you can't really transcend your culture but because, if you could, you wouldn't have any terms of evaluation left—except, perhaps, theological ones.[3]

This move will, I hope, seem reminiscent of the Wittgensteinian argument with which I began. Michaels is proposing (as Fish is) that we can interpret agents—in this case Dreiser—only if we see them as operating within the cultural structures of their place and moment (what Michaels sometimes calls the cultural "system," but more frequently crystallizes into a regularity named "logic": the logic of capitalism, the logic of naturalism, etc.). Once we so see agents, we also see that there is no other space and time from which they have access to their own worlds. What gives rise to Michaels's and Fish's suspicion of theory is the reasonable insistence that if we accept this point, we should apply it also to ourselves.

This much must be granted as a practical tautology: each of us has a perspective, and it is simply that of our place and time. But Michaels draws the further conclusion that Dreiser cannot truly endorse or question capitalism because he is enmeshed in the structures—the logic—of a capitalist society; thus, in a parallel move, Winch argued that the Zande cannot question witchcraft because, in Evans-Pritchard's memorable phrase, "they cannot think their own thought is wrong."

This position can leave us with the sort of "damned if you do, damned if you don't" that leads Stephen Greenblatt to argue, in a typically challenging moment of paradox, that the "ideal image" of the prince in *1 Henry IV* "involves as its positive condition the constant production of its own radical subversion and the powerful containment of that subversion."[4] If subversion is the always necessarily contained product of power, then here, indeed, is a prison house from which there is no escape.

Such a juxtaposition is, to be sure, one that may mislead: Greenblatt's historical arguments, which increasingly center on a dialectic of subversion and containment, are formally very different from Michaels's. Greenblatt unmasks subversion as something orthodoxy produces for its own ends; Michaels questions the possibility of real subversion on, as it were, analytical grounds. And I shall want to insist later that there is an important difference between the Wittgensteinian style of argument—whose point is essentially logical and a priori—that we find in Michaels, and the sorts of Marxian and post-Marxian claims for the pervasive authority of the social order which we find in Greenblatt. Still, these two proof texts can serve to identify a certain tendency, in these contemporary modes of historicism, to what I shall be calling "structural determinism": to the view that, once an agent's sociocultural location is fixed, his or her capacities for and in agency are fixed also; and, more particularly, that we will understand the outcome of social process only as the consequence of social structure and not "merely" as the result of individual acts.

What is common to the space of problems I have in mind is more general, however, than a structural (or discursive or material) determinism of the individual agent; for, because these theorists attend to a textual world, they tend also to be skeptical of allowing much individual effectivity for texts. Michaels's *Sister Carrie*, as we saw, cannot challenge capitalism. So too, for Greenblatt, mechanisms of containment largely prevent Shakespeare's history plays from challenging kingship:

> There are moments [Greenblatt writes] in *Richard II* in which the collapse of kingship seems to be confirmed in the discovery of the physical body of the ruler, the pathos of his creatural existence:
>
> > "throw away respect,
> > Tradition, form, and ceremonious duty,
> > For you have but mistook me all this while.
> > I live with bread like you, feel want,
> > Taste grief, need friends: subjected thus,
> > How can you say to me I am a king?" (III.ii.172-77)
>
> By the close of *2 Henry IV* such physical limitations have been absorbed into the ideological structure, and hence justification, of kingship.[5]

It is a tribute to the ease of Greenblatt's structural determinism that this last sentence does not even need to begin with a concessive "But."

Of course, this problem is one of which the new historicism is profoundly—indeed obsessively—aware. Thus Greenblatt's analysis of the Renaissance subject as "the ideological product of the relations of power in a particular society" gains part of its point by contrast to the Renaissance ideology of freedom.[6] But it will be important to remind you now that the kind of structural determinism I have in mind is not distinctive of new historicism in particular: I shall be trying to understand a tendency that is found also in culturalism; in talk of the "system"; and in Foucaultian theories in which what is determining is called "discourse," and which leave us a conception of the subject which is purely epiphenomenal. I insist on the generality of the problem not least because to recognize what is common to all these names for what is determining is already to escape a metaphorics of structure which leads us to envision a sort of Buckminster Fullerish geodesic, all flat planes and hard edges, something starkly determinate; and to remember that "structure," too, is the name of certain actually rather fluid and diffuse power relations—both material and (in those theories that have space for this contrast) ideological.

Indeed, once this is said, we can recognize in this classic antinomy of social theory—the agon of structure and agency—what is also, perhaps, the central issue in the high humanist criticism of this century, one variously formulated by Thomas McFarland (as the originality paradox), Harold Bloom (as a problematics of influence), and Walter Jackson Bate (as the burden of the past): but let us take, for auld lang syne, the Eliotic formula, "tradition and the individual talent" as its emblem.

To announce structural or cultural determinism as a problem, however, is not yet to show that it is one; nor can my simplifying account of contemporary historicism be taken as the whole story. There are always moments of genuine contradiction in, for example, the historicisms of Louis Montrose or (to cross the Atlantic) the "cultural materialism" represented by Jonathan Dollimore—moments when textual and individual agency appear to escape the constraints of the structure.[7]

Indeed, Montrose has issued a programmatic statement on the problem in an essay, "Renaissance Literary Studies and the Subject of History" in *English Literary Renaissance,* where he seems to say precisely what needs saying. Montrose begins by citing Perry Anderson to the effect that "the nature of the relationships between structure and subject in human history and society" is the "one master-problem around which *all* contenders have revolved" in social theory today.[8] And he continues:

> The freely self-creating and world-creating subject of bourgeois humanism is now (at least in theory) defunct. The recent trend in a variety of disciplines has been a perhaps overcompensatory positing of subject as wholly determined by structure. I believe we should resist the inevitably reductive tendency to think in terms of a subject/structure opposition. Instead, we might entertain the propositions that subject and structure, the processes of

subjectification and structuration, are interdependent, and thus intrinsically social and historical; that social systems are produced and reproduced in the interactive social practices of individuals and groups; that collective structures may enable as well as constrain individual agency; that the possibilities and patterns for action are always socially and historically situated, always limited and limiting; and that there is no necessary relationship between the intentions of actors and the outcomes of their actions.[9]

I remarked that this passage *seems* to say what needs saying because, it does only seem to say it: as I shall try to show, the initially correct move of challenging the subject/structure opposition is followed by a gradual series of concessions to precisely that opposition; concessions that end by conceding too much.

Notice that what Montrose proposes that we accept, in lieu of such an opposition—apart from the uncontroversial point that structure is the product of human action—is an insistence that structure is "limited and limiting" so that agency—the intentions of actors—has no guarantee of efficacy. My point is not to deny any of this; it is rather to note that in response to a legitimate sense of a "perhaps overcompensatory positing of the subject as wholly determined by structure"—the claim that structure *must* determine agency—Montrose implies that we should say only that structure *may* determine agency. This is interesting because it has a corollary that Montrose chooses not to stress: namely that there can be agency that is *not* structurally determined.

In fact, even this consequence is only implicated, not asserted; for it would be consistent with the truism that we may not succeed in doing what we intend to do to suppose that even in those cases in which we *do* succeed, we remain determined because our intentions are determined by the structure—that class position, for example, determines what we will; that ideology determines what an author desires or is able to represent. What Montrose does not say is that there can be moments when what happens—and, in particular, what is done by a text—is something that is not determined by the structure, but rather by the character—in the language of the romantic ideology of the self, one might say the genius—of the individual agent, the author; and by aspects of that character which are not themselves socially determined.

I observe, then, that Montrose, even in remarking the dangers of structural determinism, is drawn, once more, into its embrace.

The story so far is this. Humanist criticism overplayed the self-reflexive actor, the autonomous individual, the subject. Structuralism and then poststructuralism responded by overplaying structure (alias: totality, systematicity, even "discourse"). The new historicism, while inheriting a theoretical suspicion of the subject, asks for balance: yet in that very moment of synthesis it seems irresistibly drawn back toward structure, now not as determining but as primary. My object in what remains of this essay is to try to explore the problematic that generates the tar baby of structural determinism, the presuppositions that make it stick.

Let me begin again in what is for me the easiest place, namely with a Wittgensteinian argument for the "form of life" as explanatory bedrock in social thought. Let us grant, for the moment, that our common conceptual life, which Wittgenstein identifies with our ability—in a characteristically laconic formulation—to "go on in the same way," cannot be seen as founded in something else: that, so to say, there is no explanation of why it is that after a certain amount of what we call "training" most children can proceed with the number series, following 1000 by 1001 and 1002 and not, as Wittgenstein often asked us to imagine, 1002 and 1004. Wittgenstein wants us to accept that there is no explanatory force in the claim that the child who does this has "grasped the principle of adding 1"; that to say this is only to say in another way that the child knows how to go on . . . which is itself only to say that he or she goes on as all suitably equipped humans go on after the same sort of what we call "training." It is an easy step from here to the thought that there really is no place outside the practice of using numerals in the way we do from which to assess that practice. Within the practice, "4 plus 4 makes 8" is right, "4 plus 4 makes 9" is wrong; there is no question of what 4 and 4 makes outside the practice of enumeration. To understand elementary arithmetic is to participate in the practice: what is available outside the practice is not a review of arithmetical practice but only no arithmetical understanding at all.

Wittgenstein wants us to stop simply with the recognition that it is part of the natural history of our species that most of us can count.

The generalization of this point in the direction that will lead Michaels to wonder whether Dreiser can evaluate capitalism requires us first to see that the concepts through which Dreiser understands the social world of *Sister Carrie*—concepts such as *market, price* and *value*—are themselves constituted through certain practices, certain ways of going on: and to participate in the appropriate way in those ways of going on is to have concepts of price and value, to live one's life through those practices and, thus, equivalently, under those concepts. There is, then, as the argument proceeds, no place outside those practices to discuss and evaluate price: only within the world of price and value is there anything to discuss.

In particular, the concepts of *right* and *property* and *worth*, which we may use to discuss the value of particular commodities, belong to the practices of commodity capitalism; and so they cannot provide the resources for a conceptual demolition of it.

I imagine this line of thought will seem plausible to many, but there is a practical inadequacy in this Wittgensteinian argument; or rather, there are at least two.

The first is one to which the new historicists have been acutely sensitive, drawing as they do on a century of Marxist thought: and it is, of course, that the fact that a practice exists does not entail that it is without those tensions, that potential for agonistic exchange, which Marxism calls "contradiction." (Indeed, contradiction and mediation are a common focal point in the readings produced by new historicist Renaissance critics and their "cultural materialist" cousins in England.) If one were to put this point in Wittgensteinian terminology one might say, simply, that we all participate in a complex network of interacting forms of life; there may be no singular "logic" of cultural capitalism, no unitary logic of naturalism either. "Value" as we experience it as sellers of labor and as consumers of commodities is not identical; as deconstruction might lead us to recognize, we cannot sum our many practices into a single homogeneous totalized practice. (The eighteenth-century legal practices that help give meaning to the word *liberty* in the

Declaration of Independence exist in the same space as those that give meaning to *chattel-slavery*. Mill, on the "Subjection of Women," uses no concepts from outside the world, the practices, the form of life, of the nineteenth-century culture that deprives married women of rights in property.)

If that is the first inadequacy, the second is that we have not yet, nor will we ever have, exhausted the range of practices that can become possible for human beings: if there is a human nature, it will never be fully explored. Even if the conceptual resources do not exist for a challenge to existing practices, that does not mean that they cannot become possible. Technological determinists will hold that what makes these new possibilities is technological change and the changing relations of production that it makes possible; but, whatever their sources, new practices—and thus new concepts—are perpetually becoming available.[10]

To proceed with this argument, framed this way, however, is still to concede what I want finally to deny: namely, that the opposition of structure and agency has been properly framed here in the first place. Before advancing, finally, to what I believe is a more adequate framing of these issues, it is crucial, I think, to distinguish them from a confusingly similar range of considerations drawn from recent social theory. And we must begin by repeating that these arguments that I have been styling "Wittgensteinian" are logical arguments, not psychological ones. To say this is to say that (paradoxically) they are theoretical arguments of the purest sort, deriving from reflection on such *concepts* as *agent, rule,* and *social norm,* not from a posteriori explorations of the specific historical configurations in which agents live by these rules or under those norms. This is paradoxical because it is the anti–theory Michaels who is, along with Stanley Fish, most clearly committed to this most theoretical of lines of argument.

There is, however, a very different line of argument, one that depends on claims about individual and social psychology, that might lead to the view that we cannot escape the demands of our own culture. It is the argument, I think, that has sometimes tempted Montrose and

Greenblatt; and it claims that, *as a matter of fact*, the mechanisms of social reproduction—the family, the school, all the ideological apparatus—capture the thoughts (or determine the subjectivity) of all the subjects of the modern state, making it impossible as a matter not of logic but of psychology, of subject formation, for us to see and thus to escape what is going on. This claim is, *as a matter of fact*, simply hyperbolic.

As so many recent theorists have insisted—as Orwell argued through his imaginative fantasy—hegemony of this sort is never achieved: the detailed empirical examination of contemporary working-class attitudes in industrialized societies; the historical exploration by Ginzburg, for example, or by Keith Thomas, of heresy in preindustrial Europe; the anthropological exploration of the ideologies of subject peoples in Africa's feudal empires; all of them show, again and again, that the ideology of the ruling estates is not usually (perhaps not ever) simply accepted by the ruled.[11] Indeed, in a practical way, the rulers have always known this, which is why the state has claimed and exercised a certain monopoly of the coercive power of literal force.

The issues raised by this second form of argument for the inescapability of an allegedly totalizing hegemony are interesting and important for cultural studies: a proper theorizing of these issues—of the sort I believe we are beginning to see in the works of Laclau and Mouffe, or in Giddens, to take only two exemplars—is crucial and will reveal the reality of ruling ideology—the ideology of the center—at the same time as stressing its complexity, its contingent and contradictory character, and the complementary resisting ideologies of the periphery.[12]

Now it is, of course, his recognition that the view of hegemony as absolute *is* hyperbolic that accounts, of course, for the hesitations I cited earlier in Montrose.[13] But once we have distinguished these two very different arguments for structural determinism, it is tempting to offer the following diagnosis: Michaels's argument—the "Wittgensteinian" argument of the new pragmatists—accounts for the air of tautology about the claims of structural determinism; while the a posteriori claims for the power of the system give them their substance . . . too much substance. In short, I suspect that the plausibility of the logical arguments has led, through their confusion, to too much sympathy for the social-psychological arguments.

Nevertheless, these social-psychological arguments share with the Wittgensteinian ones what I shall argue is the crucial presupposition of the whole debate over structure and agency. Like Montrose, then, I believe "we should resist the inevitably reductive tendency to think in terms of a subject/structure opposition"; but unlike him, what I believe we need to substitute is not a conception of these notions as causally related in some new and subtler mode. Rather, I think, we should try to understand what it would be not to see structure and agency as competing at the same level of explanation at all.

To come, at last, to a thesis: it is my claim that the whole debate over structure and agency has tended to suppose an opposition between them in which they compete, so to speak, for the same causal space. In simpler times, the case for structure might have been put by saying that in *Native Son*, Bigger Thomas acts as he does because of his social conditioning. The case for agency, posed in terms of the same simplicity, is the case for the individual: the figure whose escape from society makes the romantic subject its most obvious epitome. To resolve this supposed tension, various dialectics have been proposed: Giddens's duality of structure, Laclau-Mouffe's insistence that "autonomy, far from being incompatible with hegemonic construction, is a form of hegemonic construction." Each of these formulations attempts to see structure as enabling agency while structure is itself constituted through action in social practices.

What I want to suggest, by contrast, is that we should see the relations between structural explanation and the logic of the subject as a competition not for causal space but for narrative space: as different levels of theory, with different constitutive assumptions, whose relations make them neither competitive nor mutually constitutive, but quite contingently complementary. If they compete for our attention, I want to argue it is as, say, *Mansfield Park* and *Childe Harold* might compete: they compete, that is, not for the truth but for our interest.

In order to make my points, let me first remind you of (a simplified view of) some familiar Habermasian apparatus. As is well known, Habermas accounts for the distinction that Dilthey had sought to establish between the *Naturwissenschaften* and the *Geisteswissenschaften* by arguing that each kind of theory is constituted by a distinct kind of interest. The natural sciences are rooted in a "knowledge-constitutive interest in possible technical control," while the knowledge-constitutive interest of the *Geisteswissenschaften* is "practical." There are many problems with this line of thought; but the idea that *interests* play a role in the constitution of areas of inquiry or of the institutions we call "disciplines," while already less specifically Habermasian, is surely something we can borrow.[14]

"Interest" here should carry both its senses: the sense in which it contrasts with disinterest and the sense in which it contrasts with a mere lack of epistemic engagement. But what should immediately draw *our* interest is the question of what it is for an interest—in any sense—to *constitute* an area of inquiry or a kind of knowledge. Here, I believe, we can draw on some recent work in the philosophy of psychology. It has been argued by many recently—Donald Davidson and Dan Dennett both, for example—that in understanding people as intentional systems—as having the beliefs, desires, intentions, and other propositional attitudes of common sense psychology—we make a certain *projection* of rationality. We ascribe beliefs and desires to people in such a way as to "make-rational" their acts.[15]

The details here are not important for what I want to say now: the crucial point is that it is also acknowledged that it is simply false to suppose that agents are generally (indeed, ever) fully rational. If this line of thought is correct, then, our psychological theories are at best implicitly conditional upon a false presupposition, at worst inevitably false.

Now at this point, it is usual to mention "idealization." As Jerry Fodor has often insisted, we should not make methodological demands of psychology that cannot be met by chemistry and physics. So, the argument goes, since it is clear that, for example, ideal gas theory is still held to be usefully explanatory because "approximately true"—we should hardly want to say that all those high school physics teachers are simply lying—why shouldn't we hold that rational psychology is useful because roughly correct also? But the crucial point here, one that often gets missed, is that what is being offered is an argument in defense of a theory that is acknowledged to be in a certain identifiable respect false: for, if I may be permitted an aphorism, being approximately true is just a special way of being false.

The same sort of problems arises for physics if, as Nancy Cartwright has argued, most of the laws of physics are false and known to be so. Here too, idealization is common; and here, as in psychological theory, the notion of approximate truth has been driven very hard. I am sure that some notion of approximate truth is needed to handle the case of psychological theory or the theory of lasers: but, as Cartwright says (apropos of idealization in physics):

> In calling something an idealization it seems not so important that the contributions from omitted factors be small [gloss: so that the theory is approximately true], but that they be ones for which we know how to correct. If the idealization is to be of use, when the time comes to apply it to a real system we had better know how to add back the contributions of the factors that have been left out . . . either the omitted factors do not matter much or we know how to treat them.[16]

There are, then, two major sources of idealization: one is approximate truth, the other is what we can call *truth under idealized assumptions*. Thus, in the case of ideal gas theory, the theory may be horribly inaccurate in its handling of a case—a gas of large molecular weight at high temperature—even though, if the explicitly counterfactual assumptions of the theory—that the gas is composed of frictionless, perfectly inelastic point masses—were true, the theory would indeed (in some sense) give the right answer.

Now the crucial point is that the question of whether we count the theory as false *simpliciter* or approximately true is a question of *judgment,* a question that may legitimately depend on our interests (in both senses). A chemistry whose practical focus is on the development of industrial dyes might, say, accept the idealizing assumption that filtered river water is H_2O; a chemistry interested in energy regulation at the cellular level probably could not. As for "approximate truth" "good enough" in the theory of, say, the laser is "good enough to build a laser that does its job."

It will have occurred to many readers, I am sure, that the alternative view—that science does not idealize—would entail the epistemological miracle of our having constructed a system of representations that fit the world, as we say, "like a glove." So that if we did not already know from the crudest epistemological reflection, we learn from recent philosophical psychology that our theories are best conceived of as idealizations, and that this means that they are both (in some sense) approximately true and conditional upon false assumptions that simplify the theoretical task. Interests constitute areas of inquiry in part by determining what sorts of falsehoods are tolerable. We do not need to keep hold of purely disinterested reasons for idealizing any more than we can insist on *un*interested ones. An idealization is a useful falsehood: if we manage disinterest and uninterest we will be left simply rejecting idealization (and thus theory) altogether; useful always means "useful for some purpose."

I would only want to add to this picture a recognition of the fact that the interests that drive theory will change—are suitable objects of historical inquiry; that they are often unlikely to be explicitly articulated, even where they are articulable; and that, in one of those many subtle dialectics that inform historical process, the ways in which they change may themselves be driven by the very theories they constitute.

We require only one more piece of paraphernalia before the argument can be made complete: namely, a distinction between ontological and methodological reductionism. The core of ontological reductionism in the social domain is a certain version of methodological individualism: it is what underlies the claim, which I earlier suggested was uncontroversial, that structure is, in a certain sense, the product of human action. Whatever form our social theories take—and especially if, as I believe, they should be in some important sense materialist—they must surely be consistent with the observation that social facts are composed out of human acts, intentions, beliefs, and their interactions with each other and with the nonhuman world.

I do not think that ontological reductionism of this sort is the only intelligible position. But I—and most modern intellectuals—have both a strong metaphysical predisposition toward it and a sense that there is a good deal of support in the history of science, and indeed of other kinds of knowledge, for continuing for the moment to subject our theories to this constraint. Ontological reductionism, like all metaphysics, must be seen as a high-level empirical hypothesis; but it is one that I am happy enough to go on with.

But methodological reductionism is altogether a different matter; for methodological reductionism is the view that we are bound to construct our social theories in such a way as to describe all social facts as the product of the interactions of individual agents—as understood by our best psychological theories—with each other and their environments—as understood by our best theories of those environments. It is this position that is usually intended by those who speak of methodological individualism.[17]

There is a number of fundamental difficulties with this position. One might first object, for example, by following those who have issued to the methodological reductionists a challenge: either explain to us what, say, *money, banks,* and *stocks* are in reductionist terms or give up the concepts of *money, banks,* and *stocks* in discussing social matters. Although this is a challenge that has hardly been met—that we might imagine hardly could be met—it is rhetorically effective at the price of leaving us with a mystery: the mystery of why such a reduction cannot be carried out, given the truth of ontological reductionism.

One might, therefore, want to make at least the subtler objection that the history of science is a catalogue of the errors that flow from premature attempts to constrain theories of one level by the demand that they postulate only phenomena that can be understood in terms of theories at a lower level. Theories are, like all our products, imperfect things—we are, after all, fallen creatures. Since we do not have perfect theories we might want to proceed with the best theories we can muster; and it may be that the best theory at some level, for some purposes, is better—for *those* purposes—than the best theory that meets this methodological demand. The irreducibility of current meteorology to the physics of atmospheric particles hardly warrants us in giving up the advantages of what little understanding of the climate we now seem to have; nor is it any reason to deny that those particles are all there is for the weather to be composed of. (Presumably, the conflation of ontological and methodological reductionism is part of the reason that the latter has seemed so plausible.)

I want, however, to suggest what I think is a new kind of argument against such methodological reductionism: an argument that begins with the interest relativity of idealization which I have taken some trouble to establish. The shape of the argument I must make is surely already apparent. I must argue that the understanding of agents and texts through the language of the subject is guided by different interests from the understanding that operates in the language of social structure, that these different interests make different idealizations appropriate, different falsehoods tolerable. In each of these languages, as I shall suggest, "subject" and "structure" operate: there is even an exchange of terms between these two different discursive economies. But precisely because the guiding interests are differently rooted, a simple equation of the terms as they occur in the two discourses entails a conflation of different meanings. It will follow then that there is space here for two independent but interconnected projects; it will follow, that is, if I can make a case for distinct constitutive clusters of interest. Let me begin then with the theoretical economy of the subject.

The thought is this. We are ourselves agents. Our theories of agency are connected in the directest possible way with what Habermas rather bloodlessly describes as a "practical" interest in mutual understanding; in other words, as one might more humanely express the matter, by our concern to live intelligible lives in community with other agents who are, first of all, lovers, families, and friends, and then, colleagues, officers, checkout counter assistants, garage mechanics, doctors, congressional representatives, strangers, and so on. This practical interest requires us to be able to articulate our own behavior in relation to theirs, and this we do through our understanding of them as having beliefs and intentions—in short as reasoning—and also as having passions and prejudices—in short as always potentially unreasonable. But the very theories that make this possible themselves provide terms—ranging from the most neutral—*belief*—to the most affectively inflected—*love*—which themselves come to constitute the objects of our projects: if I love you, I may want to hope that there will not be another Republican presidency this century, to fear that this is too much to hope for. So that here is an instance in which a primary interest in the coordination of behavior may lead to a theory that itself then plays a part in determining a further interest in developing the theory—which is only to say what we call our understanding of each other—in new directions.[18] In particular, in some, but not, apparently, all societies a crucial moment in the development of the language of the subject comes when agents, whose subjectivity is, of course, dialectically constituted with the theory, come to focus their interest on, as we say, themselves. Self-fashioning as a project is exactly the sort of possibility that the view I am developing intends to make intelligible.

It is a determining fact of philosophical anthropology that once there exists a human community possessed of the materials for our mutual theoretical understanding, it develops practices—which is to say common activities coordinated and understood through that understanding—that constitute them as a society: as having families and relationships, marriages and alliances, and, of course, in the end, social stratifications and contradictions determined by the conditions of scarcity which led Hobbes to his pessimistic conception of human potential and Marx to his materialism; and, more to our current purpose, that these social facts themselves become the objects of belief, of revulsion, and of desire.

The point of this story is twofold: first, to indicate the complexity of the interests that guide our understanding of each other; second, to insist that social facts themselves become the objects of that understanding through our recognition of them as the objects of our psychological attitudes and thus, in particular, make possible new interests by which the development of our understanding may be driven.

Let me call the body of propositional belief dialectically constituted by these developing interests "common sense psychology"; it is not everywhere the same, nor, certainly, everywhen. The literature on the psychological theories of classical Greece, or Yorubaland; or the history of "possessive individualism"; or the economistic rational psychology of the utilitarians; or of Freudian psychoanalytic theory, is a catalogue of its varieties. The story I have been telling is meant to persuade you that which of these theories is truest or even true is a foolish question; for to adhere to one of these visions is not simply to see the world and your fellows a certain way but to live a certain way, to care about certain things and not about others, to admire not this but that. The complex dialectic of interest and theory in each social formation engenders its own tolerable falsehoods.

The commonsense psychology of a social group is not necessarily the common property of a whole society; but it is, by its nature, a social product, not an individual possession. Much, but, of course, not all, imaginative literature understands the people who populate it through such theories: and to understand it is thus to seek to understand those theories. But in our practice with literature we can sometimes come to be interested in a fiction through our own theories, whether or not they are, whether or not we believe them to be, identical with the theories of its producers: a process perhaps best exemplified in our perpetual recasting of the dramas of past social formations. There are imaginable practices with the texts that we call "literary" which engage those texts in other ways, but they surely are not anything like the practice that we call "reading."

I turn now to the theoretical economy of the structure; but it may seem that I have, in a certain sense, already been within it all along, for the metatheoretical position from which I have spoken of the theoretical economy of the subject is one that naturally sees that subject as socially positioned, because commonsense psychology is, as I recently remarked, by its nature, a social product. But this is not exactly true, for by the theoretical economy of structure I mean not just any language in which to speak of social fact; it is rather a specific, historically determinate theoretical trajectory, which passes, let us say, through Saint Simon or Marx and which is guided by an interest, as Marx himself said, not in understanding society but in changing it.

I do not mean to insist that there can be no other kind of social theory. It seems to me quite generally to be unwise in the extreme—and here, perhaps I find myself in agreement with Knapp, Michaels, and Fish—to attempt to say in advance what sorts of theory (of what they would call "practice") there can be; and we have the historical example of the ambitions of behaviorism—the construction of a social psychology that was aimed primarily at the regulation of behavior—that demonstrates that other interests are possible. I do mean to insist that the specific interests that constituted the discourse that the new historicism inherits are Marxian, and to observe that although, as I have said several times, interest and theory develop dialectically so that there is no guarantee that the initiating cluster of interests which generated this discourse must persist, there is every reason to believe that, by and large, new historicists remain committed to a view of theory as rooted in a historical project of emancipation.

In this discourse, structure is central because of a series of preferences and beliefs; but above all because of a preference for social life without exploitation, originally conceived of as the expropriation of surplus labor. You will recall that Althusser argued persuasively that surplus value simply did not exist for Ricardo; it is only once this concept comes into view in Marx that we are able discursively to represent the specific character of exploitation under capitalism. It is precisely because it allows us to theorize an inchoate unease with capitalism through a specific theory of exploitation that the Marxist theory of the structure is so central to the emancipatory project. Only once we understand the character and mechanisms of exploitation can we begin to develop (and, at the same time, continuously to retheorize) nonexploitative practices within capitalist societies. It would be enough of an argument for the project in my view that it makes such understanding and such action possible. But I would not want to neglect the role of socialism in the constitution and the analysis of many of the emancipatory projects of decolonization. Capitalism has changed, of course;

and so the specific form of the theory of exploitation that we need to understand and to act in our world must change also. Even if it was adequate to the capitalism of his own day, the specific understanding of exploitation that underlies the Marxisms of Marx must therefore develop dialectically with capitalism and with socialist practice and theory.[19]

I hope I have said enough to justify the claim I made earlier that although agent (or subject) and structure (or society) occur in what I have been calling "commonsense psychology" and "the discourse of structure," these terms must not be seen as simply equivalent in these different contexts. In the discourse of the subject—of commonsense psychology—references to social structure must be seen as references to that structure as ordinarily conceived by agents in a specific social formation; in the discourse of structure, references to agents must be seen as references to persons largely as occupants of social positions; subject-positions as we say. Further, the range of tolerable falsehood determined by the different (developing) clusters of interest of the two discourses will mean that what is for the purposes of one project—living with a spouse of a different social class, say—an intolerable falsehood, is for the purposes of the other—deciding as a couple to work for emancipation—an acceptable simplification.

Thus, I am precisely not drawing Perry Anderson's "lesson" that structure and subject "have always been interdependent as categories."[20] To the contrary, my point is that there is much to be gained by disconnecting these concepts from each other analytically, by proceeding with the discourse of structure without seeking always an individualist, subject-based reduction. I am insisting, in fact, as perhaps in our culture only a philosopher—raised in the most totalizing of disciplinary heritages—respectably can, that there is much to be said for the noncoherence of our different theoretical practices, for the existence of theories that empower and illuminate certain projects in ways that simply say "So what" to the fact that they contradict other theories that belong to other projects.[21] Once motivated, this noncoherence can be seen as both necessary and desirable.

Indeed, we might even revise Greenblatt's remark that there can be no "exhaustive and definitive cultural poetics,"[22] and assert that there can be *many* such "exhaustive and definitive" practices, each adequate to the degree that any theoretical practice can be adequate to its own distinct constitutive project, challenging each other not for the one truth but for our time, our interest, our passion.

Still, of course, this is all too simple. In a society in which the discourse of structure is operative, the discourse of agency will have to take account of that discourse as the object of the attitudes of social agents; and the discourse of structure will be bound to acknowledge the discourse of agency because the only plausible view is that it is through this discourse that emancipation will be acted out by agents. In the end, the analytical separation of levels of theory will always be blurred in the lives of human beings who construct and are constructed as subjects by those theories.

Still, this analytical distinction does suggest a diagnosis for the problem with which I began: the problem of the irresistible attraction of structural determinism (or, I think I can now say, of the discourse of structure *tout court*, since without the notion of structure as at least partly determining, this concept lacks its distinctive content). Everything that a theory of the structure claims to explain belongs to the language, the discourse, of the structure; to insist on autonomous agency within this discourse is, if I may say so, simply to change the subject.

What my analysis also allows is an understanding of why it is that what that discourse stigmatizes as bourgeois humanism remains inescapable also. For the call of humanism in what we hopefully label "late capitalist" society is the call of our everyday affections. To tell the full story of the articulation of theory and interest in the discourse of structure would be to report the history of socialist thought; and that we cannot spin that story out of our heads is a reflection of our not living our lives through socialist theory—which is to say, equivalently, that we do not have a socialist practice. That we all know so much more about the discourse of agency is a reflection of the fact that the possession of our commonsense psychological theory is a condition in our society of being socialized (or interpellated) subject at all.

This suggests a final thought before I return to the more specific concerns of literary theory. It is only this: the fault lies not in our theories but in our praxis. To develop an emancipatory discourse that was also adequate to our everyday lives—if we were, so to speak, fully to abolish the distance between the personal and the political—would have been already to have emancipated ourselves, already to have established a liberated form of life (however this is to be theorized). In this sense theory can only proceed in a dialectical relation to practice: emancipation has to be made as well as thought.

Now, many historicist scholars today insist that the critic should acknowledge his or her own historicity, his or her own inscription in history. If this is a familiar call, it is also one usually more honored in the breach than the observance. But I hope this is just the sort of diagnosis I am gesturing toward when I claim that the tension between the individualism of late capitalist culture on the one hand, and the necessity for structural modes of explanation within the discourse of emancipation (characteristic of poststructuralist theory, as of the social theory it displaced) on the other, is displayed in the irresolvable antinomies of structure and agency that have come to plague our historicist accounts.

If there is a consequence for literary theory it is surely only this: that the dialectic between the language of genius or of individual talent and the language of tradition or of the death of the subject, the dialectic inscribed in the history of literary studies in our century, reflects the dialectic *tout court,* which is to say, reflects history. Our task would then be to learn how to find in our own histories in theory and in praxis new ways of transcending an experience of these poles as opposed: modes of experiencing them first as distinct levels of theory, competing practices rather than competing causalities; so that through the dialectic of theory and praxis we can develop toward a form of life in which they are truly unopposed because we have left both of them behind.

NOTES

1. Peter Winch, "Understanding a Primitive Society," reprinted in *Rationality*, ed. Bryan R. Wilson (Oxford: Oxford University Press, 1979), 82. (Originally published in the *American Philosophical Quarterly* 1 [1964].)

2. Franco Moretti, *Signs Taken for Wonders* (London: Verso, 1988), 2.

3. Walter Benn Michaels, *The Gold Standard and the Logic of Naturalism* (Berkeley and Los Angeles: University of California Press, 1987), 18.

4. Stephen Greenblatt, "Invisible Bullets: Renaissance Authority and Its Subversion, *Henry IV* and *Henry V*," in *Political Shakespeare: New Essays in Cultural Materialism*, ed. Jonathan Dollimore and Alan Sinfield (Ithaca: Cornell University Press, 1985), 30.

5. Ibid., 40.

6. Stephen Greenblatt, *Renaissance Self-Fashioning: From More to Shakespeare* (Chicago: University of Chicago Press, 1980), 256; cf. also 1–9.

7. Despite a broad commonality of sympathies, Dollimore's upbeat interpretations of Renaissance drama are comedies (the plays turn out to advance just the sort of radical critique Dollimore would have, had he been around); Greenblatt's readings are tragedies. But it would be a mistake to see the distance between them as one of temper: the distance, say, between Eeyore and Pooh. For Greenblatt, Dollimore's stories may be right as far as he goes, but he has only told the half of it. Dollimore, on his part, implicitly chides Greenblatt for his pessimism: "If we talk only of power producing the discourse of subversion we not only hypostatise power but also efface the cultural differences—and contexts—with the very process of containment presupposes." Besides, "although subversion may indeed by appropriated by authority for its own purposes, once installed it can be used against authority as well as used by it." Jonathan Dollimore, "Introduction: Shakespeare, Cultural Materialism and the New Historicism," in *Political Shakespeare* ed. J. Dollimore and A. Sinfield (Ithaca: Cornell University Press, 1985), 12.

8. Perry Anderson, *In the Tracks of Historical Materialism* (Chicago: University of Chicago Press, 1984), 33.

9. Louis Montrose, "Renaissance Literary Studies and the Subject of History" *English Literary Renaissance* 16, no. 1 (1986): 9–10.

10. Hence we cannot rule out what Michel Pêcheux has termed "disidentification."

11. Keith Thomas, *Religion and the Decline of Magic* (New York: Charles Scribner's Sons, 1971); Carlo Ginzburg, *The Cheese and the Worms* (Baltimore: Johns Hopkins University Press, 1980); for attitudes of the working classes in industrialized democracies, see M. Mann, "The Social Cohesion of Liberal Democracy," *American Sociological Review* 35, no. 3 (1970); cited in Alex Callinicos, *Making History* (Ithaca: Cornell University Press, 1988), 146; for an African example, see Chapter 5 of Thomas J. Lewin, *Asante before the British* (Lawrence, Kans.: Regents Press of Kansas, 1978). One should read these empirical claims in the light of such theoretical formulations as Anthony Giddens's, in which power is on *logical* grounds a reciprocal, albeit asymmetrical, relation. In this "relational sense," power, Giddens stipulates, "concerns the capabilities of actors to secure outcomes where the realization of these outcomes depends upon the agency of others . . . Social systems are constituted as regularised practices: power within social systems can thus be treated *as involving reproduced relations of autonomy and dependence in social interaction.* Power relations therefore are always *two-way*, even if the power of one actor or party in a social relation is minimal compared to another. Power relations are relations of autonomy and dependence, but even the most autonomous agent is in some degree dependent, and the most dependent actor or party in a relationship retains some autonomy." Anthony Giddens, *Central Problems in Social Theory* (Berkeley and Los Angeles: University of California Press, 1979), 93.

12. A. Giddens, *Central Problems;* E. Laclau and C. Mouffe, *Hegemony and Socialist Strategy* (London: Verso, 1985); of course I dissent from Laclau and Mouffe in accepting the topology of center and periphery.

13. It accounts, too, for Greenblatt's cautioning us—in a recent essay for a work of introductory pedagogy—against construing culture as a unified body and against presuming a straightforward relation between orthodoxy and artistic production: "I have written at moments as if art always reinforces the dominant beliefs and social structures of the culture, as if culture is always harmonious rather than shifting and conflict-ridden, and as if there necessarily is a mutually affirmative relation between artistic production and other modes of production and reproduction that make up society. At times there is precisely such an easy and comfortable conjunction, but it is by no means neces-

sary. Indeed in our own time most students of literature reserve their highest admiration for those works that situate themselves on the very edges of what can be said at a particular place and time, that batter against the boundaries of their own culture." ("Culture," in *Key Words in Contemporary Literary Studies,* ed. Frank Lentricchia and Tom McLaughlin [Chicago: University of Chicago Press, 1990], 231.)

Notice that the qualification is followed by a concession that ends not by remarking on what is not limiting in culture, but by adverting to edges, to boundaries, to a sense of structure if not as determining, then as constraining. Of course there is a good deal to say about the romance of the margins in this metaphorics, but here I want to remark only the way that the primacy of structure is always allowed "in the last instance."

In fact, the distance between Greenblatt's historical arguments and what I have been calling the "logical" argument for structural determinism may be more apparent than real if (as, for example, Carolyn Porter suggests) the relation between power and subversion which Greenblatt describes is an intrinsic one, vouchsafed by a shifting analytic of "power" as such. "It is," Porter argues, "built into a procedure which frames the discursive field in such a way that sites of potential or actual resistance are either excluded from that field or incorporated within it in terms that confirm the tautology's rule." Carolyn Porter, "Are We Being Historical Yet?" *South Atlantic Quarterly* 87, no. 4 (1988): 769.

14. J. Habermas, *Knowledge and Human Interests,* trans. J. Shapiro (Boston: Beacon Press, 1972), 135, 176. Without dwelling on the difficulties here, let me say that the distinction between a "practical" interest in mutual understanding and a "technical" interest in control is far from clear; nor is it clear how these differences in interest "constitute" a field of inquiry (though I seek to contribute to the answer to this question later); or that we should seek to understand differences between domains of knowledge at the perilous level of abstraction at which natural, social, and critical knowledge are supposed to be differentiated.

15. See, for example, D. Davidson, *Inquiries into Truth and Interpretation* (Oxford: Oxford University Press, 1984); D. Dennett, *Brainstorms* (Cambridge: Bradford Books, 1978).

16. Nancy Cartwright, *How the Laws of Physics Lie* (Oxford: Oxford University Press, 1983), 111. (The idea of ignoring factors for which we know how to account is very old: consider Anselm's discussion of the existence of God

remoto Christo. Here, removing Christ from the picture is plainly not meant to be a trivial move, a move that leaves the world "approximately" as it was. But the point of considering whether we can prove the existence of God, *remoto Christo,* is that Anselm is clear enough that he knows "how to add back the contributions of the factor[s] that have been left out.")

17. Methodological individualism is usually taken to be committed at the same time and independently to the view that the best versions of psychological theory are those of rational psychology of the sort implicit in neoclassical economics. There is a substantial body of recent argument, including, perhaps surprisingly, the arguments of a substantial group of what are called "analytical Marxists," which is committed to the both of these propositions. But, of course, the structure-agency agon has emerged in contemporary Marxism in other guises as well. Recall, for example, the crucial debate twenty years ago between Nicos Poulantzas and Ralph Miliband over the nature of the capitalist state, whose terms, you will observe, have carried over precisely in the debates that marked the emergence of contemporary New Historicism. Poulantzas objects that Miliband thinks that "social classes or 'groups' are in some way reducible to *inter-personal relations,*" and thus introduces the *"problematic of the subject,"* a "problematic of social actors, of individuals as the origin of *social action*"; Miliband, for his part, complains that Poulantzas thinks "that the structural constraints of the system are so absolutely compelling as to turn those who run the state into merest functionaries and executants of policies imposed upon them by 'the system,'" a view that leads "straight to a kind of structural determinism, or rather a structural super-determinism, which makes impossible a truly realistic consideration of the dialectical relationship between the state and 'the system.'" Nicos Poulantzas, "The Problem of the Capitalist State," and Ralph Miliband, "Reply to Nicos Poulantzas," in *Ideology in Social Science,* ed. Robin Blackburn (New York: Pantheon Books, 1973), 242, 258–59. (Reprinted from the *New Left Review* no. 58 (November–December 1969) and no. 59 (January–February 1970.)

18. You will notice here how I have been driven to narrativize this theoretical point as if these different interests, which we can presume developed historically in parallel, in fact came in succession. But to tell the tale without this misleading temporal implication is a feat beyond my narrative capacity.

19. It is in the context of this project that what I earlier called the psycho-

logical argument for structural determinism is relevant; and, since some of the original formulations of this position were, as I said, hyperbolic (which is to say, for these purposes, false in a way that did not forward the project of emancipation), the newer theories of Giddens or Laclau–Mouffe provide hope, within this discourse, of an analysis that is more adequate to its constitutive emancipatory task.

20. Anderson, *Tracks of Historical Materialism*, 54.

21. Harold Garfinkel has famously objected to Parsonian styles of explanation, that they posit the actor as a "cultural dope"; and an Althusserian account of interpellation can certainly put one in mind of an *Invasion of the Body Snatchers*, a world of mindless pod-people. Yet, in a way, these are not admissible criticisms. As I have tried to suggest, explanations inhabit particular theoretical registers; and there is often no easy currency of exchange between them. A lot that is useful to say about the Puritan revolution in England is virtually unsayable in the language of a strictly atomistic (individualist) account; it is not a weakness of biology that it has little to say about physics—which is why I have been insisting that structure and agency inhabit distinct theoretical registers, each with different explanatory and practical yields.

22. Stephen Greenblatt, *Shakespearean Negotiations: The Circulation of Social Energy in Renaissance England* (Berkeley and Los Angeles: University of California Press, 1988), 19.

Lynn Hunt

History as Gesture; or,
The Scandal of History

"Let us, from now on, be on our guard against the hallowed philosophers' myth of a 'pure, will-less, painless, timeless knower'; let us beware of the tentacles of such contradictory notions as 'pure reason,' 'absolute knowledge,' 'absolute intelligence.' All these concepts presupposed an eye such as no living being can imagine, an eye required to have no direction, to abrogate its active and interpretative powers—precisely those powers that alone make of seeing, seeing *something*. All seeing is essentially perspective, and so is all knowing. The more emotions we allow to speak in a given matter, the more different eyes we can put on in order to view a given spectacle, the more complete will be our conception of it, the greater our 'objectivity.'"

I begin with this rather long quote from Nietzsche's *Genealogy of Morals* because it very precisely and persuasively foretells the death of the transcendental knowing subject in postmodern thought. I want to focus, however, on an earlier, related statement in the same paragraph, which suggests, to me at least, the problems of this view: "'objectivity' is not meant here to stand for 'disinterested contemplation' (which is a rank absurdity) but for an ability to *have one's pros and cons within one's command and to use them or not, as one chooses*" (emphasis mine).[1] What interests me is the "as one chooses," its implications for history, for the relationships between history and literature, and more generally for disciplinary boundaries.

It is in the "as one chooses" that the gesture and the scandal of this paper can be found. But to get at this I will have to do what historians almost always do: talk about some particular histories. I am struck by the historical coincidence of a series of disputes that I hope to link together (perhaps scandalously) in an interpretive gesture of my own. On one side are the scandals of de Man and Heidegger and the dispute over the new historicism; I put these together because they all, in various ways, involve the question of how history (personal history or the history of a culture) might change our understanding of the standing of theory. On the other side are to be found a series of less well-known but nonetheless professionally public conflicts, some of them scandalous in one way or another, over the historical interpretations of Nazism, cat massacres, and false identities in the sixteenth century. The disputes among historians involve the issue of the historical discipline's relationship to theory—that is, of how theory might change our understanding of history.

The stakes in these various controversies appear on the surface to be very different, and their differences are instructive. Indeed, some might argue that the mere juxtaposition of them is a scandalous gesture; but taken together these disputes reveal shared concerns with the significance of the past, with the link between history and fiction, and especially with the status of what I will call the *gesture toward history*, by which I mean the effort to ground the truth of an analysis in a reference to historical context.

I do not intend to comment on the merits of the various positions in any of these instances, for judgment about them is not germane to my focus on the gesture toward history. Moreover, I make no claim to give anything remotely resembling an exhaustive account of any of the quarrels that I will discuss. I am more interested in the status of history in certain modes of argument and in history's relationship to fiction and theory more generally, than I am in the moral particulars of each of these cases.

At issue in the broadest sense in the Heidegger and de Man affairs is the old-fashioned question of the relationship between the ideas of an author and the circumstances of his writing. Various responses have been given to the question; but the violence, agony, and exaggeration on all sides are themselves perhaps at least as interesting as the merits of the cases made. A good example of the variety of responses can be found in the essays by Tzvetan Todorov and J. Hillis Miller in the *Times Literary Supplement* in 1988. Todorov argued that the Heidegger and de Man affairs attracted so much attention because they involved a "reassessment of the meaning of our recent past." Following this unremarkable and apparently sensible beginning, the tone of the article quickly shifts. A brief review of the strategies of the apologists for the two writers turns into a summary denunciation of postmodern intellectuals, indeed, of "a large proportion" of all intellectuals in the West for their support of violent and tyrannical political systems. "If, in [the Western countries] the franchise had been restricted to intellectuals, we would now be living under totalitarian regimes." Thus our recent past, as taught by Todorov, is a warning against the dangers of totalitarianism, which he traces in turn to the aestheticization of politics by the intellectuals. He concludes that "moderation is a more reliable virtue than extremism" (though critics might well find his style of argument anything but moderate).[2]

J. Hillis Miller takes issue with the "violence of the reaction" to the discovery of de Man's writings of 1941-42, calling this the "new moment in the *collaboration* between the university and the mass media" (emphasis mine). His willingness to compare implicitly de Man's collaborationist efforts with contemporary, journalistic accounts of the de Man and Heidegger affairs works against his important—and I think partially true—claim that the real target in the de Man affair is critical theory more generally. Surprisingly, in the contortions of his attempt to make de Man's past acceptable and especially to reread the work in order to make even de Man's earliest authorial *intentions* palatable, Miller finds himself trapped in the terms of debate as set by the critics of de Man. Both Todorov and Miller write from the premise that the past of an author matters, thereby aligning themselves with precisely the terms that postmodernist thought has most fundamentally contested: the unity and historicity of authorial property, individuality, and intention. These unities (and the conflicts between Todorov and Miller over their meaning in this instance) are rooted in a sense of the importance of the individual past and the way it intersects with broader social forces in history.

The leaps of logic, *ad hominem* arguments, false analogies, and conflation of positions are not confined to literary critics whose defects in historical argumentation might be written off to inexperience with the true methods of historical analysis. The most egregious example of rhetorical sleight of hand in the de Man affair that I have seen is a little sentence in a brief piece in *The Nation* by an historian, Jon Wiener. In an attempt to show that de Man had systematically misrepresented his own past to friends and colleagues, Wiener includes a reference to de Man's relationship to Hans Robert Jauss: "He wrote about Jauss in *Blindness and Insight* and brought Jauss to Yale as a guest lecturer in the mid-1970s; Jauss is now known to have served in the S.S."[3] [It is important for me to emphasize that I have left out no intervening sentence or word in this quote.] Wiener's deliberate conflation is reminiscent of the first notorious example of the totalitarian prosecutorial voice, that of Saint-Just in his report urging the arrest of Danton. In his endeavor to examine everything that Danton had done since the beginning of the Revolution and find in it the seeds of treason, Saint-Just included the infamous charge that the traitorous general Dumouriez had praised Fabre-Fond, who was the brother of Fabre d'Eglantine, who was the friend of Danton. This showed, Saint-Just concluded, that there was a "criminal concert to overthrow the Republic."[4]

My point in reviewing these few examples is simply to show that history now matters in literary and philosophical circles in a way that it had not previously seemed to matter. The misuses of historical argument—including the striking use of totalitarian styles of argument by those interested in denouncing Nazism—should alert us to the fact that something profound is going on beneath the surface of charges and countercharges, of rhetorical violence and agony. Just what is at issue is less clear. To say that it involves a reassessment of our recent past, as Todorov does, is too general, for as Thomas Sheehan points out in his long review of the Victor Farias book about Heidegger in the *New York Review of Books* in 1988, most of the facts about Heidegger's involvement with the Nazi party have been common knowledge for forty years. Sheehan himself offers little in the way of a general assessment of the situation; indeed, the last section of his review seems singularly lacking in direction or decisiveness, as if the meaning of the issues raised still eluded him. He contents himself with an admonition to reread Heidegger while raising political questions: "The question remains," Sheehan concludes, "about how greatly he thought."[5]

Sheehan's vagueness indicates the difficulty faced by literary and philosophical critics when confronting the role of history in these affairs. At issue is not the recent past, but rather the consequences of actions further in the past for more recent or present authorial voices. In short, the issue is the *contamination* of history. Here the de Man case is instructive, for the facts have not "been known" in his case until recently. The facts were, of course, always there and in some sense always knowable and perhaps even always known, but they had little significance for us until they were activated within the circles of public opinion. The activation of historical facts in the de Man and Heidegger cases has served many purposes, not the least of them being to challenge the legitimacy of deconstruction as a literary method of analysis. However, I think that the concern with history goes further than that: it involves a reconsideration of the ways in which texts of all sorts might be understood within historical webs, which in turn entails a reevaluation of the ethical and political choices involved in textual analysis. But the road one must travel from history as contamination to history as moral foundation is a rocky one without much in the way of markers.

A look at some of the disputes associated with the rise of the "new historicism" will shed light on these issues. It may seem rather a long distance to travel from the Heidegger and de Man affairs to the new historicism, but they have in common the issue of how a text can be read with and against its history. Stephen Greenblatt has most persuasively described the endeavor of the new historicist critics as "investigating both the social presence to the world of the literary text and the social presence of the world in the literary text."[6] Essentially, the new historicism aims to put the text back into the historical context, and in the process, it tends to efface the boundaries between literary texts as canonically circumscribed and other cultural texts thrown up willy-nilly in various historical processes. The new historicism may be especially relevant to the Heidegger and de Man affairs because in its origins the new historicism was defined in part as a reaction to the formalist and decontextualizing moves of deconstruction, which had in Heidegger one of its most important fathers and in de Man one of its leading practitioners.[7]

It might seem then that a new historicist view would be just the kind of corrective that critics such as Sheehan and Todorov had in mind. At issue in those affairs has been the importance of historical context (i.e., the past of the authors) in evaluating the texts and the significance of writings and actions not usually described as literary (e.g., Heidegger's actions as rector of Freiburg University). But the new historicism itself has been under attack, in large measure for its limited view of history. Although Louis Montrose insists that the new historicism is new "in resisting a prevalent tendency to posit and privilege a unified and autonomous individual—whether an Author or a Work—to be set against a social or literary background," critics claim that new historicists replace this authorial unity with another one of their own: power or cultural hegemony.[8] As Edward Pechter complains in reference to an essay by Greenblatt, "The flow here is markedly one way, from the cultural to the literary text, and the effect again is to privilege the cultural text as the stable and determining point of reference." Pechter traces this problem to the new historicists' tendency to assume "that their version of history is the thing itself, as if they were doing history."[9]

Jean Howard has expressed a similar criticism in slightly different terms. She questions the way in which the new historicists choose their examples and juxtapose their cultural texts.

> It assumes answers to the very questions that should be open to debate: questions such as why a particular context should have privilege over another in discussing a text, whether a work of art merely reflects or in some fundamental sense reworks, remakes, or even produces the ideologies and social texts it supposedly represents, and whether the social contexts used to approach literary text have themselves more than the status of fictions.[10] [There are echoes, I hope, of Nietzsche's "as one chooses."]

These are fundamental questions, and I will return to them later because they effectively summarize the criticism that new historicists simply make a gesture toward history without really questioning its ontological and epistemological status in their discourse. For now, however, I want to note that like many of the critics of the new historicism who share an interest in developing the historical end of criticism rather than simply rejecting its premises, Howard herself can only offer a dose of Marxism in answer to these difficult questions. It is not clear to me how the recognition "that the ideological is everywhere and traverses literature as surely as other modes of representation" is really much of an advance beyond new historicism.[11] Ideology functions in just as pervasive and all-determining a way in this kind of formulation as does power or cultural hegemony in a new historicist one.

In the introduction to his most recent collection of essays, Stephen Greenblatt documents the development of his own position on history. He had intended to write a book about "a sublime confrontation between a total artist and a totalizing society," but he recognized that he was mistaken in thinking that he "would hear a single voice, the voice of the other." Here Greenblatt seems to be conceding a major point to his critics. Power and cultural hegemony are no longer all pervasive, as in his Foucaultian past: "For the circulation of social energy by and through the stage was not part of a single coherent, totalizing system." This movement away from totalizing systems certainly does not bring Greenblatt closer to Marx, however, and it leaves many serious problems of method. As he concludes, "Under such circumstances, there can be no single method, no overall picture, no exhaustive and definitive cultural poetics."[12] It is not clear whether this position offers a method other than individual virtuosity, in which history is simply a storehouse of interesting anecdotes available to an exceptionally talented writer.

The status of history is not just a problem for Greenblatt and the new historicists. A recent review, "History and Postmodern Literary Theory," ends on an almost disconsolate note. The author, Daniel Stempel, concluded that "There appear to be only two paths for the literary historian who wishes to move beyond the limits of traditional scholarship . . . : the dialectical history of Hegel and Marx or Foucault's discontinuous periods penetrated by the filiations of genealogy." He then lamely suggests that "The most useful theory of history may come from the history of science and technology," but provides no evidence that this is actually taking place or likely to happen and no argument for its merits.[13]

If we turn now to the disputes within history, we will find some interesting resonances with these debates. They are not strictly analogous controversies, but this very lack of parallelism may be instructive. Whereas the literary and philosophical debates have concerned the contamination of history, whether through the authorial past or through the structures of an ill-defined context, the historical debates have concerned the apparently more narrowly defined issue of the ways in which facts have been presented and interpreted. In a sense, the scandal in history is not the scandal of an author's past but rather the scandal of an author's overweening presence. In literature and philosophy as disciplines, theory is contaminated by history; in history as a discipline, history is contaminated by theory.

The only "affair," properly speaking, that has gained widespread attention within the American historical discipline in recent years is the Abraham affair. David Abraham wrote a book on the origins of Nazi rule—the subject matter is not irrelevant—*The Collapse of the Weimar Republic* (first published in 1981), which appeared to favorable reviews. Before long, however, it was attacked by a noted Yale historian of the same period, who was joined in his criticism by another well-known historian from Berkeley. [An ethnographically and politically interesting analysis might be done of the academic location of the principals in all of these disputes, but that goes beyond the purview of this essay.]

The critics attacked Abraham for errors of fact: mistranslations, mistranscriptions, incomplete archival references, and deliberate distortions of evidence. These vitiated, they claimed, Abraham's neo-Marxist account of the structural problems of Weimar political economy. Needless to say, many of the defenders of Abraham saw political motives (i.e., anti-Marxism) behind the screen of the discussion of factual errors. Rejoinders and amplifications, defenses and diatribes, including lists of purported errors running to scores of pages, all streamed forth from presses on both sides of the Atlantic. A recent review of the corrected second edition tried to strike a balanced note. The reviewer acknowledged the past errors that the author himself had attributed to haste and carelessness but defended the book's central structural arguments.[14] The two original critics, Henry Turner and Gerald Feldman, immediately fired off letters insisting that Abraham had continued to violate "the most elementary scholarly ethics." The reviewer,

V. R. Berghahn, replied with the observation that the critics had lost sight of the difference between factual errors and issues of interpretation.[15]

In a recent issue of *The American Historical Review,* the most widely circulated journal in history in America, another very prominent debate raised similar kinds of questions about fact and interpretation, albeit in the much less charged arena of sixteenth-century history. At issue was Natalie Zemond Davis's *Return of Martin Guerre,* which the author wrote as a companion piece to the French film of the same name. Natalie Davis came to the debate in a position very different from that of David Abraham, although both were at one time members of the same history department (Princeton). Abraham was an untenured assistant professor taken to task by two of the leading scholars in his field; he was subsequently denied tenure and left the field. Davis is one of the leading practitioners of the new cultural history and a recent past-president of the American Historical Association. Her critic, Robert Finlay, was an assistant professor of history at the University of Arkansas, Fayetteville.

One happy consequence of this difference from the Abraham affair is that the debate between Davis and Finlay focused more clearly and consistently on interpretive issues than on the professional competence of the scholar in question. Finlay's piece, significantly titled "The Refashioning of Martin Guerre," criticized Davis's account in particular for making Bertrande, Guerre's wife, into "a heroine, a sort of proto-feminist of peasant culture." "Such arguments," he concluded, "make footnotes to sources quite beside the point. If historical records can be bypassed so thoroughly in the service of an inventive blend of intuition and assertion, it is difficult to see what distinguishes the writing of history from that of fiction." In response to Davis's own question about where self-fashioning ends and lying begins in the Guerre story, Finlay countered with what he called "a more pertinent question: In historical writing, where does reconstruction stop and invention begin?"[16]

With this debate, we have come full circle, for what bothers Finlay in particular—besides the feminism of Davis's account, to which it is linked—is Davis's explicit use of Greenblatt's analysis of Renaissance self-fashioning. "Pervasive and tendentious," Finlay proclaims, "the concept is merely imposed on the historical record as an ingenious assertion, a modish way of viewing sixteenth-century peasants. Viewed through the lens of self-fashioning, Arnaud [the false Martin Guerre] is an audacious forger of self, not simply a clever fraud, while Bertrande is an assertive molder of identity rather than an unfortunate dupe."[17]

The contrast between these charges and the criticism of the new historicism is telling. Critics such as Howard and Pechter accuse the new historicists of gesturing toward history as if it were an unproblematic ground of truth without paying adequate attention to the ways in which history itself was constructed and reconstructed both by those who framed the original documents and those who later interpreted them. The critics of the new cultural historians regret the influence of those very new historicists on historical writing, but rather than reminding us of the constructed nature of all historical interpretation, the critics bemoan the ways in which this awareness has changed the writing of history. Critics like Finlay, Turner, and Feldman hold out a utopian ideal of the historian who sticks closely to the documents and inserts as little of him- or herself as possible. The quote I cited from Finlay above and the exchanges among Turner, Feldman, and Berghahn show that many historians believe in the existence of history standing outside of interpretation. Their criticisms were based on the possibility of a clear distinction between the ontological status of history and the status of fiction. Gertrude Himmelfarb, one of the most polemical commentators on current historical practice, argues that the new social and cultural historians attack the reason "inherent in the historical enterprise itself," which she describes as the "search for an objective truth that always eludes the individual historian but that always (or so it was once thought) informs and inspires his work."[18]

I have no intention of moving on to a self-satisfied jeremiad against the still dominant antitheoretical, anticonstructionist wing of historians, however. The stakes are higher than that, for even the most theoretically sophisticated of historians have to admit to intractable problems with grounding their methods. For the most part, we ignore this issue by writing within the confines of conventional types of interpretation and with the conventional tools of the trade. Natalie Davis was forced to confront these issues in her reply to Finlay, but what she leaves out in her reply is as interesting as what she includes.

Davis affirms the difference between herself and Finlay in "mental habits, cognitive styles, and moral tone," but she organizes her response largely in terms of research method and documentation: "Throughout, I worked as a detective, assessing my sources and the rules for their composition, putting together clues from many places, establishing a conjectural argument that made the best sense, the most plausible sense of sixteenth-century evidence." There follows a cogent, tightly reasoned, and copiously documented defense of her conclu- sions about the characters and their motives, including an impressive defense of the use of the notion of self-fashioning: "I am thus engaging in the historian's common practice of conjecturing from evidence on the basis of assumptions about psychological process. The processes assumed here—of identification and ambivalence—are simple ones and quite transportable across five hundred years of West European his- tory; Rabelais has equivalent ways of talking about the same thing."[19]

Davis's rejoinder is convincing in its documentary thoroughness but perhaps most revealing in its very brief theoretical introduction. In order to decide what "made the best sense, the most plausible sense" of the evidence, she makes use of two important techniques: "embedding this story" in the social and cultural context and deriving new kinds of literary evidence from the overall organization and operative rules of the central texts at her disposal. Yet it is not obvious how these two techniques go together or, even more important, how the social and cul- tural context can be fixed in any way. In other words, Davis is faced with the same intractable problems confronting the new historicists with whom she aligns herself.[20] We have indeed come full circle.

The third historical dispute—the debates surrounding Robert Darnton's interpretation of a massacre of cats in eighteenth-century Paris—is one of the most extensive and also one of the most sophisti- cated. It has attracted extended commentary from leading new cultural historians, Roger Chartier in France and Dominick LaCapra in the United States, and from a prominent anthropologist, James Fernandez.[21] In this exchange, all of the participants were practiced commentators on history as reconstruction. Revealed by the debate itself, however, were fundamental disagreements about what follows from this insight. In short, it is difficult to get beyond Greenblatt's indecision about method: "There can be no single method, no overall picture, no exhaustive and definitive cultural poetics."

Anxiety about this undecidability informs all of the debates that I have so briefly sketched. Nietzsche's "ability to have one's pros and cons within one's command and to use them or not, as one chooses" worries us—at least it worries me—because in its most extreme version it seems to open the door to a kind of deliberately distorted argumentation that we associate with repugnant political regimes. Yet the rejection of the idea that history like literature is constructed (hence full of choices, as Nietzsche reminds us) leaves only the most traditionally defined modes of explanation. Thus, Gertrude Himmelfarb argues for the importance of traditional political history on the grounds that "the political realm is more conducive to rational choice, compared with the social realm," and "it is in politics that the potentiality for freedom lies."[22] Too bad if this leaves out women, children, the lower classes, and the nonwhite races. The only way to move forward from this dilemma is to confront a set of difficult, interrelated questions.

A review of what I have done here will make those questions more evident. Like the new historicists, I have cobbled together a set of unlikely texts (though I have certainly included no piece of canonically inscribed "great" literature). There has to be some question about how representative my choices have been, since this is always the critical question in historical research. Whatever questions one might raise on those grounds, I nonetheless hope to have succeeded in raising the question of whether there is a story to be told here about the current concern with history.

History is about telling stories. It is not a repository of facts or anecdotes because it has no ontological status whatsoever. No particular fact or anecdote that comes from the past can be presumed to have any particular truth status just because it comes from the past. History is "out there" in some sense, but its thereness is not fixable. If we were to paraphrase Himmelfarb in such a way as to change her meaning, we could get at a formulation that I at least would find acceptable. History is a search for a truth that always eludes the historian but also informs her work, but this truth is not an objective one in the sense of a truth standing outside the practices and concerns of the historian. History is better defined as an ongoing tension between stories that have been told and stories that might be told. In this sense, it is more useful to think of history as an ethical and political practice than as an epistemology with a clear ontological status. On the other hand, a concept of a history that is "out there" does inform most historians' work and for good reason: it stands as a constant reminder that we cannot get at the "real" truth and yet that we must always continue to try to do so. This concept of history makes possible Nietzsche's belief that many eyes will tell us more than one: "the more different eyes we can put on in order to view a given spectacle, the more complete will be our conception of it, the greater our 'objectivity.'"[23]

History is a process of telling stories about the consequences of actions in the world (needless to say, this applies to analytical as well as to narrative forms of history). The de Man and Heidegger stories, now that they are being more fully told, are so compelling to us because they vividly demonstrate the importance of actions in the world. Even Jacques Derrida, when confronting the de Man affair, finds himself under "the obligation to tell a story," despite what he has learned from de Man himself about the dangers of allegory which are associated with narrative.[24] History is not an unproblematic ground of truth, but it is unavoidable because actions do have consequences in the world (they have a before and after and therefore an inherent narrative structure).

It was important to revive and elaborate the stories of de Man and Heidegger in order to remind ourselves that even intellectuals have responsibilities. (Indeed, one of the lingering questions about de Man is why he did not tell more stories himself about his experiences in the war.) But the histories of de Man and Heidegger cannot lead us to

incontrovertible moral and political conclusions except that there
should be such conclusions because those histories, like all stories, are
far from unified and coherent. Beyond the question of the individual
responsibilities of Heidegger and de Man, some have concluded that
intellectuals bear all the responsibilities; others believe that intellectuals bear hardly any at all. The stories are, consequently, a field of moral
and political struggle in which we learn to define ourselves in the
present. The struggle will continue because power is control over the
storytelling function (which, by the way, is another reason that history
matters).

The disquieting rhetorical sleights of hand that have marked the
retelling of the de Man story on both sides remind us that the discipline of a discipline, by which I mean the rules of conduct governing
argument within a discipline, does have a worthy function. Such rules
make a community of arguers possible. The concern for rules of conduct has been one of the motivating forces in all the historical disputes
that I have mentioned. In the Abraham affair, Turner and Feldman
were able to engage the attention of so many historians because they
raised issues about trust; when reading history, one assumes that the
quotes have been correctly transcribed and translated and that the
sources, such as they are, have not been deliberately distorted. In other
words, we assume that the historian is both competent and acting in
good faith.

More difficulty arises, however, when we move from rules of trans-
cription and translation to issues of interpretation. When questioning
Davis's conclusions, Finlay argued that she had taken too many liber-
ties with the available documentation. Similarly, critics of the new historicism often complain that too much is being made of unrepresenta-
tive anecdotes. Trust is still at issue in these cases, but now trust is
shown to depend in large measure on adherence to conventions. The
Nietzschean "as one chooses" is not so very individual after all; it sig-
nals another field of tension, this time between individual retellings
and collective constraints. When the collective constraints of the current community of interpreters and past traditions of interpretation
are too radically challenged, objections will arise. Such is the operation

of disciplinary maintenance; but if the collective constraints are too successfully enforced, the work of a discipline rapidly becomes banal. Disputes over deconstruction, the new historicism, Marxism, or feminism are conflicts over disciplinary maintenance.

The stories that I have told here ought also to prompt a rethinking of what may be the most insidious of collective constraints: our ingrained professional reticence about talking about the broader meaning of our work. Although we may be now content with "no overall picture," as Greenblatt terms it, in the end this will prove at least as intolerable as "the poverty" that Karl Popper attributed to the "old" historicism.[25] To tell a story, you have to have a beginning and an end and a plot line, and for that story to have any resonance, it has to fit into some kind of overall picture. Those who get and maintain power have an overall picture. Gertrude Himmelfarb is willing to say in public that a meaningful past depends on "a conception of *man* as a rational, political animal" (emphasis mine).[26] If we want to live in a world in which the consequences of her views are not dominant, then we will have to be willing to say what kind of conception of the past—and of storytelling—is going to take the place of hers.

NOTES

1. Friedrich Nietzsche, *The Birth of Tragedy and the Genealogy of Morals*, trans. Francis Golffing (New York: Doubleday Anchor, 1956), 255.

2. *Times Literary Supplement*, no. 4446, 17–23 June 1988, 676, 684–85.

3. *The Nation*, 9 January 1988, 22.

4. "Rapport sur la conjuration ourdie pour obtenir un changement de dynastie; et contre Fabre d'Eglantine, Danton, Philippeaux, Lacroix et Camille Desmoulins," *Oeuvres complètes de Saint-Just*, 2 vols. intro. and notes by Charles Vellay (Paris: Librairie Charpentier et Fasquell, 1908) 2:319. When I use the word *totalitarian* here, I do not mean to say that the French Revolution was itself an example of totalitarianism, but rather that there are certain styles of argument which I consider totalitarian. By *totalitarian*, I mean the willingness

to use any distortion of logic or history in order to defend the purity and solidity of a regime that will tolerate no opposition.

5. "Heidegger and the Nazis," *New York Review of Books,* 16 June 1988, 47.

6. Stephen Greenblatt, *Renaissance Self-Fashioning: From More to Shakespeare* (Chicago: University of Chicago Press, 1980), 5.

7. In the short piece that succinctly introduced the "new historicism" as a concept, Greenblatt made at least one explicit connection between a critical position and historical context. In his introduction to a special issue of *Genre* on *The Forms of Power and the Power of Forms in the Renaissance,* Greenblatt focused on a lecture by Dover Wilson on *Richard II* which was given before the German Shakespeare Society, at Weimar, in 1939. He tied Wilson's ideas about the text to "the eerie occasion" of the lecture. "Introduction," *Genre* 15 (Spring 1982): 3–6.

8. Louis Montrose, "Renaissance Literary Studies and the Subject of History," *English Literary Renaissance* 16 (1986): 5–12.

9. Edward Pechter, "The New Historicism and Its Discontents: Politicizing Renaissance Drama," *PMLA* 102 (May 1987): 293, 296.

10. Jean E. Howard, "The New Historicism in Renaissance Studies," *English Literary Renaissance* 16 (Winter 1986): 31.

11. Ibid., 28.

12. Stephen Greenblatt, *Shakespearean Negotiations: The Circulation of Social Energy in Renaissance England* (Berkeley and Los Angeles: University of California Press, 1988), 2, 19, 20.

13. Daniel Stempel, "History and Postmodern Literary Theory," in *Tracing Literary Theory,* ed. Joseph Natoli (Urbana, Ill.: University of Illinois Press, 1987), 101. It is strange to me that this book includes nothing on the new historicism and discusses historicity only in the context of hermeneutics.

14. For the review of David Abraham, *Collapse of the Weimar Republic: Political Economy and Crisis,* 2d ed. (New York: Holmes and Meier, 1986), see V. R. Berghahn, "Hitler's Buddies," *New York Times Book Review,* 2 August 1987, section 7, 12–13.

15. For the exchange of letters among Henry Turner, Jr., Gerald Feldman, and V. R. Berghahn, see *The New York Times Book Review,* 13 September 1987, section 7, 60–61.

16. Robert Finlay, "The Refashioning of Martin Guerre," *American Historical Review* 93 (1988): 570, 569.

17. Ibid., 564.

18. Gertrude Himmelfarb, *The New History and the Old: Critical Essays and Reappraisals* (Cambridge, Mass.: Harvard University Press, 1987), 21.

19. Natalie Zemon Davis, "On the Lame," *American Historical Review* 93 (1988): 574, 575, 597.

20. See Davis, "On the Lame," 573. I am indebted to Natalie Davis for her response to an earlier version of this essay and especially for drawing attention to this important passage in her argument.

21. Roger Chartier, "Text, Symbols, and Frenchness," *Journal of Modern History* 57 (1985): 682–95; Dominick LaCaptra, "Chartier, Darnton, and the Great Symbol Massacre," *Journal of Modern History* 60 (1988): 95–112; James Fernandez, "Historians Tell Tales: Of Cartesian Cats and Gallic Cockfights," *Journal of Modern History* 60 (1988): 113–27.

22. Himmelfarb, *The New History and the Old*, 31–32.

23. I am indebted to Randolph Starn for his many helpful comments on this point, although I know that I have not done justice to them here.

24. Jacques Derrida, "Like the Sound of the Sea Deep within a Shell: Paul de Man's War," trans. Peggy Kamuf, *Critical Inquiry* 14 (1988): 595.

25. Karl R. Popper, *The Poverty of Historicism* (New York: Harper and Row, 1964).

26. Himmelfarb, *The New History and the Old*, 25.

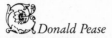

Donald Pease

Toward a Sociology of Literary Knowledge

GREENBLATT, COLONIALISM,
AND THE NEW HISTORICISM

The title for this essay arose from my interest in emergent academic disciplines and the larger social or political movements with which they are sometimes related. My interest can be phrased as a series of questions. How can the process of discipline formation (its theoretical and self-rationalizing process) be related to the formation of political movements? Can an academic discipline find itself implicated in different but not necessarily incompatible directions when developed within the environment of a political movement? Conversely, can a discipline simply invoke its relationship to an emancipatory social movement to claim greater authority as an academic discipline?

In what follows I want to explore the relationship between the political discourse that a new academic discipline borrows to describe its formation within the academy and the quite different uses to which that discourse can be put in a political movement. The academic discipline I will be most interested in here is what Stephen Greenblatt calls the new historicism[1]; and since the discourse of colonialism plays an important role in the formation of that discipline, I will frame a consideration of that discipline's formation in the different terms to which Frantz Fanon puts the discourse of colonialism.

THE DISCOURSE OF COLONIALISM, SHAKESPEARE, THE DISCOURSE OF THE OTHER

With the publication of *Peau Noire, Masques Blancs* in 1952 Frantz Fanon initiated an unprecedented cultural conversation. This conversation, which should have taken place centuries earlier, included the colonized and the colonizer within a shared dialogue. In opening up this dialogue, Fanon could not speak in the primitive voice of his native Antilles. That voice had been thoroughly distorted following the Antilleans' first encounter with European colonists. But neither did he speak with any explicit dialogue partner separable from himself. Instead, he spoke from within an articulate and extremely sophisticated use of the French language. I say "from within" because, as the title of the book suggests, Fanon consistently splits himself into two speakers: one speaks the language as if it were an essential aspect of his identity, and the other experiences this linguistic identity as a form of colonization.

Fanon's terms for these two speakers are in the title. The speaker who says "I speak" and does not recognize any difference between himself and the language he uses is a "white mask," whereas the speaker who experiences himself misrepresented by a language that speaks in his place is a "black skin."

Fanon identifies the native speaker in a colonialist context as a theatrical effect, the production of a white mask rather than an authentic identity. He intends by way of this description to violate the ordinary understanding of the terms *authentic identity* and *theatrical self.* Although two figures from Western theater will play crucial roles in this conversation, Fanon does not violate ordinary usage for a merely theatrical effect. Instead he does so to insist on the difference between who speaks and what gets spoken whenever anyone in French culture (white or black) speaks. Fanon describes what gets spoken in the neo-colonialist French culture of 1952 as a white mask, and he believed that everyone who spoke was compelled to wear this mask. He elaborates this belief in terms borrowed from the French psychoanalyst Jacques Lacan and by means of Caliban and Prospero, characters from Shakespeare's *The Tempest.*

The reason he chose Lacan's subdiscipline of psychoanalysis as a way of understanding these Shakespearean characters requires some explanation. Two years before Fanon wrote *Black Skin, White Masks,* another French psychoanalyst, Mannoni, had written a study of colonialism entitled *Prospero and Caliban: The Psychology of Colonization.*[2] In that work, Mannoni uses the Caliban/Prospero relationship as the model for two interdependent psychological complexes crucial to the colonial encounter. Caliban represented a "dependency complex" characteristic of primitive people. The lore of these people included legends about the return of powerful white ancestors who would bring about the recovery of a primordial inheritance. Mannoni argued that such legends indicated the natives' psychological need for colonization, after the manner in which Caliban's identity depended on his submission to Prospero. Similarly, Mannoni described Prospero's character in terms of an "authority complex": he needed to exercise the authority that Caliban required. Prospero's own recognition of his authority consequently depended on the signs of Caliban's submission to it.

Fanon, as you might imagine, found this account contemptible, an ideological continuation rather than a disinterested explanation of the psychology of colonialism.[3] In proposing another, he turned to Jacques Lacan's account of identity formation. Lacan explained the development of an infant's identity in terms of miming the coherent image of another. However, whereas Lacan intended the description as an alternative to the Oedipal model (which recently had been appropriated by American ego psychologists), Fanon found in it an alternative explanation of the psychology of colonialism. Like the infant, the primitive organized his official identity by miming the language, customs, and judiciary system (versions of what Lacan calls "*le nom du père*") of the colonizers.

In correlating Lacan's account of the white infant's process of identity formation with the colonization of primitive peoples, Fanon proposed a social relationship the white infant shared in common with primitive peoples. Fanon established the basis for this relationship where Mannoni did: on Prospero's relationship with Caliban. But Fanon's description of this relationship was quite different from Mannoni's. In articulating this difference Fanon put one of Jacques Lacan's more slippery notions, "the discourse of the Other," to strategic use.

The discourse of the Other is Jacques Lacan's phrase for the difference between what does the speaking in ordinary conversation and what must of necessity remain speechless. For Lacan, what does the speaking is not a speaker, but the endlessly reiterated motions of linguistic displacement which produce what Lacan calls the *Symbolic*. The Symbolic is Lacan's shorthand description for the entire set of a culture's symbol systems, developing its legal, religious, artistic, political, and philosophical registers. What gets displaced by these linguistic operations is another realm (Lacan refers to it as the *Imaginary*) in which biological processes (whether the mother's or the child's), in their undifferentiated state, make words (which depend on differentiation) unnecessary.[4] Lacan, in his various analyses of the difference between the Imaginary and the Symbolic, designates this difference as the discourse of the Other, and he locates the inception of this in the speechless past of the human infant. Lacan stages the appearance of the discourse of the Other between a time when the infant, utterly identified with its mother, does not need words (the Imaginary) and a time when the infant loses this identification and needs words to mediate between itself and its world (the Symbolic). He calls these mediating words the discourse of the Other to call attention to the different kind of signification that results when the child must change its orientation from the mother to the world, and he describes the operation of this discourse in terms of displacement because of the lost identification with the mother.

In the use to which he puts Lacan, Frantz Fanon first relocates this discourse within the context of the language instruction of colonized peoples: following a colonial encounter, the native speaker (like the white infant) must articulate his identity in another's language. Then Fanon provides a different account of the origin of the discourse of the Other in the Frenchman's psyche.

In their discovery of the new World, Fanon argues, European explorers encountered cultural realms quite different from their own. These encounters would later entail the loss of belief in European culture as the materialized utterance of a divine speaker, the *Logos*. But during their initial contact with native cultures, European explorers denied authority to the languages of the natives as antithetical to the speech authorized by the Christian *Logos*. In the process of colonizing these native lands, Europeans supplanted the natives' speech with their own, but they thereby left the traces of this other speech in the wake of this displacement. In a practice that Stephen Greenblatt refers to as "linguistic colonialism,"[5] the Europeans covered over the native languages they heard spoken in the New World with what they believed were their own enlightened discourses.

One effect of the Europeans' language lesson, Fanon maintains, was the production of the discourse of the Other, in themselves as well as in the natives. Redefined as what did the displacing whenever the Europeans' "enlightened discourses" took the place of native speech, the discourse of the Other became for Fanon representative of the master discourse of law and order which articulated itself through the relationship between the colonizer and the colonized.[6] Although this discourse remains unvocalized in most conversations, it became startingly audible in the conversations between Prospero and Caliban, especially when Caliban claims that the only true lesson he has learned from his European master is "how to curse." Caliban means that the language he learned educated him in how to be properly colonized and thereby alienated him from his former way of life. That is why the instruction itself seems to Caliban a form of cursing. The lesson Caliban learns is not the one Prospero teaches; nevertheless, the lesson Caliban learned instructs Prospero in a different way to understand what he was doing as well. In his initial encounter with the New World, Prospero had also experienced another dimension of his own character in internal exile from Europe which could have resulted in a transformation of his identity. By choosing instead to identify with the master discourse of his homeland, Prospero also experiences his colonial identity as a curse (the discourse of the Other); or to recover Fanon's vocabulary: he experiences his colonial identity as a white mask, the role he was condemned to play in place of becoming himself.

By experiencing the European language (and the cultural system it conveyed) as a way of cursing rather than a form of enlightenment, Caliban recognizes counterenlightenment forces in his character that were opposed to the structure of the colonial relationship with Prospero. Learning the master language of Europe only as a vivid lesson in what they were compelled *not* to speak leads both Caliban and Prospero to another, as yet inarticulate discourse. When it developed its emancipatory potential centuries later, this other discourse enabled Frantz Fanon to write *Black Skin, White Masks*.

For Fanon, then, the colonial encounter produced alternative discourses in both Caliban and Prospero. Positioned between two different discourses—the colonialist one they spoke, and the one critical of colonialism, which they suppressed by speaking—their identities depended upon Caliban's and Prospero's very different relations to these discourses. As the colonizer, Prospero is the subject of the colonialist discourse; as the colonized, Caliban is subjected to the discourse. But these social roles do not exhaust the subject positions that Caliban and Prospero occupy. Their mutual experience of linguistic colonialism as a way of cursing produces the extraordinary state of mind wherein both recognize themselves as displaced from within the very language that (as the Lacanian Symbolic) should have positioned them as identities. In recognizing the colonial situation they shared, Fanon maintains, Caliban and Prospero experience the difference between the language that colonized them (a white mask) and a different language through which they could emancipate themselves from colonialism. This new language could neither be Prospero's master discourse of colonialism nor Caliban's native speech, but a conversation arising out of their jointly recognizing the limitations in both of those language systems. This cultural conversation is inseparable from the critical consciousness and the emancipatory political practices that arise after Caliban and Prospero recognize "linguistic colonialism" as their shared cultural estate. It is also inseparable from their shared resolve to free themselves from a world imprisoned within the discourse of colonialism.

This explicit resolve does not appear in Shakespeare's play, nor does the emancipatory political practice appear within Lacan's new psychoanalytic discipline. For Lacan, the discourse of the Other, insofar as it covered the entire field of culture, designated the impossibility of such a collective social practice rather than an enabling instance of one.[7] By putting Lacanian analysis to work within a worldwide political movement directed against colonialism, Fanon developed an intellectual environment other than the institutional for this discipline. Here it led to the formation of a coherent account of collective praxis.[8]

That account did not appear in Fanon's or Lacan's writings but in Jean-Paul Sartre's *Critique of Dialectical Reason*. Jean-Paul Sartre found in Fanon's *Black Skin, White Masks* a devastating critique of the Hegelian master/slave dialectic that had influenced Sartre's account of the existential phenomenology of the authentic self. Fanon enabled Sartre to understand that work as the symptomatic effect of his own experience of colonialization. Sartre worked out the political implications of significant portions of *Being and Nothingness* during the German occupation. The structure of colonial relations in the form of totalitarian rule formed the backdrop for Sartre's account of human freedom in *Being and Nothingness*. Sartre equated the colonial power with the capacity to impose fixity (*en soi*) on an otherwise fluid subjectivity (*pour soi*); and he theorized human freedom in terms of a subject's ability to evade these impositions. In ways too complex to do justice to here, Sartre's subsequent reading of Fanon led him to recognize that this utterly free subjectivity was itself only another version of the unself-consciously exercised power of the colonial master. Instead of evading that master, the Sartrean subject had merely rationalized the master's will to absolute mastery. Having realized that the master/slave dialectic within colonialism had been reduplicated in his speculations on free subjectivity, Sartre proposed an alternative dialectic in *Critique of Dialectical Reason*,[9] a dialectic that includes a discussion of what Sartre called "groups-in-fusion." In the years of France's occupation of Vietnam and Algeria, such groups were composed of two constituencies: Frenchmen who felt victimized by the discourse of colonialism, and the colonized people of Vietnam and Algeria. The political practices these groups developed resulted from the give and take, the ongoing discussion engaged in by these two constituencies, and those discussions resulted in the experience of a cultural personality quite different from that of either master or slave.

Like Lacan's emergent discipline of psychoanalysis, Sartre's *Critique* took on a life of its own within the movement of anticolonialism.[10]

However, whereas Sartre worked out the implications of *Black Skin, White Masks* in philosophical terms, Aimé Césaire worked out these implications for Shakespeare's play. Césaire occupies a central place in the anticolonialist movement. A student of Mannoni's, Césaire spelled out his differences with his mentor in *Discourse on Colonialism*, a work that virtually identified colonialist practices with the Lacanian discourse of the Other. This work in turn influenced the work of Frantz Fanon, who was Césaire's student. However, Césaire registered the radical significance of his project by rewriting Shakespeare's *The Tempest*. Altering Shakespeare's title slightly to *Une Tempête*,[11] he recharacterized Caliban as a rebellious slave who not only recovers his island but persuades Prospero to remain and help him in the process of decolonization.

By concentrating on the emancipatory potential in Prospero's relationship with Caliban, Césaire and Fanon insisted on the relationship between Shakespeare's play and anticolonialism.[12] In "Learning to Curse: Aspects of Linguistic Colonialism in the Sixteenth Century," Stephen Greenblatt follows their line. The article turns on Greenblatt's interpretation of a line from Prospero. In his reading of Prospero's "this thing of darkness I / Acknowledge mine," Greenblatt teases out Prospero's conflicting loyalties to colonialism by way of the line's ambiguity. In acknowledging "this thing of darkness," Caliban, as his own, Greenblatt argues that Prospero tacitly acknowledges a division in his own character: the Prospero who is agent and the Prospero who is victim of colonialism. Greenblatt begins his account with a stipulation of this internal division, "Prospero's words are ambiguous,"[13] then he offers two accounts of the line that "colonize" (in the sense that they render it continuous with the structure of colonialism) this ambiguity. The first of these readings turns the lines into an example of the superiority of Prospero's claim to colonial mastery over Alonso's: "They might be taken as a pure statement that the strange demi-devil is one of Prospero's party as opposed to Alonso's." A second reading, that Caliban is Prospero's slave, "would only absorb the lines,"[14] Greenblatt notes, back into slavery, which Greenblatt earlier condemned as the most peculiar and abominable institution of colonialism. Greenblatt refuses both readings as insufficient in their empathy. He concludes by dislodging both of these readings from their place within the structure of colonialism and absorbing them within an evangelical anticolonialism. Prospero's words "acknowledge a deep if entirely unsentimental bond" with Caliban, Greenblatt concludes, and to underscore his belief in an ethical imperative underwriting this bond, Greenblatt proposes a moral lesson that almost turns into a curse: "Perhaps, too, the word 'acknowledge' implies some moral responsibility, as when the Lord, in the King James translation of Jeremiah, exhorts them to 'acknowledge thine iniquity, that thou hast transgressed against the Lord thy God' (3:13)."[15]

If Greenblatt concludes his discussion by borrowing on biblical wrath, he does so both because he never loses sight of the continued power of the discourse of colonialism to repossess the relationship between Caliban and Prospero and because he feels himself bound to oppose this appropriation. To foreclose this colonialist repossession, Greenblatt first finds it generalized in the work of another Shakespeare scholar, Terence Hawkes, into the interpretive master plot for all of Shakespearean drama. The colonist, in Hawkes's reading, parallels the dramatist. "Like the dramatist, a colonist imposes the shape of his own culture, embodied in his speech, on the [New World]."[16] But the colonist cannot articulate the New World into one recognizable as his own without the help of the dramatist, whose language, Hawkes says, "expands the boundaries of our culture, and makes the new territory over in its own image. His raids on the inarticulate open up new worlds for the imagination."[17] To hear colonialism described in these terms is precisely *not* to acknowledge it as a dark thing; and it is this refusal on Hawkes's part to acknowledge the immorality of colonialism that compels Greenblatt to continue his jeremiad: "To read such glowing tribute, one would never know that there had been a single doubt whispered in the twentieth century about the virtues of European colonialism. More important one would never know that Prospero and the other Europeans leave the island at the end of the play. If *The Tempest* is holding up a mirror to colonialism, Shakespeare is far more ambivalent than Terence Hawkes about the reflected image."[18]

Greenblatt directs this jeremiad against Terence Hawkes because he finds him weak in his criticism of colonialism. Greenblatt intends the righteous wrath he invokes to seal the bond of reciprocity between Caliban and Prospero against reappropriation by the discourse of colonialism. But Greenblatt's jeremiad is stronger in its condemnation than are Shakespeare's words. Shakespeare, as Greenblatt reminds us, was not unambiguously opposed to colonialism. At the time he wrote *The Tempest,* neither the discourse of colonialism nor its critique had been developed. Nor had Shakespeare been elevated to the status of England's national poet. That elevation took place in the nineteenth century and led to Shakespeare's plays being used throughout the British colonies to instruct native speakers in the King's English and thereby turn them into British subjects. As the "universal" poet who had developed the master language into its highest cultural form, Shakespeare, as uniformly taught throughout the British Empire, gave "linguistic colonialism" great cultural authority.[19] Indeed, Shakespeare's plays, as the chief instrument for instruction in the King's English, achieved linguistic colonialism throughout the British Empire.

Mannoni acknowledged Shakespeare as a colonial authority when he developed his own psychological justification for colonialism in terms of Caliban's need to depend on Prospero. In the use to which Mannoni puts him, Shakespeare seems to endorse Prospero's colonial subjection of Caliban without any ambiguity. Following this usage, Shakespeare's play became identified with the discourse of colonialism, and Prospero and Caliban became sociopolitical symbols in that discourse.

In conducting his argument with Mannoni by rewriting Shakespeare's play, Aimé Césaire does not intend to offer a new reading of *The Tempest.* A new reading of Shakespeare would remain within the British education system and endorse the use to which Shakespeare was put in the discourse of colonialism. By rewriting *The Tempest,* Césaire does not continue, but decolonizes that discourse from within its definitive cultural wording. Not Shakespeare but a colonial subject claims in *Une Tempête* the power to determine the political implications of colonialism for himself and the native speakers he represents.

In the critique of colonialism he developed along with Fanon, Sartre, and other, politically committed intellectuals, Césaire appropriated the characters of Shakespeare's *The Tempest* to address the political needs of an anticolonialist political movement. He did so because these characters had already been used to justify colonialism. When it suited the needs of this emancipatory political movement, Césaire and these other intellectuals also appropriated other concepts (like Jacques Lacan's discourse of the Other) that had been used previously to justify colonialism. Greenblatt's critique of linguistic colonialism implicitly depends on the critical consciousness developed by this political movement.

Whereas Greenblatt depended on the anticolonialist movement for his critique, he did not identify his writing with any specific political movement. By 1975, the United States had completed its troop withdrawal from Vietnam, thereby ending its official policy of neocolonialism. A partial explanation for the animus in Greenblatt's critique derives from the international consensus condemning U.S. involvement in Vietnam. After Vietnam, the United States entered a postcolonial era, thereby relegating colonialism to the status of a political anomaly from which Renaissance scholars like Greenblatt (and their academic disciplines) could remain free. In reading a postcolonial bond into the relationship between Caliban and Prospero, Greenblatt read the discourse of colonialism out of Shakespeare's play. Moreover, he did so in an approved academic manner: he found a correspondence between Shakespeare the dramatist and British colonists insufficiently criticized in another Shakespeare scholar, Terence Hawkes.

BREAKING THE BOND:
THE FOUNDING OF THE NEW HISTORICISM

In a dramatic reversal of the imperative informing his jeremiad directed against Hawkes, Greenblatt, in the essays following "Learning to Curse," restored Hawkes's relation between the colonist and the dramatist. More precisely, he reinstituted this relation with an essay that he first read at the 1978 English Institute. This essay, entitled "Improvisation and Power," constitutes a watershed moment in Greenblatt's career. It was collected in Edward Said's edition of selected papers for the English Institute 1977–1978. As the last chapter in *Renaissance Self-Fashioning: From More to Shakespeare,* it marked the conclusion of one interpretive schema, "self-fashioning," and the inauguration of a new discipline. In different contexts and on different occasions, Greenblatt described this new discipline either as "cultural poetics" or "the new historicism." The flexibility in naming just what it is you do when you follow the rules of this new discipline only enhances its applicability. Whatever they choose to call it, the new discipline supports many followers, most of whom are sufficiently revisionary (or improvisatory) in their handling of new historicist matters to produce the internal differentiation constitutive of the discipline's rationality. In 1982, Greenblatt with Svetlana Alpers founded a new journal, *Representations,* which often features the work of new historicists; and the new discipline has become the subject of books as well as of issues of journals and academic conferences. In what may be the most reliable sign of its status as a burgeoning critical enterprise, the new historicism has become the target of critics who, in some cases, are defectors from the new discipline.[20]

On one level, what I have to say about Greenblatt's new historicism is the result of what this new discipline has taught me. "The new historicism," in Greenblatt's description of it, "erodes the firm ground of both criticism and literature. It tends to ask questions about its own assumptions and those of others." It might even "encourage us to examine the ideological situation not only of a play but of a critic on that play," as well as the relationship "between a critical reading and its occasion."[21]

In the remainder of this discussion I hope to follow this rule for examining the "ideological situation" of the new historicism; but I shall also add one more feature: the relationship between the new historicism and linguistic colonialism. I will add that feature by now risking an assertion: the ideological ground of Greenblatt's new historicism corroborates in its formation as an academic discipline the enterprise of linguistic colonialism which he earlier questioned.

For the purposes of this discussion, Greenblatt's continuation of the colonialist enterprise constitutes his definitive break from the anticolonialism Frantz Fanon called for in *Black Skin, White Masks*. This break necessarily involves him in a reinterpretation of the relationship between Prospero and Caliban. Curiously, this reinterpretation does not appear in "Improvisation and Power" (at least not explicitly) but in two essays following it: "Invisible Bullets: Renaissance Authority and Its Subversion, *Henry IV* and *Henry V*" and "Martial Law in the Land of Cockaigne."[22] These essays, I will argue, are important for their revisionary readings of the Caliban/Prospero bond and for the relationship between these revised readings and the emergence of the new historicism.

Greenblatt organizes "Improvisation and Power" by establishing a linkage between an obscure anecdote from the archives of colonialism and Shakespeare's *Othello*. The anecdote, which is Peter Martyr's account of the exploitation of Lucayan natives by Spanish conquistadors, might be described as the story of a Caliban who does not know how to curse. It seems the Lucayans believed that their dead would one day return to them in boats from across the sea. When the Spaniards learned of this belief they identified themselves with the Lucayan dead in order to persuade the living to work for them in the gold mines. According to Greenblatt's recounting of Martyr's narrative, "the entire population of the island . . . thus deceived . . . passed 'singing and dancing' . . . onto the ship and were taken to the gold mines of Hispaniola."[23]

What differentiates this account of cultural contact from the earlier ones in "Learning to Curse" is the potential for reciprocity, the "entirely unsentimental bond" missing from the exchange. In what we might call the *Fanonian moment* in Greenblatt's earlier treatment of colonialism, he did not eliminate accounts of duped natives; but he carefully balanced such accounts with counterexamples. These contrary accounts often assumed the form of reciprocal exchanges between colonists and natives rather than forms of linguistic colonialism. For example, in "Learning to Curse," Greenblatt cites a report from a Spanish captain in which he includes the Cenu Indians' refutation of the Europeans' ideological claim to their land: "'When I said,' the captain began, 'that the Pope, being the Lord of the universe in the place of God, had given the land of the Indies to the King of Castille,' the Indians' chief responded, 'The Pope must have been drunk when he did it, for he gave what was not his.'"[24]

Whereas the anticolonialist in Greenblatt carefully included such accounts of reciprocity, the new historicist in him is more interested in the absence of reciprocity in the Spaniards' exchanges with the Lucayans and the Spaniards' use of nonreciprocity to increase their own power; for it is in exercising their right to nonreciprocal exchanges that the Spaniards exemplified what Greenblatt means by an "improvisational self." Improvisation results from the ability that Greenblatt, following the lead of the sociologist Daniel Lerner, calls "empathy".[25] The ability to identify, no matter how briefly, with the role of another, the capacity for empathy usually results in the understanding of the other person; but in improvisation, empathy is deployed strictly for the purpose of exploitation. The Spanish conquistadors displayed a gift for improvisation when, in the interest of exploiting their labor in the gold mines, they identified themselves with the Lucayans' belief in the resurrection of the dead.

In the course of this improvisation, the Spaniards put into operation the two activities that Greenblatt believes essential for a felicitous improvisation: displacement and absorption. In Greenblatt's interpretation of the line, "This thing of darkness I / Acknowledge mine," his displacement of two colonialist readings of the line prevented the line's absorption within the language of colonialism. Absorption and displacement produced multiple interpretations of the line. The differences in these interpretations resulted in the ambivalence Greenblatt found in Prospero's attitude toward Caliban, and Greenblatt's empathy with Caliban was the result. However, Greenblatt's new historicist definitions of these terms assign to them different linguistic functions. By *displacement* he now means "the process whereby a prior symbolic structure (such as the Lucayans' belief in the resurrection of the dead) is compelled to coexist with other centers of attention (such as the Catholic faith of the Spanish conquistadors) that do not necessarily conflict with the original structure but are not swept up in its gravitational pull."[26] This final qualification is the key to a successful improvisation, for without it, the conquistadors could find their Catholicism susceptible to a counterdisplacement onto the symbolic structure of the Lucayans; that is, they might recover their empathy in a nonimprovisational and non–new historicist sense. Such a mutual displacement would restore reciprocity to this exchange, rendering it akin to Prospero's relationship with Caliban in "Learning to Curse." As if in acknowledgment of this danger, absorption, the second improvisational gesture, completes the defense against reciprocity. Greenblatt defines it "as the process whereby a symbolic structure is taken into the ego so completely that it ceases to exist as an external phenomenon."[27] In terms of the Lucayan episode, absorption refers to an assimilation of the Lucayan beliefs into the Roman Catholic faith that is so thorough that nothing remains of those beliefs other than the traces of their displacement into the Spaniards' state of mind.

The necessity of this activity becomes clearest when we consider the danger against which it defends. This danger can be expressed as a question: If the Spaniards can treat the Lucayans' belief structure as an ideology vulnerable to exploitation, why do they not treat their own beliefs as an exploitable ideology? J. G. A. Pocock, for example, implicitly asks this question in *The Machiavellian Moment*, a different account of similar materials.[28] Pocock correlates colonial encounters in the New World with related experiences in fifteenth-century Europe: fear of invasion by barbarians from without, and subjection to tyrannical rule from within. Pocock maintains that the conjunction of these events led to a dramatic transformation in the political organization of Europe. When conjoined with the experience of coercive monarchical rule at home, colonial encounters as a displaced reflection of monarchical rule enabled Europeans to interpret feudal monarchy as a form of colonial subjection. As the feudal structures to which their beliefs once adhered either collapsed or were gutted in civil strife, European subjects, Pocock argues, became citizens who developed a new political belief—in a social contract theory of government with reciprocal rights and duties. In the course of their development, these citizens would question the Catholic faith that legitimated feudal monarchy, and their opposition to monarchy would eventually lead to the civil wars that brought the Renaissance to a conclusion.[29]

Pocock affiliates colonial encounters with related historical events that resulted in the demystification of monarchic rule. The result of this "Machiavellian Moment" in European history was the transformation of the people of Europe from the status of subjects who obeyed the rule of monarchs to citizens who formulated different rules.

Greenblatt does not corroborate Pocock's understanding of these events. The improvisations he describes did not lead the Spanish conquistadors to question either their ruler or their religion. Greenblatt explains why the Spaniards' improvisations did not undermine their religious beliefs in two different ways and two different contexts.

He provides the first explanation within the context of the Lucayan episode. "The Spanish were not compelled to perceive their own religion as a manipulable human construct," Greenblatt asserts; "on the contrary the compulsion of their own creed was presumably strengthened by their contemptuous exploitation of an analogous symbolic structure."[30] The key word here is *compulsion*. By identifying the basis for the Spaniards' successful improvisation as a *compulsion*, Greenblatt transposes colonial subjection out of its place within history and into the Spaniards' psyche. This transposition is crucial to an understanding of the different use to which Greenblatt will put materials from colonial archives in the new historicism.

A reading of Shakespeare's *Othello* is the new use to which Greenblatt puts the materials from the colonial archives and the second explanatory context for the Spanish compulsion. In the transit from the colonial archives to Shakespeare's *Othello*, Greenblatt's interpretation of what strictly is at issue in colonial exploitation undergoes a startling transformation. In *Othello*, the improvisational self does not simply serve the state, but turns into a double-agent who serves two different colonial powers.

We can begin to sort out the differences between these colonial powers by considering the different rationales for the improvisations. The Spaniards want the Lucayans' physical labor in the gold mines; but Iago wants to ensnare Othello within a social discourse whose terms he controls. The Spaniards succeed in their exploitation by absorbing the Lucayans' beliefs within their own Catholic faith; but Iago's successful manipulation of Othello depends on Iago's skepticism about the Catholic doctrines that Othello needs to believe. Like the Spaniards, Iago does not want a reciprocal exchange, but rather a manipulative relationship. Unlike the Spaniards, however, he does not derive the authority for his manipulation from the Catholic faith. His ability to manipulate Othello derives from Othello's previous belief in Church doctrine covering sexuality. Greenblatt tellingly describes Othello's belief in terms of his submission to the Church's "colonial power".[31] Iago's power lies elsewhere: just where requires an analysis of his manipulation.

Iago succeeds in his manipulation by persuading Othello that his bond with Desdemona is not a reciprocal one. In the course of this persuasion, Iago exploits an internal division within Othello: a black Moor who is a stranger to society, and also a military leader whose duties identify him with Venice's ruling class. The outsider in Othello fears Desdemona loves him for the wrong reason. The insider fears she loves another. Iago decides on adultery as the narrative plot device equipped to give both of these fears their full development. The insider's fear readily lends itself to Iago's control. To gratify Othello's fear that Desdemona loves another of her own kind, Iago offers him Cassio. The outsider's fear is more subtle: according to its logic, Othello fears Desdemona loves his "other" self—Othello the black Moor, not Othello the defender of Venetian society. To capture this fear, Iago, Greenblatt claims, exploits Othello's prior belief in a peculiar Church doctrine equating a husband's uncontrolled sexual attraction for his wife with adultery.

Greenblatt devotes most of his discussion of Shakespeare's *Othello* to this material from Church archives, which he treats in the same manner as he treated materials from the colonial archives—that is, as raw data for his reading of Shakespeare. As a result of the reading that follows from Greenblatt's identification of Church doctrine with colonial power, he is able to discard one key concept, "self-fashioning," and take up another, "improvisational self," as his fundamental analytical category. Othello's need to fashion a social self out of a Church doctrine alien to his human needs makes him a representative instance of all the other Renaissance self-fashioners (More, Wyatt, Tyndale, Spenser, Marlowe) Greenblatt had discussed previously. Like Othello, these other Renaissance self-fashioners felt ambivalent about their need to identify with cultural institutions (like Church doctrine on sexuality) that they found coercive. Their writings, Greenblatt argued, expressed this ambivalence by designating two different selves within the self-fashioner; the self who constructed roles out of Renaissance institutions, and the self who felt a victim of them. The self-fashioners' internalization of this ambivalence produced an "internal distance"[32] that rendered them unable to identify with the true agency of colonial power in the Renaissance.

Whereas self-fashioners felt colonized by these institutions, Greenblatt claims that neither Shakespeare nor Iago did. Instead of colonizing Othello in the name of the Church, as did the Spaniards, Iago successfully exploits Othello's belief in Church doctrine because he considers religious beliefs as well as the selves fashioned out of them to be manipulable fictions. For Iago (and Shakespeare), every structure of belief represents a power designed to colonize anyone willing to accept the structure. Although Iago may enunciate symbolic structures in which others believe, he himself accepts no structure. Consequently, Iago can be said to be colonized by another's beliefs only as long as it takes him to colonize the other who holds those beliefs. Iago founds his power not on any structure or credo but upon the structure of colonial relations he embodies and acts out. By refusing to identify with any of the belief structures out of whose terms Renaissance subjects fashioned their identities, Iago identifies himself with the master code, the cultural system out of whose generative grammar every Renaissance cultural structure spelled itself out.

In our earlier discussion of Frantz Fanon, we described as the discourse of the Other the master code in whose terms all other cultural institutions positioned their structures of belief. Fanon would have found Greenblatt's use of *displacement* and *absorption* to explain the operations of the discourse of the Other compatible with his understanding. Like Fanon, Greenblatt equates the discourse of the Other with the master code of the colonizing power. Following colonial instruction in this code, every native structure of belief was displaced from native culture and absorbed within the master code. Unlike Iago, however, Fanon did not believe himself empowered to speak the discourse of the Other; he felt himself spoken for by this master code. The claim to speak the master code entails the speaker's disclaimer of identification with any other cultural discourse, no matter whether legal, religious, political, or cultural and his consequent identification with the practice of displacing these other discourses. To believe oneself represented by the terms provided in any of these discourses is, like Othello and Renaissance self-fashioners, to find oneself displaced and absorbed by a colonial power. To be able to speak the master code is, like Iago and improvisational selves, to do the displacing and absorbing.

Earlier we encountered Shakespeare's representation of a scene of instruction in the discourse of the Other. It took place during the language lesson Prospero gave to Caliban. The result of that language lesson was the identification of the discourse of the Other with the discourse of colonialism. Like Iago's improvisation of Othello, that instruction was not reciprocal. Greenblatt cited it as an instance of linguistic colonialism, and he cited Caliban's curse as the first critique of linguistic colonialism. In reaction to the absence of reciprocity in that scene of instruction, Greenblatt discerned in Prospero a compensatory ambivalence binding him to Caliban.

Greenblatt finds no ambivalence in Iago's send-up of Othello. Iago experiences no bond of attachment to Othello. He exploits the ambivalence in Othello's love for Desdemona in order to break that bond as well. However, although Iago may believe in nothing, Greenblatt conducts his reading of Iago's relationship with Othello as if his own beliefs still condemn all forms of colonial power.

I say "as if" because Greenblatt's reading of *Othello* colonizes Iago within quite modern belief structures about sexuality and sexism. Greenblatt does so because he could not otherwise persuade a modern audience of the felicity of Iago's improvisation. For example, what preserves Iago from colonization by a Church doctrine analogous to

Othello's is apparently a consensus about liberated sexuality he shares with "modern" readers.[33] That shared belief itself gets threatened, however, in the remainder of his reading of Othello, in which Greenblatt multiplies the positions of the colonial power: not just the Church occupies the position of colonial power over sexuality, but a sexist male (not Iago but Othello) whose "brutish violence is bound up with his experience of sexual potency"[34] over a submissive woman.

As we witness Othello colonized by sexual repression and sexism, Greenblatt would have us effortlessly decolonize these forces. Instead, we experience problems with displacement. The centers of attention into which the Catholic doctrine covering adultery has been displaced do not peacefully coexist, but rather conflict with one another. Two modern structures of belief (that is, liberated sexuality and feminism) instead come into open conflict here. As they conflict with one another, these two modern belief structures cannot be said to decolonize Renaissance superstitions, nor do they absorb Iago's manipulation into a coherent state of mind. As symbolic structures that demand belief, these modern dogmatisms about sexuality and gender cannot be distinguished from Renaissance dogmas that Greenblatt identifies with forms of colonial power.

The similarity between Othello's colonization by Church doctrine and Iago's decolonization by these modern consensuses becomes startlingly clear when we consider the result. The outcome of the decolonization engaged by Greenblatt's reading is a colonial subject; a representation of Othello as "thick lips," an oversexed black male from whose sexual violence no white woman can believe herself safe.[35] This colonial version of Othello marks the return of Caliban to Greenblatt's new discipline; or rather it marks the return of the version of Caliban upon which linguistic colonialism depended to justify its operations.

LINGUISTIC COLONIALISM AND
THE NEW HISTORICISM

That Caliban returns in the displaced form of Othello indicates Greenblatt's continued ambivalence about linguistic colonialism. Given Greenblatt's identification of Shakespeare with Iago's improvisations and both of them with the discourse of the other, it is not surprising that Caliban returns to haunt his new academic enterprise.[36] In reaction to Caliban's complaint that he felt cursed by the language he felt compelled to speak, Greenblatt earlier expressed his empathy. Although the new historicist in Greenblatt may have emptied out Shakespeare's empathy through his redefinition of the word, the reappearance of Caliban to the scene of Greenblatt's new venture indicates Greenblatt's continued ambivalence (if not quite empathy) about Caliban; and this ambivalence requires from Greenblatt an explicit reinterpretation of the Caliban/Prospero bond.

This explicit reinterpretation takes place in "Invisible Bullets: Renaissance Authority and Its Subversion, *Henry IV and Henry V.*" This essay also depends upon a linkage between an anecdote from colonialist archives and Shakespeare's plays. It is not this time the story of the exploitation of Lucayan ideology by Spanish faith (Greenblatt's use of that anecdote contained an implicit critique of colonialism or what is more to the point he took the critique for granted), but the exploitation of the Algonquin Indians' faith by Thomas Harriot, a British subject, suspected of atheism. The difference between these two anecdotes carries with it a change within the character of the improviser—from a Spanish believer to a British nonbeliever. This change in character implies an equally important shift in the conditions covering a successful displacement. The Spanish conquistadors had fairly obvious reasons for their exploitation of the Lucayans' beliefs: they needed cheap labor for work in the gold mines. But Thomas Harriot, in his *Brief and True Report* of an encounter with Algonquin Indians, expresses a more subtle need: he uses their religious beliefs as a way to displace his own religious doubts.

In this turn to Harriot, Greenblatt intends to eliminate the difficulties in displacement which he encountered in Iago. Iago presents modern readers with difficulties because he believes in nothing but his power to manipulate belief, and modern readers have difficulty believing in manipulators. But Harriot believes in doubt about religion, and his religious skepticism remains a pervasive symbolic structure for modern readers. In displacing Iago with Harriot, Greenblatt finds a state of mind into which he can absorb the improviser's manipulation. In manipulating the Algonquins' religious beliefs, Greenblatt contends, Harriot turns his profound doubts about religion into opportunities for control. In a brilliant and perverse reading of *Brief and True Report,* Greenblatt argues that Harriot, when in the New World, neither expressed nor surrendered his doubts about state religion, but elevated them onto a plane of Machiavellian insight. Unlike his fellow colonists, Harriot located the origins of religion in the imposition of coercive doctrines by a priestly ruling caste.

Initially, Harriot might appear unable to do the work of improvisation because, unlike the Spanish colonizers, he doubts that the symbolic structure is capable of absorbing the natives' displaced beliefs. But in Greenblatt's remarkable reading, Harriot's doubt turns out to be an even more effective resource for the colonialist practices than either the Spaniards' unquestioned belief or Iago's endless manipulations. Doubt enables Harriot to experience religious belief itself as a coercive power. His experience of being victimized by power leads him to wish to become the agent rather than the dupe of this structure of coercion. In converting the Algonquins to Christianity, Harriot turns his previous experience of being coerced by religious belief into the power to coerce through his religious doubts.

The colonialist enterprise turns out to be more resourceful in its use of Harriot's religious doubt than it was previously in its use of the Spaniards' religious belief. As long as Harriot's doubts remain directed against religious beliefs, he does not need to question the master code of colonialism as the supervening structure of dominance that turns both religious belief and religious doubt into aspects of its power. In converting the Indians to a religious system that Harriot believes only to be coercive, Harriot treats religion as an exploitable ideology rather than a dominative structure. Consequently, Harriot's subversion of religion can assume the form of a manipulation of the Algonquins' beliefs.

As a psychological explanation of Harriot's peculiar solution to a difficult problem, I find this argument quite compelling. Greenblatt does not read the *Report* in terms of Harriot's biography; instead he elevates it into exemplary instance of subversion in a colonial context and then generalizes its applicability: "One may go still further," he writes, "and suggest that the power Harriot both serves and embodies not only produces its own subversion but is actively built upon it: in the Virginia colony, the radical undermining of Christian order is not the negative limit but the primitive condition for the establishment of the order. And this paradox extends to the production of Harriot's text. *Brief and True Report,* with its latent heterodoxy, is not a reflection upon the Virginia colony nor even a simple record of it—not, in other words, a privileged withdrawal into a critical zone set apart from power—but a continuation of the colonial enterprise."[37]

This is an unusual passage in Greenblatt's criticism. In it he does not depend on any agent other than himself for the display of improvisational power, and he does not oppose but rather celebrates colonialism. The source of Greenblatt's improvisation, the symbolic structure capable of displacing and absorbing potentially subversive counterexamples, has nothing to do with Thomas Harriot's doubt. Harriot consigned his doubts to a particular aspect of the Renaissance power structure—that is, religious belief. Harriot believed enough in the dominant religion to *need* to doubt it. That his doubts were turned into a form of colonial domination only indicates the presence of a power more pervasive than the displacement of his doubts.

This power finds its expression in what we might call Greenblatt's elevation of the discourse of colonialism into a more inclusive power than religion. Unlike religious discourse, colonialism is capable of transforming both belief and doubt into its own manifestation of a power which includes its own subversion as one of its operations. This elevation serves a purpose: it provides the new historicist with a symbolic structure strong enough to outlast either orthodox religious faith or monarchy as a belief structure. When in these lines Greenblatt invokes a power that Harriot "both serves and embodies," he addresses a power that transcends the entire symbolic structure of organized religion and that continues to exert its influence to this day. This transcendent power can displace and absorb the Christian belief structures as readily as Christianity absorbed the Algonquins'.

Before Harriot could convert the Algonquins to Christianity, Greenblatt suggests that he had to undergo his own conversion experience. Unlike the Algonquins', Harriot's conversion involved giving up religion as a matter of belief or doubt and treating it as a fiction to be manipulated. Once he treated religion as such, Harriot's dissent no longer took place within the structure of religious belief, but within the discourse of colonialism to which he had been converted. Following this conversion, Harriot could identify (for purposes of improvisation) with a transcendent power that produced the symbolic structures in which others believed; and Harriot himself need believe only in this power to make believe.

Following his representation of Harriot's conversion, Greenblatt uses the language of religious faith to articulate a significant change in his understanding of Prospero's bond with Caliban. "It is tempting," Greenblatt begins, "to focus such remarks on Shakespeare's *Tempest* where Caliban, Prospero's salvage and deformed slave, enters cursing the expropriation of his island and exits declaring that he will be wise hereafter and seek for grace."[38] In "Learning to Curse," Greenblatt identifies as the reason for Caliban's cursing his prior experience of having been deprived of his language as well as his island. After citing an example of Caliban's unusual language, Greenblatt writes that it "compels us to acknowledge the independence and integrity of Caliban's construction of reality. We do not sentimentalize this construction . . . but we cannot make it vanish into silence."[39] Greenblatt seals his determination not to ignore Caliban's needs with a jeremiad; but in "Invisible Bullets," Greenblatt writes that he is "tempted" to break that resolve, and his use of this word readies us for a change in his understanding of colonialism. Greenblatt makes Caliban's constructions as well as his own empathy with him vanish by turning Caliban himself into an unequivocal sign of the power of colonialism to "contain" Prospero's dissent: "What better instance, in the light of Harriot's Virginia, of the containment of a subversive force by the authority that has created that force in the first place: 'This thing of darkness,' Prospero says of Caliban at the close, 'I acknowledge mine.'"[40]

In this passage, Greenblatt breaks the "entirely unsentimental bond" between Prospero and Caliban by reading the ambiguity out of the line. If the line was previously an indication, for Greenblatt, of Shakespeare's ambivalence about colonialism, that ambivalence about colonialism as well as Greenblatt's earlier opposition to it have now been transformed into an example of colonialism's power to license and contain forces subversive of it. In explaining colonialism's power to subject any apparent opposition to it within its operation, Greenblatt has displaced his own previous reading of the line's ambivalence and absorbed it within the discourse of colonialism.

THEATRICAL COLONIALISM

Earlier we heard Greenblatt voice his opposition to the entire colonialist enterprise; but "Invisible Bullets" does not continue that opposition. Instead, it turns colonialism into so pervasive a structure that "Learning to Curse," his previous critique of colonialism, now seems a colonial anecdote, an exemplification of a "privileged withdrawal into a critical zone set apart from power" and thereby discontinuous with everything else in the colonialist enterprise.

In understanding why Greenblatt withdraws his previous criticism, we should recall that "Learning to Curse" was written before Greenblatt developed the two concepts crucial to his new discipline: Renaissance self-fashioning, and improvisation. These two concepts produced a critical persona whose relationship with both literature and history was quite different from the Greenblatt of "Learning to Curse." The new historicism was the result of Greenblatt's terminological shift from self-fashioning to improvisation as the explanatory framework for understanding Elizabethan and Tudor England. That shift entailed a revaluation in Greenblatt's attitude toward colonialism. A direct result of Greenblatt's application of the improvisation model to Shakespeare's plays was a startling recognition: Shakespeare turned linguistic colonialism into a means of taking theatrical possession not merely of the New World but of the entirety of Renaissance culture. His new historicist reading of Shakespeare's plays in turn becomes Greenblatt's means of taking possession of the entire field of Renaissance studies.

In his reading of Shakespeare's plays, Greenblatt identifies them as a crucial part of the ideological apparatus of the theater state. Shakespeare's theater enabled Tudor subjects to misrecognize the colonialism the Tudor state had internalized as theatrical improvisation. As the absolute authority that replaced religion as a pervasive belief structure in Renaissance England, colonial power as internalized by Shakespeare became in the essays following *Renaissance Self-Fashioning* the basis for the improvisations needed to operate the new discipline. However, the colonialism operating within the essays following "Improvisation and Power" was not the oppressive force directed against native population. It was indistinguishable from the pervasive theatricalization of Tudor society—the conversion of everyone in it into two social categories: either self-fashioners who could be manipulated, or improvisational selves who did the manipulating. Here's where new historicist practices and rule in the theater state become metaphors for one another. Both Tudor subjects and new historicists are produced out of this misrecognition of colonialism as improvisation. Following the demotion in power of the symbolic structure of religion in modern time, only colonialism could solicit the deepest beliefs about freedom and constraints needed for the new historicists' and Tudor subjects' empowering improvisations, while theatricality remained the safeguard against identifying with those deep beliefs.

We begin to understand how theatricality provided such a safeguard if we reconsider Greenblatt's reading of the Harriot episode. By treating the structure of religious belief as a fully articulated arrangement of persons and their activities, Harriot, in Greenblatt's reading, produced a gigantic *mise en scène* that captivated the Algonquins' culture.

As he ensnared the Algonquins within this scenario, Harriot was able to reinterpret religion in terms of the theatrical illusion it empowered him to produce. As he witnessed the effect this illusion produced in the Algonquins, he at once recognized the power of this illusion and that this power was an illusion he could control. Like linguistic colonialism, theatricality manipulated the Algonquins' beliefs; but unlike linguistic colonialism, theatricality exposed the effects of manipulation (the absorption and displacement of deeply held beliefs) as manipulable illusions. Once described as a theatrical ruse rather than a coercive force, the colonialist enterprise need not arouse Harriot's (or Greenblatt's) opposition.

In order to oppose theatrical colonialism, one first needed to believe in its activities as something other than the effects of theatrical illusion. Greenblatt demonstrates the relationship between Harriot's theatricalized colonialism and the Renaissance by applying it to Shakespeare's *Henriad*. Like Harriot, Prince Hal subsumed the subversive energies he enacted as an unruly youth within the power of rule he exercised over England as king. His internalized misrule gave him the license to rule his unruly colonies. Including misrule within his persona as a ruler, Hal, like Harriot, contains subversive forces within a theatrical form. "To understand Shakespeare's whole conception of Hal from rakehell to monarch, we need," Greenblatt writes, "in effect a poetics of Elizabethan power, and this in turn will prove inseparable, in crucial respects from a poetics of the theater."[41]

Theatrical colonialism enabled Prince Hal and Thomas Harriot not to believe in anything but the power of belief structures to induce belief in the colonized. It also enabled Greenblatt no longer to disagree with Terence Hawkes's claim that the dramatist and colonist were homologous to one another.

NEW HISTORICISM AND ANTICOLONIALISM

While the new historicism subsumed Greenblatt's opposition to linguistic colonialism within the operations of theatrical colonialism,

Greenblatt's anticolonialism did not entirely disappear. The new historicism redesignated the appropriate object for this anticolonialism narrative in the old historicism's demotion of literature itself into one of history's linguistic colonies. History had become the culturally dominant academic discipline in the nineteenth century when it detached from literature and identified its purposes with those of social scientists intent on describing (and strengthening) developing nation states. Historians turned literature (such as Shakespeare's *The Tempest*) and colonial anecdotes (such as Martyr's account of the Lucayans and the Spaniards) into marginal texts—more or less equivalent raw material for historical illustrations. On the other hand, *as historical evidence,* an archival narrative such as Martyr's would have priority over a play by Shakespeare. In the contestation between the old and new historicisms, then, colonialism existed in two different registers: it designated a specific conjuncture of events and forces about which historians wrote, but it also referred metaphorically to the relationship established between history and related disciplines.

As a movement within the humanistic disciplines, the new historicism was emancipatory in relation to the old historicism. In the course of its operations, it claimed the power to release literary studies from the "dominant historical scholarship of the past."[42] To realize its emancipatory effect, we need only recall the prior relationship between history and literature in Renaissance studies: the Elizabethan world picture approach that read complex literary texts in terms of a stable historical world view that at once guaranteed the autonomy of those texts and their irrelevance to the way in which the world organized itself.[43] In Greenblatt, history no longer authoritatively represents past cultures, but becomes an aspect of literary studies, a colony of literary historicism, or more precisely, one of its theatrical productions. Like Prince Hal and Harriot, the new historicist produces history as part of a vast cultural *mise en scène.* Greenblatt's treatment of colonial anecdotes represents a cogent example of this production. In the course of "Improvisation and Power" and "Invisible Bullets," he lifted them from their marginal status in the old historicism (where their very irrelevance to any larger social narrative turned them into metaphors for literature) and treated them as episodes in a much vaster historical drama whose means of production they clarified. In producing the linkage between colonial anecdotes that would otherwise remain marginal to history and the rest of what should now be called the social text, Greenblatt displaces them from history then absorbs them within a more pervasive symbolic structure, not this time the colonialist enterprise but the new historicism; and he uses the pervasive structure and social logic of colonialism as his means of establishing and expanding the field of the new historicism.

The linkage Greenblatt produces between materials from the colonial archives and Shakespeare's plays also *re*produces the homology between the colonist and dramatist which he criticized earlier in Terence Hawkes. Once reproduced within the context of Greenblatt's criticism, that homology constitutes the true inaugural moment of the new historicism.

In linking colonial materials with Shakespeare's plays by way of homology, Greenblatt binds these otherwise unrelated contexts together with all the force of a logical entailment. This linkage changes the nature of the colonial materials. By abstracting the activities at work within the colonial encounter from their specific historical location, Greenblatt turns them into metaphors for colonialism. He then uses these metaphors as analytical categories symbolic of social actions. Following this transcoding of colonial displacement and absorption into metaphors for a socially symbolic action, improvisation, the violence in the historical colonial exchange becomes virtually unrecognizable.

What is historical about the colonial encounters (that is, the developing relations between the colonists and natives) remains of only marginal interest, but the formal use to which Greenblatt puts these colonial materials makes them symbolically central to the formation of his new discipline. As he displaces these materials from the colonial archives onto the contexts of an emergent academic discipline, Greenblatt reenacts at a highly abstract level the Spaniards' displacement and absorption of the Lucayans' belief structure.

Greenblatt also significantly transforms the power authorizing these activities. As he moves from a discussion of the Spaniards' exploitation of the Lucayans to Iago's manipulation of Othello, Greenblatt generalizes the applicability of these colonialist practices until colonialism becomes the internalized norm descriptive of all of Renaissance culture. Having identified this metaphoric colonialism with the belief structures of Renaissance culture, Greenblatt turns to Iago in order to misrecognize internalized colonialism as if it were theatrical improvisation. Greenblatt then turns Iago's improvisations and Shakespeare's dramatic power into homologies for one another: he represents both Iago and Shakespeare as cultural figures able to transform their relationship to colonial power from that of subject to master. This transformation in their relationship to colonial power, however, only takes place within the homologies to colonialism produced by the new discipline's analytical categories. Having turned Renaissance structures of belief into metaphors for actual colonialism, Greenblatt makes a metaphor of anticolonialism as well. Like the anticolonialism at work in the relationship between the new historicism and the old, the overthrow of colonial powers, by means of which Greenblatt articulates the workings of his new discipline, remains a merely symbolic action.

Both forms of symbolic anticolonialism provide Greenblatt with an imaginary relationship (that is, an ideological relation) to his new discipline. This imaginary relationship enables him to misrecognize the colonialist practices that the new historicism symbolically continues—as if they are subversive of the colonialist enterprise. As the new historicist produces his linkages between colonialistic encounters and Shakespeare's plays, he transforms the discourse of colonialism into a different level of abstraction, where it too seems a symbolic activity. Following a new historicist reading of a colonial encounter, colonialism no longer refers to the activity of subjecting native peoples to coercive rule, but instead refers to the formation of discursive knowledge for Renaissance subjects.

In the archives, colonialism refers to a dominative political relationship between colonists and settlers; in the new historicism, colonialism refers to the structure of relations in a cultural field. In transferring the structure of relations within an actual colonial encounter into metaphoric equivalents for the social relations constitutive of Renaissance culture, Greenblatt tacitly turns Renaissance subjects into models for practitioners of an academic discipline. Like individuals who follow a discipline's rules, Renaissance subjects, in Greenblatt's account, do not raise questions about social justice or reciprocal rights but readily submit themselves to the generalizable control of discursive norms. Instead of asking questions about the rights of subject peoples or striving to produce their own laws and standards, Greenblatt's self-fashioners identify themselves with roles that eliminate from recognition their subjection to a central theatrical ruler. These theatrical subjects never develop into citizens because they identify with no public but an audience, and no agent but an actor.

Greenblatt's new historicism activates a series of interlinked homologies holding together, in the transfer of their metaphors, colonial subjection, Renaissance subjects, theatricalized society, and academic discipline formation. The basis for these linkages inheres in a similarity between the way knowledge is ordinarily produced in an academic discipline (through a generalized structure of domination and subjection), the way native peoples are subjected to the generalized control of colonists, and the way actors submit to the control of a script. Having joined together these otherwise unrelated realms, through the transits of his metaphors, Greenblatt defines the new historicism as different. Unlike colonialism or other academic disciplines or Renaissance culture, but like the ruler of a theater state, the new historicist, Greenblatt would claim, does not subject his practitioner to a dominative structure but instead enables him to practice the evasion of all these interlinked homologies.

Since it defines all other cultural discourses as colonial powers, the new historicism possesses virtually limitless explanational range. The only governing rule for the new historicist is that he displace these structures from their own context and absorb them within the new historicist's practices (and thereby exploit their cultural labor). New historicism is able to include within its field all other symbolic structures, no matter whether from Renaissance England (such as the Church doctrine on sexuality or exorcism rituals) or from the most recent intellectual trend (such as Althusserian Marxism or Foucaultian genealogy). That endlessly assimilative practice can be briefly described as the demystification of every cultural discourse as a theatrical illusion produced by colonial power.

The standard designation for the theatricalized colonialism at work in the new historicism is the masque, whose power to demystify illusions inheres in the homologous power to impose its power as an illusion. A society organized in terms of a theatrical masque differs significantly from the actual colonial society Greenblatt described in "Learning to Curse." There, the colonizer could recognize his authority only by way of the colonized's submission to it. Before either the colonizer or the colonialism, they must first be able to experience their relationship to one another as theatrical rather than authentic. In Greenblatt's description of theatrical colonialism, however, only the colonizer can experience colonialism as a masque; and he can do that only after undergoing the same modernization process as has Greenblatt's new historicist. But since that process depends upon the colonizing figure's denial of a reciprocal relationship with the colonized, the one who knows he is wearing a mask can never let in on the show the one who does not know. If the colonized exists only as the basis for a display of the power to manipulate him, then the colonized must experience as just plain old colonial subjection what the new historicist in Greenblatt calls improvisation.

Throughout this account I have juxtaposed Greenblatt's new historicist reading of theatrical colonialism with Fanon's quite different account of the colonial encounter. I have done so to call attention to a figure who condemns the theatricality that Greenblatt celebrates as complicit with the coercive forces of colonialism. When Fanon described the theatrical component of colonialism as a white mask, he meant to identify theatricality as an ideological mystification of colonial rule.

Unlike Greenblatt, Fanon did not equate political liberation with the exposure of colonial rule as the power of an illusion. Such an equation would only perpetuate a politics of disillusionment instead of engaged political action. Moreover, unlike Greenblatt, Fanon did not identify his anticolonialism with the practices of an academic discipline. For Fanon, colonial relations were not metaphoric of the knowledge/power relations at work in an emergent discipline, but referred quite literally to his lived experience of a coercive culture whose conditions he wanted desperately to transform.

RELEARNING HOW TO CURSE

In Greenblatt's writing, the new historicism exists simultaneously in two conflicting registers. Within the humanistic disciplines, it functions as an anticolonialist emancipatory movement, liberating literary studies from colonization by history. As a new discipline, it produces a set of disciplinary practices which cannot be distinguished from colonialist practices. Neither the discipline formation of the new historicism nor that of the theatrical colonialism Greenblatt describes acknowledges any opposition to its operations which cannot be subsumed into a continuation of the colonialist enterprise. For all of its claim to infinite inclusiveness, however, the new historicism is founded on an internal contradiction. As a discipline formation, it performs its operations in terms of a metaphoric anticolonialism even as, contrary to common sense and the historical record, it denies actual anticolonialism any effectiveness external to the workings of the discipline.

Throughout this account I have repeatedly used Greenblatt's pre-new historicist essay "Learning to Curse" as a kind of political unconscious for the emergent academic discipline. That essay lends itself to such usage because in it Greenblatt expresses his unequivocal opposition to both the structure of political enterprise as well as the policy of linguistic colonialism in alliance with the enterprise. Greenblatt argues there that Shakespeare dramatized his own ambivalence to colonialism by way of Caliban's relationship to Prospero in *The Tempest*. To uncover signs of this ambivalence I read Greenblatt's new historicist essays in terms of the bond of ambivalence which Prospero shared with Caliban. To demonstrate the political effectiveness of this bond I discussed the different uses to which Fanon, Césaire, and Sartre put it in the anticolonialist political movement.

In "Learning to Curse," Greenblatt turns to the bond of ambivalence Prospero shared with Caliban to express his opposition to such domination in all its forms. I have discussed the return of that bond of ambivalence (in the displaced form of Othello) as if it were material from Greenblatt's political unconscious; and I have suggested a way to understand Greenblatt's rediscovery of the homology between the colonist and the dramatist as a "denial" (in the Freudian sense) of this repressed material. I want to conclude this discussion of the new historicism with a reading of the essay in which Greenblatt returns to the scene of this repressed material because in it theatrical colonialism becomes indistinguishable from colonial subjection.

Before I begin that reading, however, I propose as the ideological location for Greenblatt's new historicism the "culture of spectacle" that enabled Ronald Reagan to pursue neocolonialist policies in Latin America and elsewhere. Reagan's media politics, in explicitly linking theatricality with colonialism, turned theatrical colonialism into national policy. He did so moreover in the same period (the 1980s) in which Greenblatt worked out the implications of the new historicism.

In "Martial Law in the Land of Cockaigne," Greenblatt takes up the topics he discussed in "Learning to Curse" as well as *The Tempest*, where he located those topics. Instead of offering a revisionist account of these topics, however, Greenblatt does not successfully renegotiate them into the terms of the new practice. As a result of this failed negotiation, Shakespeare's play turns into a "white mask" for economic and political domination. Among the many forms this failed negotiation assumes are three of particular significance for this discussion: the loss of the homology between the colonist and the dramatist; a breakdown in the linkage between the colonial anecdote and the Shakespeare play; and a fissioning in the bond of ambivalence between Prospero and Caliban.

All of these failed negotiations result from the literalization of colonialism as a metaphor. Greenblatt literalizes that metaphor in two related ways. By observing a remarkable number "of social and profes-

sional connections linking Shakespeare and the stockholders and direc-
tors of the Virginia Company,"[44] Greenblatt makes quite explicit the
historical connection between Shakespeare's drama and an actual
(rather than theatrical) colonial encounter. What links Shakespeare to
the Virginia Company is his status as a shareholder in a joint-stock
company, The King's Men, with corporate and institutional interests
in the Virginia Company. Those interests in turn depend on the economic success of the Jamestown colony. Consequently, what Shakespeare found of greatest interest in William Strachey's account of the
wreck off the coast of Bermuda of the *Sea Venture* with members of the
Virginia Company on Board was the threat to his economic interest in
the enterprise.

In transcoding into *The Tempest* the materials he found in the
Strachey account, Shakespeare, Greenblatt now claims, began with a
recognition of the world of difference between this colonial incident
and his theatricalization of it. Unlike other anecdotes Greenblatt cites
from the colonial archives, this one entails an account of a colonist,
Henry Paine, whose subversion could not be "contained" within the
structure of theatricalized colonial relations. Instead of finding his role
within it, Henry Paine condemned the entire colonialist enterprise.
Following the shipwreck, he declared himself free of colonial authority that remained binding only as long as the condition of his contract
remained in effect. Shipwreck nullified his contract, setting him free of
colonial authority, Paine argued. However, the threat his rebellion
posed to colonial authority proved so great that the governor ordered
him shot.

By cursing the colonial authorities rather than improvising upon
their structures, Paine too literalizes the colonial metaphor. He refuses
to play the part assigned him by the Virginia Company, and his refusal
threatens as well the homology between theater and colonialism underwriting Greenblatt's new historicist project. Instead of finding his
opposition acted out by others, Paine simply identifies himself as an
anticolonialist *tout court*.

In moving from the Paine material to *The Tempest*, Greenblatt argues
that Shakespeare reenacts the Paine rebellion but in the displaced form

of his containment of Sebastian's murderous treachery directed against his older brother through Prospero's mask. Greenblatt then goes on to claim that Prospero's art, in thwarting such rebellious activity, becomes a version of martial law in the colonies. "A crisis of authority," Greenblatt concludes, "gives way through the power of his art to a full restoration. From this perspective Prospero's magic is the romance equivalent of martial law."[45]

The trouble with this account is related to this ultimate claim. By making Prospero's art the equivalent of martial law, Greenblatt thereby equates theatrical mystification with the most coercive structure of dominance in the Renaissance. If Prospero's mask compels the other colonists to obey his colonial authority, this theatrical colonialism can no longer be described as a demystification of colonial power, but rather its artistic representation. Prospero's mask invests colonial authority with the mystery it needs to command the fear and respect of the other colonists. Greenblatt refinds in Prospero's magic, we might say, the homology between the dramatist and the colonist he could not find in Henry Paine. When he refinds this homology in Shakespeare's Prospero rather than in Henry Paine, Greenblatt once again underscores the crucial difference between Paine's rebellion and Shakespeare's play. No magic and no mystification could persuade Henry Paine to submit to the structure of colonial relations. His rebellion exposed the theatrical colonialism of colonists such as Thomas Harriot as a mystification of the actual structure of colonial relations.

Greenblatt cannot displace into his new historicist practice this source material from the colonial archives because the historical content of the Paine material is *not* simply one more symbolic structure for theatrical colonialism to manipulate. It exists outside this structure of colonial relation. Paine believes enough in his opposition to colonialism to give up his life in exchange for his refusal to embody or enact the structure of colonial relations. Paine refuses Governor Gates's demand that he displace his anticolonialism then, and Greenblatt cannot cover over this opposition with theatrical colonialism now. Instead of being displaced. Paine's rebellion exposes what is "theatrical" in colonialism as an ideological cover, what Fanon centuries later would call a

"white mask," for the murderous brutality at the heart of the colonialist enterprise.

Unlike Greenblatt, Paine does not demystify colonial relations as a
form of theater. Such a demystification, insofar as it takes place within
the structure of theatricalized colonial relations, only validates that
structure. Like Fanon, he opposes that structure of relations, thereby
recharacterizing what is theatrical in colonialism as a purely imaginary
relation to the real thing.

Greenblatt tries to displace Paine's anticolonialism into his new historicist practice by way of Prospero's magic. But when Greenblatt
does, Paine's anticolonialism turns Prospero's make-believe back into
martial law. Undisplaced, Paine's execution literalizes out what is imaginary in Shakespeare's (and Greenblatt's) colonialism as pure theater,
leaving us with a real corpse.

Earlier we pointed out the ways in which Greenblatt's new historicism transformed literal anticolonialism into two metaphoric equivalents: the evasion of domination by Renaissance belief structures, and
the decolonization of history's dominance of literary studies. We also
claimed that once he metaphorized anticolonialism into these symbolic equivalents, Greenblatt could misrecognize the ideology of colonialism at work in the new historicism. However, Paine did not
accept any other Renaissance structure of belief (no matter whether
Catholicism or religious skepticism) as an equivalent location for his
opposition. He opposed colonialism; and the account of his opposition, insofar as it cannot be eradicated from mind by Shakespeare's art
(or Greenblatt's revisionary account), remains in the colonialist archives. The literal anticolonialism at work in the incident exposes the
anticolonialism in the new historicism as a mere metaphor. Instead of
affiliating itself with the new practice at any level of abstraction, this
colonial anecdote eliminates from it the misrecognition of the new
historicism's affiliation with actual colonialist practices.

If the Paine incident literalizes the imaginary anticolonialism out of
the new historicism, it also gives back something to Greenblatt—
namely, the literal anticolonialism of "Learning to Curse." In "going
native" in Bermuda, Henry Paine finds a Caliban in his own nature. He

embodies that bond of ambivalence Greenblatt found earlier in Prospero's relationship with Caliban. In "Learning to Curse," Greenblatt bases his opposition to colonialism on that entirely unsentimental bond; but in "Martial Law in the Land of Cockaigne," Greenblatt provides a reading of that bond which enables him to misrecognize his anticolonialism. He identifies his earlier reaction as that of "modern reader." A Renaissance audience might have been more ambivalent about "the ambiguous status of magic,"[46] Greenblatt claims, than about Caliban. Following this division in audience reaction, Greenblatt identifies any anxiety over the dispossession of Caliban, the brutality directed toward him, and even Prospero's ambivalence about his relationship to the figure who stands "anxious and powerless before him" with a modern reader's sensitivity to "implied criticisms of colonialism."[47] Having identified anxieties about colonialism with a modern readership and anxieties over magic with a Renaissance audience, Greenblatt then rejoins Renaissance to modern anxieties in a final sentence, "At the play's end the princely magician appears anxious and powerless before the audience to beg for indulgence and freedom."[48]

Greenblatt obviously expects a lot from this concluding sentence. By describing Prospero as anxious and powerless as he stands before the (Renaissance and modern) audience, he links him metaphorically with the Caliban Greenblatt described earlier as anxious and powerless before Prospero. If a modern audience directed its sympathies toward a Caliban, why not toward such a Prospero? And if that sympathy entails believing in his theatrical magic, why not?

In linking (modern) anxiety over Prospero's colonial subjection of Caliban with (Renaissance) anxiety over the power of make-believe Greenblatt intends the sentence to join Renaissance (theatrical) anxiety with modern (colonial) anxiety. He also intends as a result to rejoin theatrical colonialism to its powers of make-believe. There is one other figure Greenblatt does not mention, however, who also stood anxious and powerless before both Renaissance and modern audiences: Henry Paine. In the figure of Paine, the homology between Shakespeare's drama and colonialism upon which Greenblatt founded the new historicism had already come unhinged. Moreover, it had done so within the context of a colonial anecdote whose narrative he could not renegotiate into the terms of the new historicist practice. Instead of offering itself as a manipulable fiction, the Paine material turns the new historicist account itself into pure fantasy. Without the power to (de)mystify Paine's anticolonialism, Prospero (and Greenblatt) ask for belief in his (their) power to make believe.

That final image of Prospero standing anxious and powerless before an audience would be a moving sight, and it might have evoked as a sentimental response a need to believe in his magic had Greenblatt not previously identified Prospero's art with martial law. To withstand that sentimental response, we might recall that Greenblatt, in "Learning to Curse," described as entirely unsentimental the bond Prospero shared with Caliban. Then we might recall what Fanon claimed: that this bond enabled both Caliban and Prospero to experience the discourse of colonialism as a curse. When Henry Paine, who embodied this bond, was asked by Governor Gates to believe in the discourse of colonialism, he is reported to have said, "Let the Governor kiss . . . ."[49]

This curse connects Henry Paine with the Caliban in Greenblatt's earlier essay.[50] Like Paine's, Caliban's curse enabled him to experience the difference between himself (black skin) and his colonial identity. This difference, once articulated, would become the basis for the related transformation in the history of colonial relations—from a subject with no rights to a citizen with reciprocal rights and duties. Paine's curse in "Martial Law in the Land of Cockaigne" echoes Caliban's in "Learning to Curse." Their reciprocated curses restore the deep and entirely unsentimental bond between Caliban and Prospero to Greenblatt's new historicist practice. That bond of ambivalence, if we gave it voice, might encourage Greenblatt to apply his earlier critique of Hawkes to his new practice and thereby become ambivalent about an academic discipline that reenacts as its new historicist practice the system of colonial domination he earlier cursed.

NOTES

1. Greenblatt first uses the term *new historicism* in his introduction to *The Forms of Power and the Power of Forms in the Renaissance.* "Yet diverse as they are, many of the present essays give voice, I think, to what we might call the new historicism, set apart from both the dominant historical scholarship of the past and the formalist criticism that partially displaced this scholarship in the decades after World War II" ("Introduction," *Genre* 15 (Spring 1982): 5).

2. O. Mannoni, *Prospero and Caliban: The Psychology of Colonization,* trans. Pamela Powesland (New York: Praeger, 1956).

3. For Fanon's discussion of Mannoni's use of Caliban and Prospero, see Frantz Fanon, *Black Skin, White Masks,* trans. Charles Lam Markmann (New York: Grove Press, 1967), 83–108.

4. Fanon also uses Lacan's mirror phase to explain the origins of racism: "It would be interesting, on the basis of Lacan's theory of the *mirror period,* to investigate the extent to which the *image* of his fellow built up in the young white at the usual age would undergo an imaginary aggression with the appearance of the Negro." Fanon, *Black Skin, White Masks,* 161.

5. Stephen Greenblatt, "Learning to Curse: Aspects of Linguistic Colonialism in the Sixteenth Century," in *First Images of America: The Impact of the New World on the Old,* ed. Fredi Chiapelli (Berkeley and Los Angeles; University of California Press, 1976), 561–80.

6. For a remarkably similar analysis of the origins of modern man in the discourse of the Other, see Michel de Certeau, *Heterologies: Discourse in the Other,* trans. Brian Massumi (Minneapolis: University of Minnesota Press, 1986), 3–34, 67–79, 225–236; Homi Bhabha, "Of Mimicry and Man: The Ambivalence of Colonial Discourse," *October* 28 (Spring 1984): 124–35.

7. This feature of Lacan's theory may be related to its origins amid the infighting of competing schools of psychoanalysis, described by Sherry Turkle in *Psychoanalytic Politics: Freud's French Revolution* (New York: Basic Books, 1978), 47–140.

8. For an example of the way in which a Caribbean intellectual can put Shakespeare's *The Tempest* into the service of anticolonialist struggles, see Roberto Fernandez Retamar, "Caliban: Notes toward a Discussion of Culture in Our America," trans. Lynn Garafola, David Arthur McMurray, and Robert

Marquez, *Massachusetts Review* 15 (Winter/Spring 1974) 11–16. Alden T. Vaughan in "Caliban in the 'Third World: Shakespeare's Savage as Sociopolitical Symbol'" *Massachusetts Review* 29 (Summer 1988): 289–313 explores the anticolonialist use to which Caliban was put by Latin America and African intellectuals in the late nineteenth and twentieth centuries.

9. Sartre brings his previous work into relationship to the question of colonialism in his preface to Frantz Fanon's *The Wretched of the Earth,* trans. Constance Farrington (New York: Grove Press, 1966), 7–26. For an analysis of Western self-consciousness and the master/slave dialectic, see Mitchell Aboulafia, "Self-Consciousness and the Quasi-Epic of the Master," *The Philosophical Forum* 18 (Summer 1987): 304–28. For a brief discussion of Sartre's relationship to the politics of anticolonialism, see Fredric Jameson, *The Syntax of History* vol. 2 of *Ideologies of Theory-Essays 1971–1968* (Minneapolis: University of Minnesota Press, 1988), 187–88.

10. For an interesting version of this different life, see O. Onoge, "Caliban on the Couch," in *African Social Studies: A Radical Reader,* ed. Peter C. W. Gutbind and Peter Waterman (New York: Monthly Review Press, 1977), 32–43. For a useful reading of the transformations in Sartre's critique, see Ronald Aronson, "Vicissitudes of the Dialectic," *The Philosophical Forum* 18 (Summer 1987): 358–91.

11. Aimé Césaire, *Une tempête: d'apres "La Tempête" de Shakespeare,* adaptation pour une théâtre nègre (Paris: Editions du Seuil, 1969).

12. Rob Nixon provides a fine critical account of these matters in "Caribbean and African Appropriations of *The Tempest,*" *Politics and Poetic Value,* ed. Robert von Hallberg (Chicago: University of Chicago Press, 1987), 185–206.

13. Greenblatt, "Learning to Curse," 570.

14. Ibid.

15. Ibid.

16. Terence Hawkes, *Shakespeare's Talking Animals* (London: Routledge and Kegan Paul, 1973), 211.

17. Ibid. Interestingly, Terence Hawkes has changed his reading of Shakespeare and colonialism in ways consonant with Greenblatt's in "Learning to Curse." See Terence Hawkes, "Swisser-Swatter: Making a Man of English Letters," in *Alternative Shakespeares,* ed. John Drakakis (London: Methuen, 1985), 26–47.

18. Greenblatt, "Learning to Curse," 570.

19. See Hawkes, "Swisser-Swatter," 30–31.

20. For good accounts of the new practice, see Jonathan Dollimore, "Introduction: Shakespeare, Cultural Materialism and the New Historicism," in *Political Shakespeare: New Essays in Cultural Materialism*, ed. Jonathan Dollimore and Alan Sinfield (Ithaca: Cornell University Press, 1985), 2–17. Louis Montrose, "Renaissance Literary Studies and the Subject of History," *English Literary Renaissance* 16 (Winter 1986): 5–12; Greenblatt, *Genre* 15 (Spring 1982): 3–6; Howard Horwitz, "I Can't Remember: Skepticism, Synthetic Histories, Critical Action," *South Atlantic Quarterly* 87 (Fall 1988): 787–820. The numbers of dissenters from the new practice are by now legion. Among the many fine critiques are: Edward Pechter, "The New Historicism and the Its Discontents: Politicizing Renaissance Drama," *PMLA* 102 (May 1987): 292–303; Jean E. Howard, "The New Historicism in Renaissance Studies," *English Literary Renaissance* 16 (Winter 1986): 13–43; Jonathan Goldberg, "The Politics of Renaissance Literature: A Review Essay," *ELH* 49 (Summer 1982): 514–42; Judith Newton, "History as Usual?: Feminism and the 'New Historicism,'" *Cultural Critique* 9 (Spring 1988): 87–121; Walter Cohen, "Political Criticism of Shakespeare" in *Shakespeare Reproduced: The Text in History and Ideology*, ed. Jean Howard and Marion O'Connor (New York: Methuen, 1987), 18–46; Carolyn Porter, "Are We Being Historical Yet?, *SAQ* 87 (Fall 1988): 743–86, and especially Frank Lentricchia in *Ariel and The Police: Michel Foucault, William James, Wallace Stevens* (Madison: University of Wisconsin Press, 1987), 86–102. As an example of its prominence, at the 1988 Modern Language Association convention I counted more than thirty papers in which the new historicism figured in the title. Since most of these critiques agree to the structure of relations at work within the practice, the new historicism has little trouble "containing" these subversions.

21. Greenblatt's original sentence includes a specific example: "in the present case, for example it might encourage us to examine the ideological situation not only of *Richard II* but of Dover Wilson in *Richard II*. The lecture from which I have quoted—'The Political Background of Shakespeare's *Richard II* and *Henry IV*'—was delivered before the German Shakespeare Society at Weimar in 1939. We might, in a full discussion of the critical issues at stake here, look closely at the relation between Dover Wilson's reading of *Richard II* . . . and the eerie occasion of his lecture," *Genre* 15 (Spring 1982): 5–6.

22. The version of "Invisible Bullets: Renaissance Authority and Its Subversion, *Henry IV* and *Henry V*," which I will cite appears in *Political Shakespeare,* 18–47. It is reprinted in a substantially revised form along with "Martial Law in the Land of Cockaigne" in *Shakespearean Negotiations: The Circulation of Social Energy in Renaissance England* ed. Stephen Greenblatt (Berkeley and Los Angeles: University of California Press, 1988), 21–65, 129–64. "Invisible Bullets" has also appeared in other forms, among them, *Glyph* 8 (1981): 40–61.

23. Stephen Greenblatt, "The Improvisation of Power," *Renaissance Self-Fashioning: From More to Shakespeare* (Chicago: University of Chicago Press, 1980), 226.

24. Greenblatt, "Learning to Curse," 571. Greenblatt's point here was that the Europeans, in translating the native speech into their own diction, had altered it out of recognition. He makes this point, however, as a plea for linguistic reciprocity as opposed to linguistic colonialism.

25. Greenblatt, "The Improvisation of Power," 230. Greenblatt changed the title from "Improvisation and Power" to identify the practice with Renaissance powers. Daniel Lerner's word appears in *The Passing of Traditional Society: Modernizing the Middle East,* rev. ed. (New York: Free Press, 1964), 49. Given the ideology of colonialism at work in Israeli-Palestinian relations, I am surprised Greenblatt does not consider how empathy affects the structure of colonial relations in this modern account of middle eastern society.

26. Greenblatt, "The Improvisation of Power," 230.

27. Ibid.

28. See J. G. A. Pocock, *The Machiavellian Moment: Florentine Political Thought and the Atlantic Republican Tradition* (Princeton: Princeton University Press, 1974), particularly 82–218, 353–60, 506–51.

29. Only the colonial enterprise as a symbolic structure applicable both to Renaissance England as well as the New World can establish an all-inclusive field for the new historicism to explain. Once he has saturated the entire Renaissance field with the discourse of colonialism, Greenblatt can even read the great transformations in Europe's political arrangements as renegotiations of the colonial model. "Moreover," he writes of Pocock's argument, "the 'Atlantic Republican Tradition,' as Pocock argued, does grow out of the 'Machiavellian Moment' of the sixteenth century, and that tradition . . . does ultimately undermine, in the interests of a new power, the religious and secular authorities that

had licensed the American enterprise in the first place." "Invisible Bullets," 25. But in Greenblatt's understanding of *The Machiavellian Moment*, this undermining of monarchic rule does not lead to the development of citizens who believe in civic virtue and participation in a public world (as it does for Pocock) but only to the need for more and more manipulation of other people's beliefs.

30. Greenblatt, "The Improvisation of Power," 224.

31. "This (sexual) tension is less a manifestation of some atavistic 'blackness' specific to Othello than a manifestation of the colonial power of Christian doctrine over sexuality." Greenblatt, "The Improvisation of Power," 42. But Greenblatt claims Freud was the first to point out the similarity between the political operation of colonial subjection and the mechanisms of repression in this sentence, "Civilization behaves towards sexuality as a people does which has subjected another one to its exploitation." Greenblatt, *Renaissance Self-Fashioning*, 173.

32. The phrase is Althusser's. Greenblatt cites it in explaining how a self-fashioner makes "us . . . 'perceive' . . . from *the inside*, by an internal distance the very ideology in which it is held." Greenblatt, *Renaissance Self-Fashioning*, 192.

33. Greenblatt writes of Iago on Church and sexuality "To Iago, the Renaissance skeptic, this system has a somewhat archaic urge as if it were an earlier stage of development which his own modern sensibility had cast off." Greenblatt, "The Improvisation of Power," 246.

34. Ibid., 250.

35. "Iago," Greenblatt writes, "can conceal his fallacious intention towards 'the thick lips'" (of Othello). Ibid., 234.

36. Like Iago, "Shakespeare possessed limitless talent for entering into the consciousness of another, perceiving its deepest structures as a manipulable fiction, reinscribing it into his narrative form." Ibid., 252.

37. Greenblatt, "Invisible Bullets," 24. Greenblatt depends on Foucault for this containment of subversion model. Foucault treats discourses as closed fields of knowledge and power arranged around the model of colonial subjection. For a different view of how to get out of such discourses, I have depended upon a Sartrean dialectical model of discourses as social practices.

38. Ibid., 29. Greenblatt eliminates this passage from *Shakespearean Negotiations*, but this quote appears in *Glyph* 8 (1981): 53.

39. Greenblatt, "Learning to Curse," 575.

40. Greenblatt, "Invisible Bullets," 29. This passage does not appear in *Shakespearean Negotiations*, but it does in *Glyph* 8 (1981): 53.

41. Greenblatt, "Invisible Bullets," 44.

42. Greenblatt, "The Forms of Power." For a fine account of the struggle between literary history and the history professed in history departments, see Linda Orr, "The Revenge of Literature: A History of History," *New Literary History* 18 (Autumn 1986): 1–22.

43. Given the number of times the new historicists cite Tillyard's "world picture" approach, they might site its ideological location. For an example of such a siting, see Alan Sinfield, "Royal Shakespeare: Theatre and the Making of an Ideology," in Dollimore, *Political Shakespeare,* 260–62.

44. Greenblatt, "Martial Law in the Land of Cockaigne," 149–150.

45. Ibid., 153.

46. Ibid., 157.

47. Ibid., 158.

48. Ibid., 157. In this passage Prospero asks the audience to bring back a theater state; but as soon as he has to ask for a recovery of belief in the theater state, Prospero indicates the end of its rule. At this moment as well, Greenblatt also indicates a certain incoherence in his own account of the theater state. If the theater represents the system of signs by means of which Renaissance society organizes itself, the theater, no matter whether it represents these signs as signs or not, simply expresses that sign system. When they participate in the world expressed by the sign system, that entire sign system then becomes symbolic of the nature of the state. You can stop believing in that symbol, but whether you believe in it or not has nothing to do with the system of signs.

49. Ibid., 153. Interestingly, Greenblatt characterizes Paine's crime as a violation of linguistic colonialism. In effect, Paine is killed to set an example, condemned to die for cursing authority, for a linguistic crime, for violation of "discursive decorum" (153). The discursive decorum he violates is the discourse of colonialism; and as Greenblatt uses Shakespeare to recover that discourse, he turns *The Tempest* into a way to pursue a policy of linguistic colonialism. As if to deny this usage, he writes in a footnote that Shakespeare's plays are not conceived of as agents in the work of empire. But, as we have seen, that is just how they were used in nineteenth-century education. And that's why Fanon and

Césaire and the early Greenblatt opposed that policy in their use of *The Tempest.*

50. Henry Paine's going native inverts Thomas Harriot's earlier colonization of the natives. Greenblatt, in his displacement of Paine with the figure of Prospero's art, tries to turn Paine into Harriot; or rather he tries to turn his modern readers into versions of Harriot's Algonquins.

Gayatri Chakravorty Spivak

Theory in the Margin

COETZEE'S *FOE* READING DEFOE'S *CRUSOE/ROXANA*

For somewhat more than a decade, literary criticism in the United States had been made to pay attention to the representation and self-representation of margins. So much so, indeed, that the President's Forum at the Modern Language Association annual convention in 1988 had the title "Breaking Up/Out/Down: The Boundaries of Literary Study." It is also true that, perhaps as a result of these efforts, a strong demand to keep U.S. culture purely "Western" has also been consolidated.[1] Under pressure of this debate, we tend to monumentalize something we call "margins." Yet, for the sake of the daily work at the ground level, we must still raise the persistent voice of autocritique.

As we try to shore up our defenses, we tend to leave untouched the politics of the specialists of the margin—the area studies, anthropology, and the like. Third World studies, including Third World feminist studies in English, become so diluted that all linguistic specificity or scholarly depth in the study of culture is often ignored. Indeed, works in poor English translation or works written in English or the European languages in the recently decolonized areas of the globe or written by people of so-called ethnic origin in First World space are beginning to constitute something called "Third World literature." Within this arena of tertiary education in literature, the upwardly mobile exmarginal, *justifiably* searching for validation, can help commodify marginality. Sometimes, with the best of intentions and in the name of convenience, an institutionalized double-standard tends to get established: one standard of preparation and testing for our own kind and quite another for the rest of the world. Even as we join in the struggle to establish the institutional study of marginality we must still go on saying "And yet . . ."

Consider Sartre, speaking his commitment just after World War II:

> And, diverse though man's projects [*projets*—this word has the general exis-
> tentialist sense of undertaking to construct a life] may be, at least none of
> them is wholly foreign to me, . . . Every project, even that of a Chinese, an
> Indian or a Negro, can be understood by a European. . . The European of
> 1945 can throw himself [pro-ject] out of a situation which he conceives
> towards his limits [*se jeter a partir d'une situation qu'il concoit vers ses limites*]
> in the same way, and . . . he may re-do [*refaire*] in himself the project of the
> Chinese, of the Indian or the African . . . There is always some way of
> understanding an idiot, a child, a primitive man or a foreigner *if one has
> sufficient information.*[2]

Sartre's personal and political good faith cannot be doubted here. Yet
commenting on such passages, Derrida wrote in 1968: "Everything
occurs as if the sign 'man' had no origin, no historical, cultural, or linguistic limit."[3] Indeed, if one looks at the rhetorical trace of Rome in
"none of [man's projects] is wholly alien to me" [*humani nil a me alie-
num puto* (Terence via the *philosophes*)], one realizes that the history
obliterated here is that of the arrogance of the radical European humanist conscience, which will consolidate it*self* by imagining the other, or,
as Sartre puts it, "redo in himself the other's project," through the collection of information. Much of our literary critical globalism or
Third Worldism cannot even qualify to the conscientiousness of this
arrogance.

The opposite point of view, although its political importance cannot be denied, that only the marginal can speak for the margin, can, in
its institutional consequences, legitimize such an arrogance of conscience. Faced with this double-bind, let us consider a few methodological suggestions:

1. Let us learn to distinguish between what Samir Amin long ago
called "internal colonization"—the patterns of exploitation and domination of disenfranchised groups within a metropolitan country like
the United States or Britain—and the colonization of other spaces, of
which Robinson Crusoe's island is a "pure" example.[4]

2. Let us learn to discriminate the terms *colonialism*—in the Euro-

pean formation stretching from the mid eighteenth to the mid twentieth centuries—*neocolonialism*—dominant economic, political, and cul-
turalist maneuvres emerging in our century after the uneven dissolu-
tion of the territorial empires—and *postcoloniality*—the contemporary
global condition, since the first term is supposed to have passed or be
passing into the second.

3. Let us take seriously the possibility that systems of representation
come to hand when we secure our *own* culture—our own cultural explanations. Consider the following set:

   a. The making of an American is defined by at least a desire to
   enter the "We the People" of the Constitution. One cannot dismiss
   this as mere "essentialism" and take a position against civil rights,
   the Equal Rights Amendment, or the transformative opinions in
   favor of women's reproductive rights. We in the United States cannot not want to inhabit this rational abstraction.

   b. Traditionally, this desire for the abstract collective American
   "We the People" has been recoded by the fabrication of ethnic
   enclaves, affectively bonded subcultures, simulacra for survival that,
   claiming to preserve the ethnos of origin, move further and further
   away from the vicissitudes and transformations of the nation or
   group of origin. "How seriously can we [Africans] take . . . her
   [Alice Walker's] Africa, which reads like an overlay of South Africa
   over a vaguely realized Nigeria?"[5]

   c. Our current tendency to obliterate the difference between U.S.
   internal colonization and the transformations and vicissitudes in
   decolonized space in the name of the pure native invests this already
   established ethnocultural agenda. At worst, it secures the "They" of
   development or aggression against the Constitutional "We." At
   best, it suits our institutional convenience, bringing the Third
   World home. The double-standard can then begin to operate.[6]

In the face of the double-bind of Eurocentric arrogance or unexa-
mined nativism, the suggestions above are substantive. Deconstructive
cautions would put a critical frame around and in between them, so
that we do not compound the problem by imagining the double-bind
too easily resolved. Thus, if we keep in mind only the substantive

suggestions, we might want to help ourselves by a greater effort at historical contextualization. Yet this too, if unaccompanied by the habit of critical reading, may feed the Eurocentric arrogance in Sartre's declaration: "there is always some way of understanding [the other] if one has sufficient information." The critical frame reminds us that the institutional organization of historical context is no more than our unavoidable starting point. The question remains: With this necessary preparation, to quote Sartre again, *how* does "the European"—or, in the neocolonial context, the U.S. critic and teacher of the humanities—"redo *in himself* [or herself] the project of the Chinese, of the Indian or the African?"

In the face of *this* question, deconstruction might propose a double-gesture: Begin where you are; but, when in search of absolute justifications, remember that the margin as such is wholly other. Or, as Derrida put it in 1968 in a speech given at a philosophical colloquium: "I was thinking, first of all, of all those places—cultural, linguistic, political, etc.—where the organization of a philosophical colloquium simply would have no meaning, where it would be no more meaningful to instigate it than to prohibit it."[7]

To meditate on the wholly otherness of margins, I will look at a novel in English, *Foe,* by a white South African, J. M. Coetzee.[8] This novel reopens two English texts in which the early eighteenth century tried to constitute marginality: Daniel Defoe's *Robinson Crusoe* (1719) and *Roxana* (1724).[9] In *Crusoe,* the white man marginalized in the forest encounters Friday the savage in the margin. In *Roxana,* the individualist female infiltrates nascent bourgeois society. In Coetzee's novel, a double-gesture is performed. In the narrative, Roxana begins her construction of the marginal where she is; but when her project approaches fulfillment, the text steps in and reminds us that Friday is in the margin as such, the wholly other.

I use the novel as a didactic aid to share with my students some of the problems of which I have been speaking. For the substantive provision of a historical context, I use Derek Attridge's "The Silence of the Canon: J. M. Coetzee's 'Foe,' Cultural Narrative, and Political Oppression," a much more detailed study than mine.[10] My reading attempts to be a critical supplement to his. It attends to the rhetorical conduct of the text as it stages reading and writing. It is my hope that such a reading points out that a merely historically contextualized interpretation might produce closures that are problematic even as they are reasonable and satisfactory, that "the danger to which the sovereign decision [of the historical critic] responds is undecidability."[11] Since the theory of which my intervention is the consequence is deconstruction in and on margins, I will spend a few moments on it before I turn to Coetzee's novel.

In 1972, Derrida published his *Marges de la philosophie.*[12] I was taken by the caesura in his title. In *De la grammatologie,* Derrida let the title stand by itself. Five years later, a cannier Derrida stuck the word *Margins* before a comparably structured title: *de la philosophie.* The obvious meanings: I, the philosopher, philosophize in the margins; or, philosophy lives in its own margins; or yet, here I philosophize in an unauthorized way, attending to margins. The absent word is *margin* in the singular, the wholly other.

I learned another lesson from it, as follows: if we want to start something, we must ignore that our starting point is shaky. If we want to get something done, we must ignore that the end will be inconclusive. But this ignoring is not an active forgetfulness. It is an active *marginalizing* of the marshiness, the swampiness, the lack of firm grounding at the margins, at the beginning and end. Yet those of us who "know" this also know that it is in those margins that philosophy hangs out. These necessarily and actively marginalized margins haunt what we start and get done, as curious guardians. Paradoxically, if you do not marginalize them but make them the center of your attention, you sabotage their guardianship. Perhaps *some* of the problems with *some* of what you recognize as deconstructive work has been a fixation with the stalled origin and the stalled end: *differance* and *aporia* will do as their names. On the other hand, if you forget the productive unease that what you do with the utmost care is judged by those margins, in the political field you get the pluralism of repressive tolerance and sanctioned ignorance, and varieties of fundamentalism, totalitarianism, and cultural revolution; and, in the field of writing about and teaching literature, you get both the benign or resentful conservatism of the establishment *and* the masquerade of the privileged as the disenfranchised, or their liberator.

This is *marginal* in the *general* sense, no more and no less than a formula for doing things: the active and necessary marginalization of the strange guardians in the margins who keep us from vanguardism. The *marginal* in the narrow sense is the victims of the best-known history of centralization: the emergence of the straight white christian man of property as the ethical universal. Because there is something like a relationship between the general and the narrow sense, the problem of marking a margin in the house of feminism can be stated in another way. In her influential and by now classic essay "The Laugh of the Medusa," Helene Cixous writes: "As subject *for* history, woman occurs simultaneously in several places."[13] In a minimal way, this can be taken to mean that, in a historical narrative in which single male figures or groups of men are definitive, woman or women as such cannot fit neatly into the established periodizing rubrics or categories. Maximally, as Cixous goes on to point out, this might also mean that the feminist woman becomes part of every struggle, *in a certain way.*

Proof of this can be found in the increasing interest in marginality in general within feminism in the academy. The exuberance of this interest has sometimes overlooked a problem: that a concern with women, *and* men, who have not been written in the *same* cultural inscription, cannot be mobilized *in the same way* as the investigation of gendering in our own. It is *not* impossible, but new ways have to be learned and taught, and attention to the wholly other must be constantly renewed. We understand it more easily when folks of the other *gender* inscription wish to join *our* struggle. For example, I confess to a certain unease reading a man's text about a woman. Yet, when we want to intervene in the heritage of colonialism or the practice of neo-colonialism, we take our own goodwill for guarantee.

I am ready to get on with Coetzee's actual reading of *The Life and Adventures of Robinson Crusoe.* On the threshold stands Marx's paragraph on Defoe's novel.[14] Everyone reads it as being about capitalism, but it is exactly not so. The main drift of Marx's chapter in which this paragraph occurs is that in generalized commodity production, the commodity has a fetish character. It represents the relationship between persons as a relationship between things. When commodities are not produced specifically for exchange, this fetish character disappears. *Time,* not money, is then the general equivalent. Marx chooses four examples, three precapitalist and one post-. Of the three precapitalist examples, Robinson is the first and most interesting because the other two are situations of exchange, although not of generalized commodity exchange. Robinson's example is of the production of use-values.

Marx's argument that all human beings perform that structure in exchange which is later expressed as money is not supposed to hold in cases of the production of *use*-values. But throughout the entire range of his writings, the theoretical fiction of the binary opposition between use- and exchange-value is repeatedly undone. Indeed, this may be the cornerstone of the subterranean text of socialist ethics in Marx which is still to be theorized. The undoing of the use-value/exchange-value binary repeatedly shows that for Marx, the private is defined by and contains within it the possibility of the social. The concrete individual is inherently predicated by the possibility of abstraction, and Marx's first great example of this is Robinson. *And* his critique of political economists including Ricardo is that *they* read it as literary commentators on *Robinson Crusoe* think Marx read it: applying capitalist standards.

Marx is not interested in the novel, and all the English translations hide this by rendering his introduction of Robinson as: "Let us first look at Robinson on his island." No. For Marx, the character of Robinson is a form of appearance of man in nature, and he introduces him this way: "Let Robinson first appear on his island." I need not emphasize the importance of forms of appearance [*Erscheinungsformen*] in Marx's tight argument. In his situation, of man alone in nature, producing use-values, Robinson already of "necessity" thinks abstract labor: "He knows that . . . the activity of one and the same Robinson . . . consists of nothing but different modes of human labor . . . all the relations between Robinson and the objects . . . of his own creation, are here . . . simple and clear . . . and yet . . . contain all the essential determinants of value." Time, rather than money, is the general equivalent that expresses this production. I make this digression before I enter *Foe* because, in my reading, Coetzee's book seems interested in space rather than time, as it stages the difficulties of a timekeeping investigation before a space that will not yield its inscription.[15]

Foe is more about spacing and displacement than about the timing of history and labor. This is perhaps the result of the colonial white's look at the metropolitan classic. Just as the Jamaican white Jean Rhys's rewriting of a nineteenth-century English classic cannot accept *Jane Eyre* as the paradigm woman, so can the South African white's rewriting of an eighteenth-century English classic not accept Crusoe as the normative man in nature, already committed to a constitutive chronometry.[16] This Crusoe bequeaths a lightly inscribed space to an indefinite future: "'The planting is not for us,' said he. 'We have nothing to plant—that is our misfortune . . . The planting is reserved for those who come after us and have the foresight to bring seed. I only clear the ground for them'" [*F* 33]. The theme of the transition from land to landed capital is, after all, only *one* important strand of the mission of imperialism.

Foe's Crusoe has no interest in keeping time. Indeed, the narrator of *Foe,* who is *not* Crusoe, "search[es] the poles . . . but [finds] no carvings, not even notches to indicate that he counted the years of his banishment or the cycles of the moon" [*F* 16]. She begs him to keep a record, but he resolutely refuses. Although produced by merchant capitalism, Crusoe has no interest in being its agent, not even to the extent of saving tools. Coetzee's focus is on gender and empire, rather than the story of capital.

Who is this female narrator of *Robinson Crusoe*? We know that the original had no room for women. There was the typecast mother; the benevolent widow whose role it was to play the benevolent widow; the nameless wife who was married and died in the conditional mode in one sentence so that Crusoe could leave for the East Indies in the very year of the founding of the Bank of England; and last but not least, the "seven women" he sent at the end of the story, "being such as I found proper for service, or for wives to such as would take them," together with "five cows, three of them being big with calf" [*RC* 237]. So who is this female narrator? It is time I tabulated some of the ways in which Coetzee alters Defoe as he cites him.

First, consider the title, *Foe*. We know of course that Foe is Defoe's proper patronymic. He was born the son of James and Ann Foe. But in restoring this proper name, Coetzee also makes it a common noun. Whose Foe is Mr. Foe? I will leave that question suspended for now.

The narrator of *Foe* is an Englishwoman named Susan Barton, who wants to "father" her story into history, with Mr. Foe's help. Coetzee has trouble negotiating a gendered position; he and the text strain to make the trouble noticeable. This text will not defend itself against the undecidability and discomfort of imagining a woman. Is that authoritative word *father* being turned into a false but useful analogy (catachresis) here? Or is Coetzee's Susan being made to operate a traditional masculist topos of reversal and making Foe "gestate?" We cannot know. As Attridge points out, there is talk of "free choice" in *Foe*.

At any rate, Susan Barton has written a title, *The Female Castaway*, and a memoir and many letters and sent them to Mr. Foe, not all of which have arrived at their destination,[17] "More is at stake in the history you write, I will admit, for it must not only tell the truth about us but please the readers too. Will you not bear in mind, however, that my life is drearily suspended till your writing is done?" [*F* 63]. What happens to *The Female Castaway*? Susan Barton begins the novel with quotation marks, a self-citation: "At last I could row no further" [*F*5]. This first part—the story of her discovery of Crusoe and Friday, Crusoe's death on board ship on the trip back to England, and her arrival in England with Friday—is her memoirs. As for her history, it is either the book *Robinson Crusoe* or the book *Foe*, we cannot know now. At this point, it is simply the mark of the citation and alteration which is every reading, an allegory of the guardian that watches over all claims to demonstrate the truth of a text by quotation. At the beginning of the text is a quotation with no fixed origin.

Before the story of fathering can go any further, a strange sequence intervenes. It is as if the margins of bound books are themselves dissolved into a general textuality. Coetzee makes the final episode of Defoe's novel *Roxana* flow into this citation of *Robinson Crusoe*. Coetzee's Susan Barton is also Defoe's Roxana, whose first name is Susan. (There are other incidental similarities.)

Because Crusoe and Susan/Roxana are made to inhabit the same text, we are obliged to ask a further question: What happens when the unequal balance of gender determination in the representation of the marginal is allowed to tip?

The male marginal in the early eighteenth-century imagination can be the solitary contemplative christian, earning the right to imperialist soul making even as he is framed by the dynamic narrative of mercantile capitalism elsewhere. The female marginal is the *exceptional* entrepreneurial woman for whom the marriage contract is an inconvenience when the man is a fool. (A century and a half later, Tillie Olsen will write the poignant tragedy of an exceptional revolutionary woman married to an ordinary, bewildered, merely "normally" patriarchal man.)[18] Not only because of Defoe's own patriarchal production but also because of the conventions of the picaresque, his heroine must be a rogue—a social marginal finally centralizing herself through marriage. In this enterprise, she *uses* the money *held* by men as aristocrats, *made* by men as merchants; *and* she uses her sexuality as labor power.

In the presentation of this narrative, Defoe has at least two predictable problems that raise important questions about principles and the dissimulation of principle as well as about the negotiability of all commitments through the production and coding of value.

First: the relationship between principles and the *dissimulation* of principles. Defoe cannot make his Roxana utter her passion for woman's freedom except as a ruse for her real desire to own, control, and manage money:

> tho' I could give up my Virtue, . . . yet I wou'd not give up my Money, which, tho' it was true, yet was really too gross for me to acknowledge . . . I was oblig'd to give a new Turn to it, and talk upon a kind of an elevated

strain . . . as follows: I told him, I had, perhaps, differing Notions of Mat-
rimony, from what the receiv'd Custom had given us of it; that I thought
a Woman was a free Agent, as well as a Man, and was born free, and cou'd
she manage herself suitably, may enjoy that Liberty to as much purpose as
Men do. [R 147]

Second: the representation of the affective value of mothering when
contrasted with the destiny of female individualism. Susan Suleiman
has recently discussed the immense ramifications of this binary opposition in "Writing and Motherhood."[19] I will add a theoretical explanation of Defoe's problem of representation: Sexuality used as labor
power outside of the institution of marriage (not only in the British
early eighteenth century, and not only among the bourgeoisie) produces children as commodities that cannot be legitimately exchanged
and may produce an affective value that cannot be fully coded.

I think it is for rather an important reason that none of these issues
is quite relevant for Coetzee: *He* is involved in a historically implaus-
ible but politically provocative revision. He attempts to represent the
bourgeois individualist woman in early capitalism as the *agent* of *other*-
directed ethics rather than as a combatant in the preferential ethics of
self-interest. She is a subject *for* history. It is therefore she who is
involved in the construction of the marginal—both Cruso (Coetzee's
spelling) and Friday, *and* herself as character—as object of knowledge.
The rhetoric of *Foe*, especially the last section, shows that as such an
agent, she is also the instrument of defense against undecidability. This
is the liability of the peculiarly European "sense of responsibility for
the human conscience."[20]

Thus, for Coetzee, the basic theme of marriage and sexuality, freed
on the island from heavy historical determination, becomes a radical
counterfactual: the woman giving pleasure, without the usual affective
charge, *as* use-value, *in* need. Thus also, Defoe's problem of the dissimulation of the desire for liberty as a ruse for control of money is enno-
bled in *Foe* into the *full* if unrecognized, unacknowledged, and unde-
veloped capitalist agency that we have already noticed: Susan's longing
for "freedom of choice in writing her history," Susan's desire to use

time as the general equivalent, begging Cruso to mark time, dating her own section of the book meticulously, indeed, at first living on Clock Lane; and the problem of the representation of the affective value of mothering as opposed to the ambitions of possessive female individualism is dismissed by Coetzee's Susan Barton as Mr. Foe's ideas of a woman's dilemma, as merely "father-born."

If we take the open-ended double-value or abyssality of *father* under advisement here, a decision is not easy to take. "Without venturing up to that perilous necessity," let us decide that the problem is recast from the point of view of the feminist as agent, trying at once to rescue mothering from the European patriarchal coding and the "native" from the colonial account.[21] From the point of view of an other-directed ethico-politics, in this mother-daughter subplot, Coetzee marks an aporia.

Susan Barton had gone to Bahia Blanca to search for her daughter and had been shipwrecked on Crusoe's island on her way back. (Although Defoe's Roxana is a great traveler in the northwest European world looking forward to the turmoil of the transition from mercantile and commercial capital, she does not venture into the new cartography of the space of conquest.) Now a woman who claims to be her daughter haunts her footsteps and wants to be reclaimed. Susan Barton cannot recognize her as her lost daughter and tries to get rid of her in many ways. She is convinced that this encounter and pursuit are Foe's fabrication. (Attridge clues us into the "historical" Defoe's contribution to this scenario.) We cannot be convinced of this explanation. By everyday common sense, Susan Barton's credibility or sanity would here be thrown in doubt. But what place does credibility or verifiability have in this book, which is a real and imagined citation of Defoe's real book and Barton's unreal one, in a way that resembles the dream's "citation" of waking reality? I am suggesting that here the book may be gesturing toward the impossibility of restoring the history of empire and recovering the lost text of mothering *in the same register of language.* It is true that we are each of us overdetermined, part historian, part mother, and many other determinations besides. But overdetermination can itself be disclosed when the condensed rebus in the dream has been straightened out in analytical prose. Because of this dislocation, there can be no politics founded on a continuous overdetermined multiplicity of agencies. It is merely defensive to dress up the strategic desirability of alliance politics and conscientious pluralism in the continuous space opened up by socialized capital in the language of undecidability and plurality. In the middle of *Foe*, the mysterious expulsion of the daughter can be read as marking this aporia. (In *Schibboleth*, Derrida takes Paul Celan's citation of the cry from February 1936, the eve of the Spanish Civil War—*No pasaran*—and translates it, strictly, as *aporia*.[22] One cannot pass through an aporia. Yet Franco did pass through. Celan's poem stands guardian, marking the date, 13 February 1936, reminder of a history that did not happen. The main narrative of *Foe* passes through this obstinate sequence—bits of fiction that cannot articulate as a story.) Susan Barton lures her strange daughter into the heart of Epping Forest and tells her "'You are father-born. What you know of your parentage comes to you in the form of stories, and the stories have but a single source'" [*F* 91]. Yet this too could be a dream. "'What do I mean by it, father-born?'" Susan asks herself in the letter in which she recounts this to Foe. "'I wake in the grey of a London dawn with the word still faintly in my eyes . . . Have I expelled her, lost her at last in the forest?'" But is a dream contained in a dream citation a loss of authority? This first severing is not neat. Susan writes Foe again: "I must tell you of a dead stillborn girl-child" she unwraps in a ditch some miles out of Marlborough: "Try though I might, I could not put from my thoughts the little sleeper who would never awake, the pinched eyes that would never see the sky, the curled fingers that would never open. Who was the child but I, in another life?" [*F* 105]. I read "in another life" as, also, another story, another register, and pass on to more plausible explanations offered by this text, where plausibility is plural.

We could ourselves "explain" this curious sequence in various ways. We could fault Coetzee for not letting a woman have free access to both authorship and motherhood. We could praise him for not presuming to speak a completed text on motherhood. I would rather save the book, call it the mark of *aporia* in the center, and teach my students something about the impossibility of a political program founded on overdetermination.[23]

In the frame of this peculiar aporia, the decision to keep or reject the mother-daughter story is presented in terms of the making of narratives. First, Susan is imagined as imagining Foe imagining the history of *The Female Castaway*. In my reading, these imaginings may signify no more than Defoe's idea of a woman's dilemma, here thematized as Foe's problem in writing the story. At first, Susan Barton imagines a rejection:

> I write my letters, I seal them, I drop them in the box. One day when we are departed you will tip them out and glance through them. "Better had there been only Cruso and Friday." You will murmur to yourself: "Better without the woman." Yet where would you be without the woman? . . . Could you have made up Cruso and Friday and the island . . . ? I think not. Many strengths you have, but invention is not one of them. [*F* 72]

These musings describe Daniel Defoe's *Robinson Crusoe* as we have it today, without the woman as inventor and progenitor. Yet in Coetzee's story, it is described as a road not taken. The actual is presented as the counterfactual. Defoe's *Robinson Crusoe,* which engenders *Foe,* does not exist.

Next, when Susan meets Foe, he tries to question her on the details of the plot. It is a long series of questions, and Foe supplies the answers himself and tells her the structure of his storying of *The Female Castaway:*

> We therefore have five parts in all: The loss of the daughter; the quest for the daughter in Brazil; abandonment of the quest, and the adventure of the island; assumption of the quest by the daughter; and reunion of the daughter with her mother. It is thus that we make up a book: loss, then quest, then recovery; beginning, then middle, then end. As to novelty, this is lent by the island episode—which is properly the second part of the middle—and by the reversal in which the daughter takes up the quest abandoned by her mother . . . The island is not a story in itself, said Foe gently. [*F* 117]

We do not read this projected novel in *Foe*. I should like to think that, in terms of *textual* strategy, Coetzee's text makes (De)foe's book share its own concerns. My previous remarks on the formal peculiarities of the mother-daughter subplot carried the implication that feminism (within "the same" cultural inscription) and anticolonialism (for or against racial "others") cannot occupy a continuous (narrative) space. Here, Mr. Foe is made to take a similar decision within his framework of *structural* strategy. The island is the central story of both the real *Robinson Crusoe* and this fictive projected *Female Castaway*. In the former, the frame narrative is capitalism and colony. In the latter, it would be the mother-daughter story. The two cannot occupy a continuous space. Susan Barton tries to break the binary opposition by broaching the real margin that has been haunting the text since its first page. The stalling of that breaching or broaching *is* the story of *Foe*: "'In the letters that you did not read,' I said, 'I told you of my conviction that, if the story seems stupid, that is because it so doggedly holds its silence. The shadow whose lack you feel is there: it is the loss of Friday's tongue'" [*F* 117].

In *Foe*, Friday's tongue has been cut off—by slavers, says Robinson. (Attridge provides the "real" detail of Coetzee's answer to this in an interview, a genre that is generated to bring undecidability under control.) Susan wants to know him, to give him speech, to learn from him, to father his story, which will also be her story: the account of her anguish as Friday grows dull in London; her longing for Friday's desire and her exasperation at herself; the orchestration of her desire to construct Friday as subject so that he can be her informant cannot be summarized. She asks Friday to explain the origin of his loss through a few pictures. She must recognize with chagrin that her picture of Robinson possibly cutting out his tongue, "might also be taken to show Cruso as a beneficent father putting a lump of fish into the mouth of child Friday" [*F* 68–69]. Each picture fails this way. The unrepeatability of the unique event can only be repeated imperfectly. And then, " who was to say there do not exist entire tribes in Africa among whom the men are mute and speech is reserved to women?" [*F* 69]. Susan is at her wit's end. That too is a margin. When she "begins to turn in Friday's dance," it is not a *con*-versation—a turning together—for "Friday is slug-gishly asleep on a hurdle behind the door" [*F* 104]. But her project remains to "give a voice" to Friday: "The story of Friday's tongue is a story unable to be told, or unable to be told by me. That is to say, many stories can be told of Friday's tongue, but the true story is buried within Friday, who is mute. The true story will not be heard till by art we have found a means of giving voice to Friday" [*F* 118]. Where is the guarantee of this? Where indeed is the guarantee of Attridge's convic-tion that Friday is a metaphor for the work of art?

Contrast this to Defoe's text. It was noticed rather quickly, after the first publication of *Robinson Crusoe*, that Defoe kept Friday's language acquisition skills at a rather low level. It is also noticeable that, at their first encounter, "I began to speak to him, and teach him to speak to me" [*RC* 161]. Like us, Crusoe does not need to learn to speak to the racial other. Of course Crusoe knows the savages have a language. And it is a longstanding topos that barbarians by definition do not speak lan-guage. But the contrast here is also between the colonialist—who gives the native speech—and the metropolitan antiimperialist—who wants to give the native voice. (In the interview cited by Attridge, Coetzee provides the racial difference between Crusoe's and his own Friday. I ask my students to note it, not to make it the tool to an unproductive closure.) The last scene in Susan's narrative stands as a warning to both. Before I read it I want to remind ourselves of the last scene involving Friday in *Robinson Crusoe*. Friday is not only the "domesticated anti-type," as John Richetti calls him[24]; he is also the prototype of the suc-cessful colonial subject. He learns his master's speech, does his master's work, happily swears loyalty, believes the culture of the master is bet-ter, and kills his other self to enter the shady plains of northwestern Europe. The footsore company have just escaped from wolves. It is bit-ter cold, the night is advancing. At this point Friday offers to amuse the company with a huge threatening bear, and Robinson quite surpris-ingly allows him to do so. Friday speaks to the bear *in English*. The bear understands his tone and gestures. Like two blood brothers, they dance in the trees. Finally, Friday kills the bear with a gun in his ear. He has reinscribed his savagery. This is an amusement available to the natives. He makes his masters his spectators and replaces the arrow with the gun. He is on his way out of the margin.

Now let us look at the last scene of Friday in Susan's narrative. Foe asks Susan to teach Friday to write. The discussion of speech and writing between these two European principals is of great interest. Susan thinks it is a poor idea but agrees because she "find[s] it thankless to argue" [*F* 144]. The staging of this errant scene of writing should be examined fully in a classroom reading.

One of the words Barton tries to teach Friday is *Africa*. This effort is rich in meaning and its limits. The metropolitan antiimperialist cannot teach the native the proper name of his nation or continent. *Africa,* a Roman name for what the Greeks called "Libya," itself perhaps a latinization of the name of the Berber tribe Aourigha (perhaps pronounced "Afarika"), is a metonym that points to a greater indeterminacy: the mysteriousness of the space upon which we are born. *Africa* is only a time-bound naming; like all proper names it is a mark with an arbitrary connection to its referent, a catachresis. The earth as temporary dwelling has no foundational name. Nationalism can only ever be a crucial political agenda against oppression. All longings to the contrary, it cannot provide the absolute guarantee of identity.

This scene of writing may also be an unfinished thematizing of dissemination, where words are losing their mode of existence as semes. "Friday wrote the four letters *h-o-u-s,* or four shapes passably like them: whether they were truly the four letters, and stood truly for the word *house* and the picture I had drawn, and the thing itself, only he knew" [*F* 145–146].

At this stage the only letter he seems to be able to reproduce is *h. H* is a strange letter in this book—it is the letter of muteness itself. When Crusoe had first shown Friday's loss to Susan, "'La-la-la,' said Cruso, and motioned to Friday to repeat. 'Ha-ha-ha,' said Friday from the back of his throat. 'He has no tongue,' said Cruso. Gripping Friday by the hair, he brought his face close to mine. 'Do you see?' 'It is too dark,' said I. 'La-la-la,' said Cruso. 'Ha-ha-ha,' said Friday. I drew away, and Cruso released Friday's hair." [*F* 22–23]. *H* is the failed echolalia of the mute. All through the book the letter *H* is typographically raised and separated from the line in vague mimicry of eighteenth-century type-face. It is noticeable because no other letter of the alphabet is treated in this way.

The next day Friday dresses up in Foe's clothes and proceeds to write: a packed series of *o*s. "'It is a beginning,' sa[ys] Foe. 'Tomorrow you must teach him a'" [*F* 152]. This is where Susan's narrative ends, with the promise of a continued writing lesson that never happens. One can of course say that Foe is wrong. It is not a beginning unless one forgets the previous forgetting; and *o* could conceivably be *omega*, the end.

We also remember that in *Robinson Crusoe* "saying *O*" is Friday's pid-gin translation of his native word for prayer; and it is around the accounts of praying practices that Robinson shares with us the two neg-atives of reason. Within natural law what negates reason is *un*reason. Its example is Friday and his tribe's saying "*O*." Within divine law, rea-son is sublimely negated by revelation. Its example is the inconstancies of Christian doctrine, naïvely pointed out by Friday. As Susan con-fesses that she is not a good writing teacher, so does Robinson confess that he is not a good religious instructor, for he cannot make revelation accessible to the merely reasonable/savage. In the light of this, it is par-ticularly interesting to notice what Coetzee stages between the inside margins of the first and second days of the writing lesson. "While Foe and I spoke, Friday filled his slate with open eyes, each set upon a human foot: row upon row of eyes: walking eyes . . . 'Give! Give me the slate, Friday!' I commanded. Whereupon, instead of obeying me, Fri-day put three fingers into his mouth and wet them with spittle and rubbed the slate clean" [*F* 147].

Here is the guardian of the margin. Neither narrative nor text gives pride of place to it: active marginalizing perhaps. This event changes the course of Foe's and Susan's conversation only to the extent that Susan finally says, "How can Friday know what freedom means when he barely knows his name?" [*F* 149].

Are those walking eyes rebuses, hieroglyphs, ideograms, or is their secret that they hold no secret at all? Each scrupulous effort at decod-ing or deciphering will bring its own rewards; but there is a structural possibility that they are nothing. Even then it would be writing, but that argument has no place here.[25]

It is the withholding that is of interest in terms of Susan Barton's narrative. The night before, Susan had said to Foe: "it is still in my power to guide and amend. Above all, to withhold. By such means do I still endeavour to be father of my story" [F 123]. After this Foe and Susan Barton copulate for the first time.

Yet it is Friday rather than Susan who is the unemphatic agent of withholding in the text. For every territorial space that is value coded by colonialism *and* every command of metropolitan anticolonialism for the native to yield his "voice," there is a space of withholding, marked by a secret that may not be a secret but cannot be unlocked. "The native," whatever that might mean, is not only a victim, he or she is also an agent. He or she is the curious guardian at the margin.

In a recent article in *Oxford Literary Review,* Benita Parry has criticized Homi Bhabha, Abdul Jan Mohammed, and Gayatri Spivak for being so enamored of deconstruction that they will not let the native speak.[26] She has forgotten that we are natives too. We talk like *Defoe's* Friday, only much better. Nearly three hundred years have, after all, passed since Defoe's fabrication of Friday. Territorial imperialism, in the offing then, has given place to neocolonialism. Within the broad taxonomy that I am proposing here, the murderous project of apartheid keeps South Africa caught in that earlier dispensation.[27] In the so-called decolonized context proper, among the migrant population in metropolitan space, the resistant postcolonial has become a scandal.

Postcolonial persons like ourselves from formerly colonized countries are able to communicate to each other (and to metropolitans), to exchange, to establish sociality, because we have had access to the so-called culture of imperialism. Shall we then assign to that culture a measure of "moral luck?"[28] I think there can be no doubt that the answer is "no." This impossible "no" to a structure that one critiques yet inhabits intimately is the deconstructive position, which has its historical case in postcoloniality. The neocolonial anticolonialist still longs for the object of a conscientious ethnography, sometimes gender marked for feminism: "where women inscribed themselves as healers, ascetics, singers of sacred songs, artizans and artists."[29]

I have no objection to conscientious ethnography, although I am forewarned by its relationship to the history of the discipline of anthropology. But my particular word to Parry is that her efforts (to give voice to the native) as well as mine (to give warning of the attendant problems) are judged by those strange margins of which Friday with his withholding slate is only a mark.

Does the book *Foe* recuperate this margin? The last section of the book, narrated by a reader of unspecified gender and date, is a sort of reading lesson which would suggest the opposite. To recover this suggestion, let us turn to Barton and Foe's copulation.

Coetzee plays the register of legible banality with panache. This is the second take on the misfiring of the mother-daughter story. Susan's supposed daughter is present earlier in the evening. That scene is put to rest by these noticeably unremarkable words: "Her appearances, or apparitions, or whatever they were, disturbed me less now that I knew her better" [*F* 136]. Foe detains Barton with a seducer's touch. In bed she claims "'a privilege that comes with the first night' . . . then I drew off my shift and straddled him (which he did not seem easy with in a woman). 'This is the manner of the Muse when she visits her poets,' I whispered" [*F* 139].

In the pleasant pause after this musing-cum-fathering, a deliberately staged scene of (future) writing, rather different from Friday's withheld writing, Susan grows drowsy, and Foe speaks, unexpectedly, of sea monsters and resumes, "to us [Friday] leaves the task of descending into the eye [across which he rows and is safe]" [*F* 140, 141].

It is this sea monster, an image engendered in the representation of the primal scene of writing but also dredged up from *The Tempest*, a play repeatedly read as a representation of the colonizer-colonized dialectic, that allows the indeterminate reader, the central character of this last section, to descend into "Friday's home."[30] In other words, this reading knits itself into Susan's scene of strange fathering, leaving Friday's writing lesson apart.

"At one corner of the house, above head-height, a plaque is bolted to the wall. *Daniel Defoe, Author,* are the words, white on blue, and then more writing too small to read" [*F* 155]. We have seen these plaques in London. Defoe is dead and memorialized, but the dates are too small to read.

Under the names of the dead father, we enter and discover Susan Barton's book, unpublished. The topmost leaf crumbles. Then the reader reads the self-quotation that opens *Foe,* now properly addressed: "Dear Mr. Foe."

The quotation marks disappear, and the reader is staged as filling the subject position, for Barton's text continues. This is easy reading. Nothing is cited, everything is at once real and fantastic, all the permissive indulgences of narrative fiction in the narrow sense are available to the reader, sole shifter on this trip. The ride is smooth, the trip leads not to Crusoe's island but to the second wreck, where Susan Barton lies fat and dead. *Robinson Crusoe* has not been written, and *Foe* is annulled, for now Barton will not reach Crusoe's island. Friday is affirmed to be there, the margin caught in the empire of signs. "This is a place where bodies are their own signs. It is the home of Friday" [*F* 157]. What is the guarantee of this confidence?

For *this* end, texts are porous. They go through to wish fulfillment. Yet we also know that Coetzee's entire book warns that Friday's body is not its own sign. In this end, the staging of the wish to invade the margin, the seaweeds seem to sigh: if only there were no texts. The end is written lovingly, and we will not give it up. But we cannot hold together, in a continuous narrative space, the voyage of reading at the end of the book, Susan Barton's narrative, and the withheld slate.

Perhaps that is the novel's message: the impossible politics of overdetermination (mothering, authoring, giving voice to the native "in" the text; a white male South African writer engaging in such inscriptions "outside" the text) should not be regularized into a blithe continuity, where the European redoes the primitive's project in herself. It can, however, lead to a scrupulously differentiated politics, dependent on "where you are." Coetzee's text can be taught as:

1. Correcting Defoe's imagination of the marginal, in comradeship
2. Reinscribing the white woman as agent, as the asymmetrical double of the author. (I think the problems with the figure of "fathering" mark this asymmetry)
3. Situating the politics of overdetermination as aporia
4. Halting before Friday, since for him, here, now, *and* for Susan Barton, *and* for Daniel Foe, that is the arbitrary name of the withheld limit.

At first I had wanted to end with the following sentence: Mr. Foe is everyone's Foe, the enabling violator, for without him there is nothing to cite. A month after finishing this writing, I heard Jacques Derrida deliver an extraordinary paper on friendship.[31] I suppose I can say now that this *Foe*, in history, is the site where the line between friend and foe is undone. When one *wants* to be a friend to the wholly other, it withdraws its graphematic space. Foe allows that story to be told.

It is no doubt because I heard and read Derrida's pieces on friendship and margins and read Bernard Williams's "Moral Luck," that I could work out this didactic exercise. I know that Stanley Fish has no objections to accepting the consequences of *reading* theory.[32] Theory itself has no *con*-sequence. It is autosequential rather than automatic. Theory is the production of theory, in presupposition, method, end. It is always withdrawn from that which it seeks to theorize, however insubstantial that object might be. Theory is a bit like Mr. Foe. It is always off the mark, yet it is what we undo. Without it, nothing but the wished-for inarticulation of the natural body: "a slow stream, without breath, without interruption," betrayed by the spacing of the words that wish it [*F* 157].

I should hope that my students would keep this duplicitous agent of active marginalizing—theory, our friend Foe—in mind as they read with informed sympathy interventionist writing, both fiction and nonfiction. Mongane Serote's *To Every Birth Its Blood*, is an example of interventionist fiction not "necessarily directed at the elite international readership"—ourselves—"addressed by South African writers such as J. M. Coetzee and Nadine Gordimer." *Not Either An Experi-*

mental Doll: The Separate Lives of Three South African Women is the "nonfiction" account of the unavoidable thwarting (in the middle of our century, by a metropolitan white anticolonialist activist woman and a successful black colonial female subject, both anxious to help) of the native seeking (rather than withholding) agency, Lily Moya, a poor Christian orphan "Bantu" woman in her teens.[33]

In a letter to Mabel Palmer, the white anticolonialist activist, Lily wrote her conviction: "We make people believe that civilization came with evil."[34] Less than two years later, after Mabel Palmer sent her a message "of total emotional rejection coupled with her act of generosity in funding Lily to an alternative school," Lily undid that conviction and wrote: "I was never meant to be a stone but a human being with feelings not either an experimental doll."[35] The stone is (in the) margin.

At a recent conference, Coetzee juxtaposed passages from Mothobi Motloatse and Nadine Gordimer and commented: "The white writer in South Africa is in an impossible position."[36] He stages the full range of that impossibility by claiming corrective comradeship and complicity with Foe, and Susan Barton. The novel is neither a failure nor an abdication of the responsibility of the historical or national elite.

A colleague unnerved me by suggesting that this book, like all transactions among men, left the woman anonymous. I should not like to discount the suggestion: I would rather use it to repeat my opening cautions. Does "the sign 'woman' have no origin, no historical, cultural, or linguistic limit?" Is Friday not a man? Further, said my colleague, "Coetzee has read a lot of theory, and it shows. But . . ." But what? "Theory should lead to practice." (So much for theory having no consequences.) What should the practice have been in this case? A book that did not show the reading of theory, resembling more "what a novel should be?" Should my colleague have known that her notion of the relationship between theory and practice has caused and is causing a good deal of suffering in the world? If figuration is seen as a *case* of theoretical production (one practice among many), could another politics of reading have led her to the conclusion that her desire to help racially differentiated colonial others had a threshold and a limit? "I quite like metafiction, but . . . ," she added. For what sort of patafiction of concrete experience must we reserve our seal of approval? The field of practice is a broken and uneven place. The convenient highway of a single issue is merely the shortest distance between two sign-posted exits.

NOTES

1. The obvious texts are Allan Bloom, *The Closing of the American Mind: How Higher Education Has Failed Democracy and Impoverished the Souls of Today's Students* (New York: Simon and Schuster, 1987); and E. D. Hirsch, *Cultural Literacy: What Every American Needs to Know* (New York: Vintage, 1988). The argument for reverse discrimination is sometimes ugly: "Leftist teachers have created an atmosphere in which those who question the value of women's studies and ethnic studies are labeled sexist, racist or 'cold warriors'" (Lawrence W. Hyman, "The Culture Battle," *On Campus* 8 [April, 1989]: 5). See also Lee Dembert, "Left Censorship at Stanford," *New York Times*, 5 May 1989, A35.

2. Jean-Paul Sartre, *Existentialism and Humanism*, trans. Philip Mairet (New York: Haskell House, 1948), 46–47. Translation modified. Emphasis mine.

3. Jacques Derrida, "The Ends of Man," in *Margins of Philosophy*, trans. Alan Bass (Chicago: University of Chicago Press, 1982), 116.

4. Samir Amin, *Unequal Development*, trans. Brian Pearce (New York: Monthly Review Press, 1976), 369.

5. J. M. Coetzee, "The Beginnings of (Wo)man in Africa," *New York Times Book Review*, 30 April 1989.

6. Various essays written by me in the last few months share some common themes. Some passages occur in more than one of them. The last few paragraphs, for example, are also to be found in "The Making of Americans, the Teaching of English, and the Future of Culture Studies," forthcoming in *New Literary History* (Autumn 1990).

7. Derrida, "Ends of Man," 112–13.

8. J. M. Coetzee, *Foe* (New York: Viking, 1987) (hereafter cited in text as *F*, followed by page number).

9. The editions used are Daniel Defoe, *Robinson Crusoe: An Authoritative Text/Backgrounds/Sources/Criticism*, ed. Michael Shinagel (New York: Norton, 1975) (hereafter cited as *RC*, followed by page number); and Daniel Defoe, *Roxana: The Fortunate Mistress*, ed. Jane Jack (Oxford: Oxford University Press, 1964) (hereafter cited as *R*, followed by page number).

10. This piece is forthcoming in Karen Lawrence, ed., *Cultural Politics: Modern British Literary Canons* (Princeton: Princeton University Press).

11. Werner Hamacher, "Journals, Politics: Notes on Paul de Man's Wartime Journalism," in *Responses: On Paul de Man's Wartime Journalism*, ed. Werner Hamacher, Neil Hertz, and Thomas Keenan (Lincoln: University of Nebraska Press, 1989), 439.

12. (Paris: Minuit).

13. Helene Cixous, "The Laugh of the Medusa," in *New French Feminisms: An Anthology*, ed. Elaine Marks and Isabelle de Courtivron (Amherst: University of Massachusetts Press, 1980), 252.

14. Karl Marx, *Capital: A Critique of Political Economy*, vol. 1, trans. Ben Fowkes (New York: Vintage, 1977), 169–170. All the passages from Marx are taken from these two pages.

15. Reading *Robinson* as a book for Europe, one could not do better than Pierre Macherey's study in *Theory of Literary Production*, trans. Geoffrey Wall (New York: Methuen, 1978); and Michel de Certeau, *Heterologies: Discourse on the Other*, trans. Brian Massumi (Minneapolis: University of Minnesota Press, 1986). Both of these studies emphasize timing.

16. See Gayatri Chakravorty Spivak, "Three Women's Texts and a Critique of Imperialism," *Critical Inquiry* 12 (1985): 243–61.

17. To thicken the thematics of sexual difference here, one might look at Jacques Derrida, "The Purveyor of Truth," in *The Post Card: From Socrates to Freud and Beyond*, trans. Alan Bass (Chicago: University of Chicago Press, 1987). What happens when letters do or do not arrive at their destination?

18. I am referring, of course, to Tillie Olsen, *Tell Me a Riddle* (New York: Peter Smith, 1986).

19. In *The (M)other Tongue: Essays in Feminist Psychoanalytic Interpretation*, ed. Shirley Nelson Garner, Claire Kahane, and Madelon Sprengnether (Ithaca: Cornell University Press, 1985), 352–77.

20. Zbigniw Herbert, cited in *Not Either an Experimental Doll: The Separate*

Lives of Three South African Women, ed. Shula Marks (Bloomington: Indiana University Press, 1987), epigraph.

21. Jacques Derrida, *Of Grammatology,* trans. Gayatri Chakravorty Spivak (Baltimore: Johns Hopkins University Press, 1976), 74, 75. This active marginalization is vintage Derrida.

22. Jacques Derrida, "Schibboleth," in *Midrash and Literature,* ed. Geoffrey H. Hartman and Sanford Budick (New Haven: Yale University Press, 1986), 320f.

23. Although this phrase is not coined by them, the enablement for this program is generally sought in Ernesto Laclau and Chantal Mouffe's most influential *Hegemony and Socialist Strategy: Towards a Radical Democratic Politics,* trans. Winston Moore and Paul Cammack (London: Verso, 1985).

24. John Richetti, *Defoe's Narratives: Situations and Structures* (Oxford: Clarendon Press, 1975), 56.

25. See Jacques Derrida, *Spurs,* trans. Barbara Harlow (Chicago: University of Chicago Press, 1979), 125f.

26. Benita Parry, "Problems in Current Theories of Colonial Discourse," *Oxford Literary Review* 9 (1987), 27–58.

27. Negotiations with the current conjuncture have led to various internal maneuvers that are beyond the scope of this chapter. David Atwell of the University of the Western Cape has pointed out to me the existence of the notion of a "colonialism of a special type" in South Africa, a colonialism that did not, by and large, export surplus value. He makes the interesting suggestion that this, too, might explain Coetzee's Cruso's noncommital attitude toward classic metropolitan interests. I keep to my much less fine-tuned point of territorial presence—though even there, a difference looms. Given the specificity of the situation and its imbrication with the current conjuncture, the white South African claims to be South African, whereas indigenous nationality was not generally the claim of territorial imperialists of the classic period. This makes clear, yet once again that 1) a taxonomy is most serviceable when not exhaustive, and 2) "the occupational weakness of the new and somewhat beleaguered discipline of a transnational study of culture" is that "conceptual schemes and extent of scholarship cannot be made to balance" (Spivak, "Constitutions and Culture Studies," *Yale Journal of Law and the Humanities,* forthcoming). (The Australian, Canadian, and U.S. cases are, *in only this respect of course,* some-

thing like heterogeneous exceptions to the British case.) The agenda is promise of future work and collective critique.

28. Bernard Williams, *Moral Luck: Philosophical Papers 1973-1980* (Cambridge: Cambridge University Press, 1981), 20–39.

29. Parry, "Problems," 35.

30. Attridge points at many echoes of *The Tempest* in *Foe*. See also Rob Nixon, "Caribbean and African Appropriations of *The Tempest*," in *Politics and Poetic Value*, ed. Robert von Hallberg (Chicago: University of Chicago Press, 1987), 185–206.

31. "Of Friendship: Of Democracy" (Unpublished lectures given at the University of Pittsburgh, 28–29 September 1988).

32. Stanley Fish, "Consequences," in *Doing What Comes Naturally* (Durham: Duke University Press, 1989), 315–41.

33. Mongane Serote, *To Every Birth Its Blood* (New York: Thunder's Mouth Press, 1989). The quoted passage is from William Finnegan, "A Distant Rumbling in the Township," *New York Times Book Review*, 7 May 1989, 38; Marks, *Experimental Doll*. Moya's diagnosis of "schizophrenia" is an uncanny demonstration of Gilles Deleuze's and Felix Guattari's argument in *Anti-Oedipus: Capitalism and Schizophrenia*, trans. Robert Hurley, Mark Seem and Helen R. Lane (Minneapolis: University of Minnesota Press, 1983), 166–84.

34. Marks, *Experimental Doll*, 89.

35. Ibid., 42. I have rearranged the parts of the sentence in the interest of coherence.

36. Conference on "Re-defining Marginality," University of Tulsa, 30 March 1989. This is the position he has described elsewhere as "generated by the concerns of people no longer European, not yet African" (*White Writing: On the Culture of Letters in South Africa* [New Haven: Yale University Press, 1988], 11). Coetzee juxtaposed Motloatse, "Editor's Introduction," in *Reconstruction*, ed. Mothobi Motloatse (Johannesburg: Raven Press, 1981), 6, and as quoted in N. Ndebele, "The English Language and Social Change in South Africa," *Tri-Quarterly* 69 (1987): 235, 17n.; and Nadine Gordimer, "Living in the Interregnum," in *The Essential Gesture: Writing, Politics and Places* (New York; Knopf, 1988), 275–76.

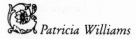 *Patricia Williams*

And We Are Not Married

A JOURNAL OF MUSINGS UPON LEGAL LANGUAGE
AND THE IDEOLOGY OF STYLE

> This, after my skin will have been peeled off; but I would behold God
> from my flesh.
>
> —Job 19:26

JOURNAL ENTRY OF 28 MAY 1988
(THE PHANTOM ROOM)

I am at a conference on race/gender/class and critical legal thought. The discussion topic is Harvard Law School Professor Derrick Bell's new book, *And We Are Not Saved.*[1] The chapter being discussed is entitled "The Race-Charged Relationship of Black Men and Black Women." The chapter deals generally with the social construction of antimiscegenation laws; forced sterilization and castration; the structure of the black family; teenage pregnancy; and the disproportionate number of black men in U.S. prisons. But the precise subject within the chapter which has caught everyone's attention is a surprising little parable entitled "The Chronicle of the Twenty-seventh-Year Syndrome." The chronicle is structured as an interiorized dream had by Professor Bell; he then tells it to an exteriorized dream-vision-anima figure named Geneva Crenshaw. In the dream, Twenty-seventh-Year Syndrome is an affliction affecting only young black professional women: if they are not married to, or have not yet received a marriage proposal from, a black man by their twenty-seventh year, they fall into a deep coma from which they awaken only after several weeks, physically intact but having lost all their professional skills.

This story has scared everyone in the room, including me, to death. The conversation is very, very anxious and abstract.

The discussion rages around my ears. Big words rush through the air, careening dangerously close to my head. Defining feminism. Undefining feminism. Women/men. Blackwoe/men. Black/white. Biology/social construction. Male creation/control of sexuality. Challenge/structure. Post–legal realist feminist/feminist. Identify/define/understand. Privilege of white womanhood/self-flagellation. Problematic/useful. Critique of patriarchy/pervasive abstracted universal wholeness. Actual/historical pathways to possibility and/or of perversion. And the cabbage head of hegemony.

I/me am sitting quietly in the vortex, trying to recall the last time I heard such definitional embattlement; suddenly a sharp voice cuts through all the rest and asks: "All this stuff about black people being socially constructed—I don't *experience* them as socially constructed. Who the hell does?" I think about that for a while; the memory that comes to me is the following:

About two years ago, New York merchants started installing buzzers and locks on the doors of their stores. Favored particularly by smaller stores and boutiques, the buzzer systems were rationalized as screening devices to reduce the incidence of robbery. When the buzzer sounds, if the face at the door looks "desirable," the door is unlocked. If the face is that of an "undesirable," the door stays locked.

The installation of these buzzers happened very swiftly in New York; stores that had always had their doors wide open suddenly became "exclusive" or received people "by appointment only." I discovered them and their meaning one Saturday in 1986. I was shopping in Soho and saw in the window of Benetton's, of all places, a sweater that I wanted to purchase for my mother. I pressed my round brown face to the store window and my finger to the buzzer, seeking admittance. A narrow-eyed white youth glared at me, evaluating me. After about five seconds, he mouthed, "We're closed" and turned his back on me. It was two Saturdays before Christmas; it was one o'clock in the afternoon; there were several white people in the store who appeared to be shopping for things for *their* mothers.

I was enraged. At that moment I wanted to break all of the windows in the store and *take* lots of sweaters for my mother. In the flicker of his judgmental gray eyes, that saleschild had reduced my brightly sentimental, joy-to-the-world, pre-Christmas spree to a shambles. He had snuffed my sense of humanitarian catholicity, and there was nothing I could do to snuff his, without simply making a spectacle of myself. His refusal to let me into the store was an outward manifestation of his never having let someone like me into the realm of his reality. He had no connection, no reference to me, and no desire to acknowledge me even at the estranged level of arm's-length transactor.

The violence of my desire to burst into Benetton's is probably quite apparent. I often wonder if the violence and the exclusionary hatred are equally apparent in the repeated public urgings that blacks understand the buzzer system by putting themselves in the shoes of white store owners[2]— that, in effect, blacks look into the mirror of frightened white faces for the reality of their undesirability, and that then blacks would "just as surely conclude that [they] would not let [themselves] in under similar circumstances."[3]

When this happened to me, I turned to a form of catharsis I have always found quite healing: I typed up as much of the story as I have just reiterated, made a big poster of it, put a nice colorful border around it, and, after Benetton's was truly closed, I stuck it to their big sweater-filled window. I exercised my First Amendment rights to place my business with them right out in the street. (I call this aspect of my literary endeavors *guerrilla writing*. I mark the spots at which I observe some racial or other indignity. In instances in which I am reduced to anonymity,[4] I do it anonymously[5]; and I always use a little piece of gum rubber with which to attach the posters so that they are easily removable without causing the slightest property damage.)

Anyway, that was the first telling of this story. The second telling came a few months later at a symposium on excluded voices sponsored by the University of Miami Law Review for which I was invited to submit an article. I sat down and wrote an essay summing up my feelings about being excluded from Benetton's and analyzing "how the rhetoric of increased privatization, in response to racial issues, functions as the rationalizing agent of public unaccountability, and ultimately, irresponsibility."[6] Weeks later, I received the first edit. From the first page to the last, my fury had been carefully carved out. My rushing, run-on rage had been reduced to simple declarative sentences. The active personal had been inverted in favor of the passive impersonal.

My words were different; they spoke to me upside down. I was afraid to read too much of it at a time – meanings rose up at me oddly, stolen and strange.

A week and a half later, I received the second edit. All reference to Benetton's had been deleted because, according to the editors and the faculty advisor, it was "defamatory"; they feared "harassment and liability"; they said printing it would be "irresponsible."[7] I called them and offered to supply a footnote attesting to this as my personal experience at one particular location and of a buzzer system not limited to Benetton's; the editors told me that they were not in the habit of publishing things that were "unverifiable." (I could not help but wonder, in this refusal even to let me file an affidavit, what it would take to make my experience "verifiable." The testimony of an independent white bystander? – a requirement in fact imposed in U.S. Supreme Court holdings through the first part of the century.[8])

Two days *after* the piece was sent to press, I received copies of the final page proofs. All reference to my race had been eliminated because "we have concluded that . . . [it] is inconsistent with our editorial policy" to permit descriptions of physiognomy. "I realize," wrote one editor, "that this was a very personal experience, but any reader will know what you must have looked like when standing at that window."[9] In a telephone conversation with them, I ranted on wildly about the significance of such an omission. "It's irrelevant," another editor explained in a voice gummy with soothing and patience; "It's nice and poetic," but it doesn't "advance the discussion of any principle . . . This is a law review, after all."[10] Frustrated, I accused him of censorship; calmly, he assured me it was not. "This is just a matter of style," he said with firmness and finality.[11]

Ultimately, I did convince them that mention of my race was a central force in making sense of all the subsequent text; that my whole story became one of extreme paranoia without the knowledge that I am black; or that it became one in which the reader had to fill in the gap by assumption, presumption, prejudgment, prejudice. What was most interesting to me in this experience was how the blind application of principles of neutrality, through the device of omission, acted either to make me look crazy or to make the reader participate in the mental habits of cultural bias.[12]

That was the second telling of my story. The third telling came last April when I was invited to participate in a conference on equality and difference sponsored by the University of West Virginia Law School. I retold my sad tale of exclusion from Soho's most glitzy and colorful boutique, focusing, in this version, on the characterization of Miami's editing process as a consequence of an ideology of style rooted in a social text of neutrality. I opined:

> Law and legal writing aspire to formalized, color-blind, liberal ideals. Neutrality is the standard for assuring these ideals; yet the adherence to it is often determined by reference to an aesthetic of uniformity, in which difference is simply omitted. For example, when segregation was eradicated from the American lexicon, its omission led many actually to believe that racism therefore no longer existed. Race neutrality in law has become the presumed antidote for race bias in real life. With the entrenchment of the notion of race neutrality came attacks on the concept of affirmative action and the rise of reverse discrimination suits. Blacks, for so many generations deprived of jobs based on the color of our skin, are now told that we ought to find it demeaning to be *hired* based on the color of our skin. Such is the silliness of simplistic either-or inversions as remedies to complex problems.
>
> What *is* truly demeaning in this era of double-speak-no-evil is going on interviews and not getting hired because someone doesn't think *we'll* be comfortable. It is demeaning not to get promoted because we're judged "too weak," then putting in a lot of energy the next time and getting fired because we're "too strong." It is demeaning to be told what we find demeaning. It is very demeaning to stand on street corners unemployed and begging. It is downright demeaning to have to explain why we haven't been employed for months and then watch the job go to someone who is "more experienced." It is outrageously demeaning that none of this can be called racism, even if it happens only to, or to large numbers of, black people; as long as it's done with a smile, a handshake, and a shrug; as long as the phantom word *race* is never used.
>
> The image of *race* as a phantom word came to me after I moved into my late godmother's home. In an attempt to make it my own, I cleared the bedroom for painting. The following morning the room asserted itself, came

rushing and raging at me through the emptiness, exactly as it had been for twenty-five years: one day filled with profuse and overwhelming complexity; the next day filled with persistently recurring memories. The shape of the past came to haunt me, the shape of the emptiness confronted me each time I was about to enter the room. The force of its spirit drifts like an odor throughout the house.

The power of that room, I have thought since, is very like the power of racism as status quo: it is deep, angry, eradicated from view, but strong enough to make everyone who enters the room walk around the bed that isn't there, avoiding the phantom as they did the substance, for fear of bodily harm. They do not even know they are avoiding; they defer to the unseen shapes of things with subtle responsiveness, guided by an impulsive awareness of nothingness and the deep knowledge and denial of witchcraft at work.

The phantom room is to me symbolic of the emptiness of formal equal opportunity, particularly as propounded by President Reagan and his Civil Rights Commission. Blindly formalized constructions of equal opportunity are the creation of a space that is filled in by a meandering stream of unguided hopes, dreams, fantasies, fears, recollections. They are the presence of the past in imaginary, imagistic form—the phantom-roomed exile of our longing.

It is thus that I strongly believe in the efficacy of programs and paradigms like affirmative action. Blacks are the objects of a constitutional omission that has been incorporated into a theory of neutrality. It is thus that omission is really a form of expression, as oxymoronic as that sounds: racial omission is a literal part of original intent; it is the fixed, reiterated prophecy of the Founding Fathers. It is thus that affirmative action *is* an affirmation; the affirmative act of hiring—or hearing—blacks is a recognition of individuality that replaces blacks as a social statistic, that is profoundly interconnective to the fate of blacks and whites either as subgroups or as one group. In this sense, affirmative action is as mystical and beyond the self as an initiation ceremony. It is an act of verification and of vision. It is an act of social as well as professional responsibility.[13]

Thus spake I to the assembled faculty and students of the University of West Virginia.

The following morning, I opened the *Dominion Post,* the Morgantown local newspaper, to find that the event of my speech had commanded two columns on the front page of the "Metro" section. I quote only the opening lines: "Affirmative action promotes prejudice by denying the status of women and blacks, instead of affirming them as its name suggests. So said New York City attorney Patricia Williams to an audience Wednesday."[14]

[Here end my journal notes for 28 May 1988. In the margin, there is a note to myself from myself: eventually, it says, I should try to pull all these threads together into yet another law review article. The problem, of course, will be that in the hierarchy of law review citation, the article in the *Dominion Post* will have more authoritative weight about me, as a so-called "primary resource" on me, than I will have; it will take precedence over my own citation of the "unverifiable" testimony of my speech.]

JOURNAL ENTRY OF 29 MAY 1988
(THE MEN'S ROOM)

Back at the Critical Legal Studies conference. For the second day in a row, the question about black women and men as social constructions hangs in the air like a fuzzy gray cloud. I think: I have always known that my raciality is socially constructed, and I experience it as such. I feel my black self as an eddy of conflicted meanings—and meaninglessness—in which my self can get lost; in which agency and consent are hopelessly relativized as a matter of constant motion. This is how I experience social constructions of race. This sense of motion, this constant windy sound of manipulation whistling in my ears is a reminder of society's constant construction, and reconstruction, of my blackness.

Somewhere at the center, my heart gets lost. I transfigure the undesirability of my racial ambiguity into the necessity of deference, the accommodation of condescension. It is very painful when I permit myself to see all this. It is terrifying when this truth announces itself to me. I shield myself from it, wherever possible. Indeed, at the conference it feels too dangerous to say any of this aloud, so I continue to muse to myself, pretending to doze. I am awakened suddenly and completely to a still and deadly serious room: someone has asked me to comment upon the rape of black women and the death of our children.

Unprepared and slightly dazed, I finessed the question with statistics and forgotten words; what actually comes to my mind, however, is one of the most tragically powerful embodiments of my ambiguous, tenuous, social positioning: the case of Tawana Brawley, a fifteen-year-old black girl from Wappinger Falls, New York. In late November 1987, after a four-day disappearance, she was found in a vacant lot, clothed only in a shirt and a plastic garbage bag into which she had apparently crawled; she was in a dazed state, responding neither to noise, cold, nor ammonia; there was urine-soaked cotton stuffed in her nose and ears; her hair had been chopped off; there were cigarette burns over one-third of her body; the words *KKK* and *nigger* had been inscribed on her torso; and her body was smeared with dog feces.[15] This much is certain—*certain* because there were objective third persons to testify as to her condition in that foundling state (and independent "objective" testimony is apparently what is required before experience gets to be labeled *truth*);[16] and this much is certainly worth the conviction that she has been the victim of some unspeakable crime. No matter how she got there. No matter who did it to her—and even if she did it to herself. Her condition was clearly the expression of some crime against her—some tremendous violence, some great violation that challenges comprehension.

It is this much that I grieve about, all told. The rest of the story is lost or irrelevant in the worst of all possible ways.

But there is a second version of this story. On 14 July 1988, New York State Attorney General Robert Abrams stated "There may not have been any crime committed here."[17] A local television call-in poll showed that the vast majority of New Yorkers—the vast majority of any potential jury pool in other words—agreed with him. Most people, according to the poll, felt either that if she were raped it was "consensual" (as cruel an oxymoron as ever was) or that she "did it to herself" (as though self-mutilation and attempted suicide are just free enterprise, privatized matters of no social consequence, with reference to which the concern of others is an invasion of privacy, an imprisoning of choice).[18] It was a surprise to no one, therefore, when a New York grand jury concluded that Tawana Brawley had made the whole thing up.[19] It is instructive to examine some of the circumstances that surround these conflicting interpretations.

When Tawana Brawley was finally able to tell her story—she remained curled in a fetal position for several days after she was found—she indicated, by nodding or shaking her head to questions posed by police, that she had been kidnapped and raped by six white men.[20] The white men she implicated included the district attorney of Wappinger Falls, a highway patrolman, and a local police officer. This accusation was not only the first, but also the last, public statement Tawana Brawley ever made.[21]

What replaced Tawana's story was a thunderous amount of media brouhaha, public offerings of a thousand and one other stories, fables, legends, and myths. A sample of these enticing distractions includes:

- Tawana's mother, Glenda Brawley (who fled to the sanctuary of a church to avoid arrest for failing to testify before a grand jury and to protest the failure of the same grand jury to subpoena the men named by her daughter)[22];
- Tawana's stepfather (with whom she was reportedly disaffected; from whom she had allegedly run away on prior occasions; by whom she had allegedly been beaten many times before; and who served seven years for manslaughter in the death of his first wife, whom he stabbed 14 times, and while awaiting trial for that much, then shot and killed)[23];
- Tawana's boyfriend (who was serving time on drug charges in an upstate "facility" and whom she had gone to visit shortly before her disappearance)[24];
- Tawana's lawyers, civil rights activists Alton Maddox and C. Vernon Mason (who advised their client not to cooperate with investigating authorities until an independent prosecutor was appointed to handle the case)[25];
- Tawana's spiritual counselor, the Reverend Al Sharpton (described variously as a "minister without a congregation,"[26] a drug informant

for the FBI,[27] a man who had a long and well-publicized history of involvement in the wiretapping of civil rights leaders,[28] yet, *mira-bile dictu,* a sudden but "trusted advisor" to the Brawley family.[29] Al Sharpton, tumbling off the stage in a bout of fisticuffs with Roy Innis on the neoconservative Morton Downey television program, brought to you Live! from the Apollo Theater.[30] Al Sharpton, railing against the court order holding Glenda Brawley in contempt, saying to the television cameras, "Their arms are too short to box with God").

It was Al Sharpton who proceeded to weave the story where Tawana left off. It was Al Sharpton who proceeded to implicate the Irish Republican Army, a man with a missing finger, and the Mafia. And it was Al Sharpton who spirited Tawana Brawley off into hiding shortly after the police officer whom Tawana Brawley implicated in her rape committed suicide.

Al Sharpton led Tawana Brawley off into hiding. More hiding. As though it were a metareenactment of her kidnap; as through it were a metametareenactment of her disappearing into the middle of her own case. It was like watching the Pied Piper of Harlem, this slowly replayed television spectacle of Tawana led off by the hand, put in a car, and driven to "a secret location"; this dance into thin air which could be accounted for by nothing less than sheer enchantment. I had a terrible premonition, as I watched, that Tawana Brawley would never be heard from again.

Tawana Brawley has not been heard from again. From time to time there are missives from her advisors to the world: Tawana is adjusting well to her new school; Tawana wants to be a model; Tawana approves of the actions of her advisors; and, most poignantly, Tawana is "depressed," so her advisors are throwing her a *party.*

But the stories in the newspapers are no longer about Tawana anyway. They are all about black manhood and white justice—a contest of wills among her attorneys, the black community, and the New York State prosecutor's office. Since Tawana's statement implicated a prosecutor, an issue was the propriety of her case being handled through the usual channels rather than having a special unit set up to handle this and other allegations of racial violence. But even this issue was not able to hold center stage with all the thunder and smoke of raucous male outcry, curdling warrior accusations, the clash and flash of political swords and shields—typified by Governor Cuomo's gratuitous offer to talk to Tawana personally; by Al Sharpton's particularly gratuitous statement that Tawana might show up at her mother's contempt hearing because "Most children want to be in court to say good-bye to their mothers before they go to jail"[31]; by television personality Phil Donahue's interview with Glenda Brawley which he began with "No one wants to jump on your bones and suggest that you are not an honorable person but"; by the enlistment of the support of the Reverend Louis Farrakhan and a good deal of other anti-Semitic insinuation; by the mishandling and loss of key evidence by investigating authorities; by the commissioning of a self-styled Black Army to encircle Glenda Brawley on the courthouse steps; by the refusal of the New York Attorney General's office to take seriously the request for an independent prosecutor; and by the testimony of an associate of Sharpton's, a former police officer named Perry McKinnon, that neither Mason, Maddox, nor Sharpton believe Tawana's story. (On television, I hear this latter story reported in a least three different forms: McKinnon says Tawana lied; McKinnon says Sharpton lied about believing Tawana's story; and/or McKinnon says that Mason and Maddox made up the whole thing in order to advance their own political careers. Like a contest or a lottery with some drunken solomonic gameshow host at the helm, the truth gets sorted out by a call-in poll: Channel 7, the local ABC affiliate, puts the issue to its viewers. Do you believe Sharpton? Or do you believe McKinnon? I forgot to listen to the eleven o'clock news, when the winner and the weather were to have been announced.)

To me, the most ironic thing about this whole bad business—as well as the thread of wisdom which runs at the heart of the decision not to have Tawana Brawley testify—is that were she to have come out of her hiding and pursued trial in the conventional manner, I have no doubt that she would have undergone exactly what she did go through, in the courts and in the media; it's just that without her, the script unfolded at a particularly abstract and fantastical level. But the story would be the same: wild black girl who loves to lie, who is no innocent,[32] and whose wiles are the downfall of innocent, jaded, desperate white men; this whore-lette, the symbolic consort of rapacious, saber-rattling, buffoonish black men asserting their manhood, whether her jailbird boyfriend, her smooth-headed FBI drug-buster informant of a spiritual advisor; her grand-standing, pretending-to-be-professional unethically boisterous, so-called lawyers who have yet to establish "a *single* cognizable legal claim,"[33] and so forth.

Tawana's awful story has every black woman's worst fears and experiences wrapped into it. Few will believe a black woman who has been raped by a white man.[34] If they believe that a white man even wanted her, no one will believe that she is not a whore. (White women are prostitutes; black women are whores.) White women sell themselves because they are jaded and desperate; black women *whore*, as a way of being, as an innateness of sootiness and contamination, as a sticky-sweet inherency of black womanhood persistently imaged as overripe fruit [e.g., melons]; so they whore, according to this fantasy script, as easily as they will cut your throat or slit open said ripe melon for said deep sweet fruit, spitting out afterward a predictable stream of blood and seeds and casual curses.) Black women whore because it is sensual and lazy and vengeful. How can such a one be raped? Or so the story goes.

It is not any easier when a black woman is raped by a black man (many of the newspapers have spun eager nets of suspicion around Tawana's stepfather[35] and/or a boyfriend); black-on-black rape is not merely the violation of one woman by one man: it is a sociological event, a circus of stereotypification.[36] It is a trial of the universalized black man against the lusty black female. The intimacy of rape becomes a public display full of passion, pain, and gutsy blues.

Tawana Brawley herself remains absent from all this. She is a shape, a hollow, an emptiness at the center.[37]

There is no respect or wonder for her silence. The world that created her oppression now literally countenances it, filling the suffering of her void with sacrilegious noise, clashing color, serial tableaux of lurid possibility. Truth, like a fad, takes on a life of its own, independent of action and limited only by the imagination of a plurality of self-proclaimed visionaries; untruth becomes truth through belief, and disbelief untruths the truth. The world turns upside down; the quiet, terrible, nearly invisible story of her suffering may never emerge from the boiling noise that overtook the quest for "what happened" and polarized it into the bizarre and undecidable litigation of "something happened" *versus* "nothing happened."

In the face of all this, there is some part of me that wants this child to stay in hiding, some part of me that understands the instinct to bury her rather than expound. Exposure is the equivalent of metarape, as hiding with Al Sharpton is the equivalent of metakidnap. It feels as though there are no options other than hiding or exposing. There is danger everywhere for her. There is no shelter, no protection. There is no medicine circle for her, no healing society, no stable place to testify and be heard, as the unburdening of one heart.

JOURNAL ENTRY OF 30 MAY 1988 (THE WOMEN'S ROOM)

The world is full of black women who have never been heard from again. Take Maxine, for example. According to one version, Los Angeles Municipal Court Judge Maxine Thomas's nervous breakdown was inexplicable.[38] She was as strong a black woman as ever conjured; a celebrated, savvy judge who presided over hundreds of mostly white male judges. Yet one day she just snapped and had to be carted from her chambers, helpless as a baby.[39]

Another version has it that Judge Thomas was overcommitted. She had bitten off more than she could chew; she had too many irons in the fire; and she just was not competent or skillful enough to handle it all.[40]

Some said that she was manic-depressive and that her endless politicking was nothing less than shamelessly irresponsible self-promotion, which is clearly the sign of an unbalanced black woman.[41]

Others said she was a woman who, like many women, thought of herself *through* other people. A woman who drained others in search of herself. A woman who criticized others into conformity; a woman who used others as substitutes for herself, as self-extenders, as personality enhancers, as screens, as crutches, and as statements. A woman who was nothing without others.[42]

A woman who had forgotten her roots.[43]
A woman who exploited her blackness.[44]
A woman who was too individualistic.[45]
A woman who could not think for herself.[46]
A woman who had the perfect marriage.[47]
A woman who overpowered her men and assaulted their manhood.[48]
A woman who was too emotional.[49]
A woman who needed to loosen up.[50]
A woman who took her profession too seriously.[51]
A woman who did not take her profession seriously enough.[52]

My mother's most consistent message to me, growing up, was that I must become a "professional woman." My only alternative, as she presented it, was to "die in the gutter." There was for me no in between. My mother was a gritty realist, a chess player always on the verge of checkmate, cagey, wary, penultimately protective. And so I became a professional woman.

According to all the best statistics available, I am the perfect average black professional woman. Single. Never married. Having bred a statistically negligible number of children.[53] I suppose I should be miserable, but in fact it is not the end of the world. The very existence of such a statistical category is against all the odds, is company enough for me. I feel like my life is a long graceful miracle, a gentle golden space through which I float on silken phoenix wings. I do not feel any inclination to marry myself off just because I am single. I like being single. (Yet as a social statistic, sometimes I feel less like I am single than socially widowed. Sometimes when I walk down the street and see some poor black man lying over a heating vent, I feel as though I am looking into the face of my companion social statistic, my lost mate—

so passionate, original, creative, fine-boned, greedy, and glorious—lying in the gutter [as my mother envisioned] lost, tired, drunk, and howling.) Nor do I feel the obligation to have children just because engineering social statisticians tell me I am "better able" to parent than the vast majority of black women who, being lower class, are purportedly "least able" to parent. (Yet sometimes I wonder what denial of the death all around me, what insistence on the Holy Grail of a certain promised form of life keeps me from taking into my arms the companions to my sorrow—real orphans, black and brown children who languish in institutional abundance and abandon, children born of desperate caring, unions of explosive love, but lives complicated at a more intimate level than I can know by guttered hopes and homelessness.)

It is early morning, the day after the Critical Legal Studies conference. Next door, as I write, my mother, who is visiting me, rises and prepares to greet the day. She makes lots of little trips to the bathroom, in developing stages of undress then dress. Back and forth, from bedroom to bath, seeking and delivering small things: washcloths, eyeliners, stockings, lipstick. The last trip to the bathroom is always the longest. It is then that she does her face and hair. Next door, I can hear the anxiety of her preparations: the creaking of the floorboards as she stands closer then farther from the mirror; the lifting and placing of infinite bottles and jars on the shelves, in the cabinets; the click of her closing a compact of blush; the running of water over her hairbrush; an anonymous fidgety frequency of sounds. She is in a constancy of small motions, like clatters, soft rattles, and bumps. When she leaves the bathroom at last, she makes one final quick trip to the bedroom, then goes downstairs, completely composed, with small brave steps.

When I get up in the morning I stare in the mirror and stick on my roles: I brush my teeth with my responsibility to my community. I buff my nails with paving the way for my race. I comb my hair in the spirit of pulling myself up by my bootstraps. I dab astringent on my pores that I might be a role model upon whom all may gaze with pride. I mascara my eyelashes that I may be "different" from all the rest. I glaze my lips with the commitment to deny pain and "rise above" racism.

I gaze in the mirror and realize that I am very close to being Maxine.

When I am fully dressed, my face is hung with contradictions; I try not to wear all my contradictions at the same time. I pick and choose among them; like jewelry, I hunt for this set of expectations that will go best with that obligation. I am just this close.

Judge Maxine Thomas's job as black female judge was to wear all the contradictions at the same time—to wear them well and reconcile them. She stretched wide and reconciled them all. She swallowed all the stories, all the roles; she opened wide to all the expectations.

Standing before the mirror, I understand the logic of her wild despair, the rationality of her unbounded rage. I understand the break she made as necessary and immediate; I understand her impatient self-protection as the incantation of an ancient and incomprehensible restlessness. Knowing she was to be devoured by life, she made herself inedible, full of thorns and sharp edges.

She split at the seams. She returned to the womb. She lay huddled in a wilderness of meaning, lost, a speechless child again, her accommodative language heard as babble, the legacy of *KKK* and *nigger* spilling from her heart, words and explanations dribbling, seeping, bursting from her. Giving birth to a thousand possibilities, she exploded, leaking fragments of intelligence and scattered wisdom.

Her clerk found her curled into a fetal position, crying in her chambers. She was singing her small songs, her magic words, her soothsayings of comfort and the inky juice of cuttlefish. She was singing the songs of meadow saffron and of arbor vitae, of eel serum and of marking nut; snowberry, rue, bitterwort, and yew. She had—without knowing, yet feeling the way of power always—invoked sea onion, shepherd's purse, red clover. In her desperation, she had called upon divinations larger than herself: pinkroot, aquilegia, jambol seeds, thorn apple, and hedge hyssop.

Her bailiff turned her in. (He, the taskmaster of the threshold world. He, the marker of the order of things. The tall protector of the way that things must be, a fierce border guard, bulldog-tough in his guarding of the gate, whose reward was not the slung scrap of salary but the satisfaction—the deep, solid warmth that comes from making-safe. How betrayed he must have felt when this creamy-brown woman rose

over her needled rim and rebuked him; told him, in her golden mad-
ness, above all to mix, mix, mix it all up. Dangerously. Such conscientious, sacrilegious mockery of protective manhood.)

Once over the edge, once into the threshold world, another sober
archangel, her attorney and spokesperson, announced to the public
that not only was it unlikely she would ever be able to rejoin the ranks
of the judiciary, she would probably never be able to rejoin the ranks
of practicing lawyers.[54] Needing so badly to be loved and lacking the
professionalism to intercede on behalf of those less fortunate than she,
it is unlikely she will ever be heard from again.[55]

ENTRY OF 31 MAY 1988
(THE LIVING ROOM)

It is two days after the Critical Legal Studies conference, and I am
finally able to think directly about Professor Bell's Chronicle of the
Twenty-seventh-Year Syndrome—this thorn of a story, this remarkable
gauntlet cast into sadness and confusion.

Here, finally, are my thoughts on the matter: giving it every benefit
of the doubt, Professor Bell's story is about gender relations as a political issue. The issue in the twenty-seventh year is not only the behavior
or lack of political black mates; the issue is also the hidden, unmention-
able secret among us: the historic white master-mate. Romantic love is
the fantasy bridge across this gap, this silent chasm. The wider the
chasm, the more desperately passionate the structuring of our compensatory vision.

The deep sleep into which the women of the twenty-seventh year
fall is an intellectual castration—they are cut off from the black community as well as from all their knowledge and talent and training. The
acquisition of professionalism is sexualized: its assertion masculinizes
as well as whitens. Professionalism, according to this construction, is
one of several ways to get marooned in an uncomprehending white and
patriarchal society; thus it sets women up to be cut off and then lost in
the profundity of that world's misunderstanding and shortcoming.

The blackness of black people in this society has always represented the blemish, the uncleanliness, the barrier separating individual and society. Castration from blackness thus becomes the initiatory tunnel, the portal through which black people must pass if they are not to fall on their faces in the presence of society, of paternity, of hierarchy. Once castrated, they have shed their horrid mortality, the rapacious lust of lower manhood, the raucous, mother-witted passion of lower womanhood, and opened themselves up to participation in the pseudo-celestial white community. Intellectual castration is thus for blacks a sign of suffering for the Larger Society's love as well as a sign to others, as in the Chronicle of the Twenty-seventh-Year Syndrome, of membership in the tribe of those who must, who need to be loved best.

For most blacks, however, this passage from closure to openness turns out not to be a passage from mortality to divine revelation but openness in the opposite extreme direction: openness as profane revelation. Not communion, but exposure, vulnerability, the collapse of boundary in the most assaultive way. White society is in the place of the blinding glory of Abraham's God. Pharaoh, not Yahweh.

Another thought I have about this chronicle is Professor Bell's "use" of the imaginary Geneva Crenshaw: throughout the whole book *And We Are Not Saved*, Geneva Crenshaw, this witchy, dream-filled wishing woman, is his instrument by which to attack the monolithism of white patriarchal legal discourse. She is an anti-Founding Father, wandering across time to the Constitutional Convention and back again, a source of aboriginal wisdom and intent. She is the word-creation by which he legitimizes his own critique, as he delegitimizes the limits of the larger body of law's literature. She is the fiction who speaks from across the threshold to the powerful unfiction of the legal order; he argues with her, but he owns her, this destroyer of the rational order. Yet the Chronicle of the Twenty-seventh Year is the one chronicle in the entire series of chronicles in *And We Are Not Saved* which is not of her telling, which Bell owns by himself. In a reversal of roles, she receives *his* story and critiques it; from this "outside position," it is easy to forget that Geneva Crenshaw is not a "real, objective" third person, but part of Bell. She is an extension of Bell, no less than the doctrines of precedent and of narrow constructionism are extensions of the judges who employ them. She is an opinion, no less than any judge's opinion, an invention of her author; an outgrowth of the text; a phantom.

As I think about this, I remember that my father would use my sister and me in that way. He would write poems of extraordinary beauty and interest; he really wanted to publish them, but did not. He gave them to us instead. In so doing, he could resolve his need for audience in safety; with his daughters as judges, he was assured a kind and gloating reception. Fears of failure or of success or of exposure motivated him I suppose; however, it placed my sister and me—or me, in any event—in a remarkably authoritative position. I was powerful. I knew what I was expected to say, and I did my duty. The fact that I meant it did not matter. What I did was a lie, regardless of how much I believed or not in the talent of his poetry. My power was in living the lie that I was all audiences. My power was in the temptation to dissemble, either out of love or disaffection. This is blacks' and women's power, I used to think: this power to lie while existing in the realm of someone else's fantasy. This power to refrain from exerting the real, to shift illusion, while serving as someone else's weaponry, nemesis, language club.

After meeting my new sisters, these inventions of Professor Bell's mind, however, I began to wonder what would happen if I told my father the truth. What would happen, I wonder, if I were to cut through the fantasy and really let him know that I am not an extension of his pen; what if I were to tell him that I like his writing (or not), but in my own words and on my own terms.

By the same token, what would happen, I wonder, if the victims of Twenty-seventh-Year Syndrome were to awaken from their comatose repose, no longer merely derivative of the black or white male experience, but sharper-tongued than ever. Whose legitimacy would be at risk? Theirs? Professor Bell's? Geneva Crenshaw's? The twenty-seven-year-olds who cannot shake the sleep from their eyes?

Or is there any risk at all?

[An undated entry in the unbounded body of sometime after May 1988: A dream. I am in an amphitheater, creeping around the back wall. I am not supposed to be there – it is after-hours, the theater is not open to the general public. On the stage, dead center, surrounded by a circle of friends, spotlighted in the quiet dark of the theater, is a vision, a version of myself. My hair is in an exaggerated beehive (a style I affected, only once, fresh from an application of the hot-comb, at the age of twelve), and I am wearing a sequined low-cut red dress (a dress I actually wore, again once, at the liberated age of twenty-three). There I am with that hair and that ridiculous cowgirl dress: it is an eye scorcher of a sparkling evening gown, my small breasts stuffed into it and uplifted in a way that resembles cleavage.

The me-that-is-on-stage is laughing loudly and long. She is extremely vivacious, the center of attention. She is, just as I have always dreamed of being, fascinating. She is showy yet deeply intelligent. She is not beautiful in any traditional sense, as I am not in real life – her mouth and teeth are very large, her nose very long, like a claymation model of myself – but her features are riveting. And she is so radiantly, splendidly good-natured. She is lovely in the oddest possible combination of ways. I sit down in the small circle of friends-around-myself, to watch myself, this sparkling homely woman, dressed like a moment lost in time. I hear myself speaking: *"Voices lost in the chasm speak from the slow eloquent fact of the chasm. They speak and speak and speak, like flowing water."*

From this dream, into a complicated world, a propagation of me's awakens, strong, single-hearted, and completely refreshed.]

NOTES

1. (New York: Basic Books, 1987.)

2. Gross, "When 'By Appointment' Means Keep Out," *New York Times,* 17 December 1986, p. B1, col. 3.

3. Letter to the Editor from Michael Levin and Marguerita Levin, *New York Times,* 11 January 1987, p. E32, col. 3.

4. My experience was based on his treating me as a generality; the person whom he excluded was not me, but the universal me; she was both everybody and nobody.

5. Although even then I always reclaim it through some other form of my writing, as now; or as in the letters I wrote to Benneton's headquarters (in New York and Italy) and to the *New York Times*. (Nothing ever came of them.)

6. P. Williams, *Spirit-Murdering the Messenger: The Discourse of Fingerpointing as the Law's Response to Racism*, 42 U. OF MIAMI L. REV. 127, 129 (1987).

7. Letters of 8 October and 13 October, on file at City University of New York Law School.

8. See generally, Blyew v. United States, 80 U.S. 581 (1871) upholding a state's right to forbid blacks to testify against whites.

9. Letter of 5 November 1987, on file at City University of New York Law School.

10. Affidavit of P. Williams (conversation with Rick Bendremer, 7 November 1987) on file at City University of New York Law School.

11. Ibid.

12. Professor Charles Ogletree has done research showing how the elimination of the race of defendants in criminal cases, like Mapp v. Ohio and Terry v. Ohio, changes one's relation to the outcome; a defendant acting "suspiciously" while walking down a public street is a perception one accepts or not based on one's knowledge of pervasive social acquiescence in theories of "inherent" suspiciousness that black as opposed to white defendants bring to bear.

13. P. Williams, *The Obliging Shell*, 87 U. OF MICH. L. REV. 2128 (1989).

14. Matesa, "Attorney Says Affirmative Action Denies Racism, Sexism," *Dominion Post*, 8 April 1988, p. B1, col. 1–2.

15. E. Diamond, "The Brawley Fiasco," *New York Magazine*, 18 July 1988, p. 22, col. 2.

16. Even this much certainty was persistently recast as nothing at all in the subsequent months: by September, the *New York Times* was reporting that "her ears and nose were *protected* by cotton wads" [emphasis added]; that it was not her *own* hair that was cut, but rather hair extensions "woven into her own short hair" which had either been torn or cut out; that only her clothes and not her body had been burned; that, from the moment she was found, "*seemingly* dazed and degraded, [she] assumed the mantle of victim" [emphasis

added]; and that her dazed condition was "ephemeral" because, in the emergency room, after resisting efforts to physically pull open her eyes, "Dr. Pena concluded that Tawana was not unconscious and was aware of what was going on around her . . . In a moment of quiet drama, Dr. Pena confronted Miss Brawley: 'I know you can hear me so open your eyes,' she commanded. Tawana opened her eyes and was able to move them in all directions by following Pena's finger." "Evidence Points to Deceit by Brawley," *New York Times,* 27 September 1988, p. A17, col. 1–3.

17. M. Cottman, "Abrams' Brawley Update: There Might Be No Crime," *New York Newsday,* 15 July 1988, p. 5, col. 3.

18. Diamond, "The Brawley Fiasco," p. 22.

19. R. McFadden, "Brawley Made Up Story of Assault, Grand Jury Finds," *New York Times,* 7 October 1988, p. 1, col. 1.

20. "Nodding or shaking her head to questions, . . . Miss Brawley gave contradictory answers. She indicated that she had been subjected to acts of oral sex, and after first indicating she had not been raped, she suggested she had been assaulted by three white men . . . Asked who assaulted her, she grabbed the silver badge on his uniform but did not respond when he asked if the badge she saw was like his. He then gave her his notebook and she wrote 'white cop.' Asked where, she wrote 'woods.' He then asked her if she had been raped, and she wrote: 'a lot' and drew an arrow to 'white cop' . . . This response was the closest Miss Brawley ever came to asserting to authorities that she had been raped; her family and advisors, however, asserted many times that she was raped, sodomized, and subjected to other abuse." "Evidence Points to Deceit by Brawley," p. A17, col. 3.

21. One may well question why she, being a minor, was ever put in the position of making public statements at all: "What first signaled to me that a black girl was about to become a public victim was hearing the *name* of an alleged rape victim—Tawana Brawley—given on a local radio news show. Since when does the press give the name of any rape victim, much less one who is underage? Obviously when the victim is black, and thus not worthy of the same respect and protection that would be given a white child. A few days later we had another demeaning first: television cameras invading the Brawley home to zoom in for a close-up of Tawana lying on a couch, looking brutalized, disoriented, almost comatose. Later, there would be published police evidence

photographs showing Tawana Brawley as she looked when she was first brought by ambulance to a hospital following her rape: unconscious, dirty, half-naked, a 'censorship band' on the pictures covering only the nipples on her otherwise exposed breasts." A. Edwards, "The Rape of Tawana Brawley," *Essence,* November 1988, p. 79, 80.

As NAACP attorney Conrad Lynn observed, moreover, "[s]tate law provides that if a child appears to have been sexually molested, then the Child Protective Services Agency is supposed to take jurisdiction and custody of that child. Now, Tawana Brawley was fifteen at the time of the incident. If that had been done, as I proposed early on, the agency would have given her psychiatric attention and preserved evidence, if there were evidence . . . But there was a state decision that the agency shouldn't be involved." "What Happened to Tawana Brawley's Case—And To Attitudes About Race and Justice," *New York Times,* 9 October 1988, p. E8, col. 1.

22. Diamond, "The Brawley Fiasco," p. 22.

23. "Evidence Points to Deceit by Brawley," p. A17, col. 2; Diamond, "The Brawley Fiasco," p. 22, col. 2.

24. "Evidence Points to Deceit by Brawley," p. A17, col. 1.

25. Diamond, "The Brawley Fiasco," p. 22.

26. "Mr. Sharpton, who is still a member of the Washington Temple Church of God in Christ, does not serve as the pastor of any church. 'My total time is civil rights,' he said. 'It's kind of hard to do both.'" E. R. Shipp, "A Flamboyant Leader of Protests," *New York Times,* 21 January 1988, p. B6, col. 3–4.

27. "The Rev. Al Sharpton, a Brooklyn minister who has organized civil disobedience demonstrations and has frequently criticized the city's predominantly white political leadership, assisted law-enforcement officials in at least one recent criminal investigation of black community groups, Government sources said.

"He also allowed investigators to wiretap a telephone in his home, the sources said." M. Farber, "Protest Figure Reported to Be a U.S. Informant," *New York Times,* 21 January 1988, p. B1, col. 5–6. "Mr. Sharpton said that he—not investigators—had put a recording device on his phone, but only to serve as a 'hot line' for people turning in crack dealers." Ibid., p. B6, col. 4.

28. "[S]enior New York City police officials said they had learned a year ago that Mr. Sharpton was an informer for the FBI—'that's the word that was used,' one official said.

"A Federal official said Mr. Sharpton had been 'introduced' to federal prosecutors for the Eastern District of New York by another law-enforcement agency more than a year ago." M. Farber, "Protest Figure Reported to Be a U.S. Informant," p. B1, col. 5–6.

29. Diamond, "The Brawley Fiasco," p. 22.

30. "Conservative black leader Roy Innis toppled Tawana Brawley advisor Al Sharpton while taping a TV program on black leadership, and the two civil rights gadflies vowed yesterday to settle their dispute in a boxing ring . . . 'He tried to 'Bogart' me in the middle of my statement,' said Innis . . . 'I said no dice . . . We stood up and the body language was not good. So I acted to protect myself. I pushed him and he went down' . . . As the rotund preacher tumbled backward, Downey and several bodyguards jumped between the pair. Neither man was hurt . . . Sharpton said he hoped boxing promoter Don King would help organize a Sharpton-Innis charity boxing match . . . but said he would promote it himself if necessary . . . 'The best part is that we will be giving a very positive lesson to young black people in this city about conflict resolution— but not on the street with guns and knives,' Innis said. 'It will be an honest, clean and honorable contest.'" "Roy Innis Pushes Al Sharpton: Fracas at 'Downey Show' Taping; Boxing Match Planned," *Washington Post,* 11 August 1988, p. D4, col. 1.

31. A. Bollinger, "Tawana's Mom to Get 'Black Army' Escort," *New York Post,* 3 June 1988, p. 7, col. 2.

32. In New York, television newscasters inadvertently, but repeatedly, referred to her as the "defendant."

33. H. Kurtz, "New York Moves against Brawley Lawyers," *Washington Post,* 7 October 1988, p. A1, col. 1.

34. In one of the more appallingly straightforward statements to this effect, Pete Hamill, while excoriating the "racist hustlers" Sharpton, Mason, and Maddox for talking "about 'whites' as if they were a monolith," asked, "After Tawana Brawley, who will believe the next black woman who says she was raped by white men? Or the one after her?" P. Hamill, "Black Media Should Tell the Truth," *New York Post,* 29 September 1988, p.5, col. 5. A slightly more highbrow version of the same sentiment was put forth in an editorial in the *New York Times:* "How can anyone know the depths of cynicism and distrust engendered by an escapade like this? Ask the next black person who is truly victimized—

and meets skepticism and disbelief. Ask the next skeptic, white or black." "The Victims of the Brawley Case," *New York Times,* 28 September 1988, p. A22, col. 2.

35. "One witness said Mr. King 'would watch her exercise' and talked to the girl 'in a real sexual way,' sometimes describing her as a 'fine fox.'" "Evidence Points to Deceit by Brawley," p. A16, col. 3.

36. "Then it was off to the airport cafeteria for a strategy session and some cheeseburgers with advisors Alton Maddox, C. Vernon Mason, and the Rev. Al Sharpton. 'The fat one, he ate the most,' said Carmen, the cashier. 'He and the skinny one [an aide] bought about $50 or $60 of cheeseburgers, orange juice, chocolate cake, pasta salad and pie,' she added." J. Nolan, "Traveling Circus has 'Em Rollin' in Aisles," *New York Post,* 29 September 1988, p. 4, col. 5; p. 5, col. 1.

37. "There is a silence that cannot speak.

"There is a silence that will not speak.

"Beneath the grass the speaking dreams and beneath the dreams is a sensate sea. The speech that frees comes forth from that amniotic deep. To attend its voice, I can hear it say, is to embrace its absence. But I fail the task. The word is stone.

"I admit it.

"I hate the stillness. I hate the stone. I hate the sealed vault with its cold icon. I hate the staring into the night. The questions thinning into space. The sky swallowing the echoes.

"Unless the stone bursts with telling, unless the seed flowers with speech, there is in my life no living word. The sound I hear is only sound. White sound. Words, when they fall, are pock marks on the earth. They are hailstones seeking an underground stream.

"If I could follow the stream down and down to the hidden voice, would I come at last to the freeing word? I ask the night sky but the silence is steadfast. There is no reply." J. Kogawa, *Obasan* (Boston: David R. Godine, 1981), 1.

38. "'I thought Maxine was a lady of unlimited potential,' said Reginald Dunn, of the Los Angeles city attorney's office." R. Arnold and T. Pristin, "The Rise and Fall of Maxine Thomas," *Los Angeles Times,* 6 May 1988, p. 1, col. 1.

39. "Clerk Richard Haines found Thomas—the first black woman to head the Municipal Court and role model for young blacks in Los Angeles—slumped in her leather chair. The 40-year-old judge's head was bowed, and she wept uncontrollably," Ibid.

40. "'She's a small, frail person,' said Johnnie L. Cochran Jr., a prominent attorney and longtime Thomas friend. 'A human being breaks . . . All these things turned in on her.'" Ibid., col. 3.

41. "Pampered, emotionally immature and unforgiving on one hand, she could also be seductively charming, selflessly kind. In public, she could inspire children with her speeches on how to succeed. In private, faced with disappointment or dissension, she could resort to temper tantrums." Ibid., p. 3, col. 1.

42. "'I think that all along there was a perception of her by a not unsubstantial group of people that there was more form than substance, that there was a lot of razzle-dazzle and not a lot to back it up,' said one of [her] critics. Like several others, this judge asked not to be identified to avoid further rancor on the court," Ibid.

43. "The only child of a janitor and a sometime domestic worker, Thomas grew up in the heart of southcentral Los Angeles in a nondescript frame house near 47th Street and Hooper Avenue. She was adored as a child, coddled as an adult . . . 'Maxine never had to do anything. She wasn't the type of girl who ever had to clean up her room," said actress Shirley Washington, Thomas's closest friend and confidante for the past 16 years." Ibid.

44. "Attorney Cochran, who now represents Thomas, characterizes her as having 'reached almost heroine status in the black community.'

"For Thomas, it was all according to plan."

"'She was a very friendly young lawyer with a great future,' said Atty. Gen. John K. Van de Kamp, who first met Thomas in the early 1970s. 'It was a time for strong and able black women.'" Ibid., col. 2–3.

45. "'I think she thought the job carried a certain power it just doesn't carry,' said retired Municipal Judge Xenophon Lang Sr. 'You're certainly not the boss of other judges . . . You're not a king of anything or queen of anything.'" Ibid., col. 4.

46. "'She wasn't able to function very well,' said Justice Joan Dempsey Klein, who reviewed Thomas's performance."

47. "Her career in chaos, Thomas focused on her private life and a new romantic interest. He was Donald Ware, a never-married cardiologist who admired her 'fighting spirit.' It seemed the perfect match, and after only a few months, Ware bought her a 4-carat diamond engagement ring.

"The pair planned a lavish May wedding, complete with 40 attendants, the bridesmaids garbed in lilac, the ushers in top hats and tails. The wedding party rode in a motorcade of Rolls-Royces, stretch limousines and vintage automobiles, and there were four soloists including Thelma Houston, Linda Hopkins and Scherrie Payne . . .

"After the nuptials, about 1,000 guests attended a reception at the Four Seasons Hotel in Beverly Hills, where they feasted on a five-tiered wedding cake iced in lavender and white . . .

"There was only one glitch in the fairly tale scenario. The wedding wasn't legal. The couple weren't married.

"They had no valid marriage license, and for that Ware blames Thomas. Thomas blames Ware." Ibid., p. 3, col. 5–6.

48. "In all, the honeymoon trip lasted three weeks, the volcanic 'marriage' about four.

"'The girl wanted everything, my money and my income,' Ware said afterward. 'Our personal life has been a tragedy. She's got a lot of problems and wanted to give me problems.'" Ibid., p. 3, col. 6.

49. "'She wasn't professional,' said one judge who observed Thomas at work. 'I remember her clapping her hands when there was a settlement . . . The way she would exclaim her glee was not very judgelike.'" Ibid., p. 3, col. 5.

50. "'People were afraid, truly afraid to confront her . . . because of a reputation, right or wrong, of vindictiveness,' one judge said. 'She probably came on the court with more political power than probably any of the other judges.'" Ibid., p. 3, col. 4.

51. "'Here's a girl who was basically a straight-A student all her life, who never knew what rejection was, never knew what failure was until she decided to run for Superior Court,' Washington said. 'After the election, I went over there and had to pull her out of bed. All she was saying, 'It isn't fair; it's not fair.'" Ibid., p. 3, col. 5.

52. "She launched a night version of small claims court and then joined her judicial colleague Richard Adler in promoting a program to process short civil cases at night and in opening a special small claims court for visitors to the 1984 Olympics. Thomas was written up in the newspapers, not part of the routine for most Municipal Court judges.

"There was rumbling among some of the judges, and in private the more critical of them began deriding her, questioning where she was trying to go with her splashy programs and complaining that she was neglecting the nitty-gritty work of the court." Ibid., p. 3, col. 3.

53. Despite persistent public images to the contrary, "[b]lack birth rates have declined from 153.5 per 1000 women in 1960, to 81.4 per 1000 women in 1984." T. B. Edsell, "Race in Politics," *New York Review of Books,* 22 December 1988, p. 24, col. 1.

54. "For now, doctors say, Thomas should not even consider a return to law, much less to the courts.

"'I think right now the doctors are saying not in the near future,' Green said. 'I'm not a doctor, but my personal view would be never.'" Arnold, "Rise and Fall," col. 7.

55. "Did you ever . . . ,
wear a certain kind of silk dress
and just by accident,
so inconsequential you barely notice it,
your fingers graze that dress
and you hear the sound of a knife cutting paper,
you see it too
and you realize how that image
is simply the extension of another image,
that your own life is a chain of words
that will one day snap." Ai, "Conversation," in *Sin* (Boston: Houghton Mifflin, 1986), 17.

The English Institute, 1988

The Program

Thursday, August 25, through Sunday, August 28, 1988

I. Sentimentality/antisentimentality
   Directed by Michael Fried, The Johns Hopkins University

Thursday, 2 P.M.	Purple Prose: Relations of Sentimentality, Relations of the Closet
	Eve Kosofsky Sedgwick, Duke University
Friday, 9:30 A.M.	True Acting and the Language of Real Feeling: *Mansfield Park*
	David Marshall, Yale University
Friday, 11 A.M.	Exploitation Cinema
	Carol Clover, University of California, Berkeley

II. Milton, Politics, and the New Historicism
   Directed by Mary Nyquist, University of Toronto

Thursday, 3:30 P.M.	Specular Structures Transhistorical?: The Problem of Narcissism in *Paradise Lost*
	John Guillory, Yale University
Friday, 2 P.M.	Portioning Blame: Domesticating the Social Discourse of Milton and the Powell Women
	Abbe Blum, Swarthmore College
Friday, 3:30 P.M.	Typology and the Ethics of Tragedy in *Samson Agonistes*
	Christoper Kendrick, Washington University, St. Louis

III. Policial Readings of Eighteenth-Century Literature
   Directed by Laura Brown, Cornell University

   | Saturday, 9:30 A.M. | The Old Order and the New Novel of the Mid-Eighteenth Century: Fielding and Smollet |
   | | *John Richetti, University of Pennsylvania* |

Saturday, 11:00 A.M.	Reading Race and Gender
	Laura Brown, Cornell University
Sunday, 9:30 A.M.	Spectral Politics: Apparition Belief and the Romantic Imagination
	Terry Castle, Stanford University
Sunday, 11:00 A.M.	Politics, Literature, and the Division of Knowledge
	Michael McKeon, Rutgers University

IV. Some Consequences of Theory (II)
   Directed by Barbara Johnson, Harvard University

Saturday, 2 P.M.	Excluding Voices: Legal Language and the Ideology of Style
	Patricia Williams, City University of New York Law School
Saturday, 3:30 P.M.	History of Gesture
	Lynn Hunt, University of Pennsylvania
Sunday, 2 P.M.	Whatever the Consequences
	Anthony Appiah, Cornell University
Sunday, 3:30 P.M.	The Marginal as Object of Investigation
	Gayatri Chakravorty Spivak, University of Pittsburgh

Sponsoring Institutions

University of Alabama, Birmingham, Amherst College, Baylor University, Bentley College, Boston College, Boston University, Brandeis University, Brigham Young University, University of California, Berkeley, University of California, Irvine, University of California, Los Angeles, University of California, Riverside, Carnegie Mellon University, Central Connecticut State University, Claremont Graduate School, University of Colorado, Boulder, Columbia University, Cornell University, Duke University, Emory University, Fordham University, Harvard University, University of Illinois at Chicago, Indiana University, The University of Iowa, The Johns Hopkins University, University of Maryland, University of Massachusetts, Amherst, Massachusetts Institute of Technology, McGill University, Michigan State University, University of Minnesota, City University of New York Graduate Center, State University of New York at Albany, State University of New York at Buffalo, State University of New York at Stony Brook, New York University, Northwestern University, University of Pennsylvania, Princeton University, University of Rochester, Rutgers University, Smith College, University of Southern California, Stanford University, Temple University, Trinity College, Tufts University, University of Tulsa, Department of the Navy, U.S. Naval Academy, University of Virginia, Wellesley College, Wesleyan University, Yale University

Registrants, 1988

Timothy J. Abraham, New York City Public Schools, Citywide Articulation Program; Marie L. Ahearn, Southeastern Massachusetts University; Janet E. Aikins, University of New Hampshire; Marcia Allentuck, City University of New York; Anthony Appiah, Cornell University; Jonathan Arac, Columbia University; Eiko Araki, Osaka City University; Alia Arasoughly, August Light Production; N. S. Asbridge, Central Connecticut State University; Michael Austin, College of St. Joseph; Roy E. Aycock, Old Dominion University

George W. Bahlke, Hamilton College; Anne H. Bailey, University of Alabama, Birmingham; Houston A. Baker, University of Pennsylvania; Evelyn Barish, City University of New York, Staten Island; Joseph F. Bartolomeo, University of Massachusetts, Amherst; James Beaton, Middlesex School; Jerome Beaty, Emory University; Jane Bellamy, University of Alabama, Birmingham; Dorothy Bilik, University of Maryland; Helen H. Black, University of Colorado, Boulder; Abbe Blum, Swarthmore College; Amy Boesky, Harvard University; Stephen Bretzius, Harvard University; Janice Broder, Brandeis University; R. H. Brodhead, Yale University; Elizabeth Brophy, College of New Rochelle; Laura Brown, Cornell University; Audrey Bruné, Concordia University; Jane Buchanan, Bentley College; Julia Budenz, Harvard University; Sanford Budick, Hebrew University; Bonnie Burns, Tufts University; Roland A. Burns, University of Maine, Fort Kent; John Burt, Brandeis University; Richard A. Burt, University of Massachusetts, Amherst; Ron Bush, California Institute of Technology

Jill Campbell, Yale University; Mary B. Campbell, Brandeis University; Mary Wilson Carpenter, Queen's University; Terry Castle, Stanford University; Stanley Cavell, Harvard University; Linda Charnes, University of California, Berkeley; Cynthia Chase, Cornell University; Gayatri Chattersee, Film and TV Institute of India/National Film Archives of India; Robert Chibka, Boston College; Jo Ann Citron; Carol Clover, University of California, Berkeley; Marjorie Condon, Fall River Public Schools; Thomas A. Copeland, Youngstown State University; José H. Córdova, Bennington College; William Corlett, Bates College; Mary Thomas Crane, Boston College; Jennifer Crewe, Columbia University Press; Robert Crooks, Bentley College; Jonathan Culler, Cornell University; Nicole J. Cunningham, Brown University; Krystian Czerniecki, Cornell University

Marie Danziger, Havard University; Lisa Davis, Harvard University; Robert Adams Day, City University of New York, Graduate Center; Apryl Denny, University of Colorado; Scott Derrick, George Mason University; Carolyn Dever, Harvard University; Linda Dittmar, University of Massachusetts, Boston; Michael Dobson, Oxford University; Daria Donnelly, Brandeis University; Jorg Drewitz, Boston College; Heather Dubrow, Carleton College; Dianne Dugaw, University of Colorado

Lee Edelman, Tufts University; Evelyne Ender, University of Geneva, Switzerland; David Erdman, State University of New York, Stony Brook; Virginia Erdman, State University of New York, Stony Brook; Betsy Erkkila, University of Pennsylvania

George Fayen, Yale University; Patricia Maria Feito, University of California, Irvine; Mary Anne Ferguson, University of Massachusetts, Boston; Henry Finder, Cornell University; Stanley Fish, Duke University; William Flesch, Brandeis University; Monika Fludernik, University of Vienna; Carol Flynn, Tufts University; Joyce Flynn, Harvard University; Carol Forney, Harvard University; Mark Francioli, Case Western Reserve University; Mike Frank, Bentley College; Debra Fried, Cornell University; Michael Fried, The Johns Hopkins University; Bettina Friedl, University of Stuttgart; Herwig Friedl, University of Duesseldorf

Marjorie Garber, Harvard University; Burdett Gardner; Julia Genster, Connecticut College; Jennifer Georgia, Harvard University; William P. Germano, Routledge; Albert Gilman, Boston University; Karen C. Gindele, Brown University; Anita Goldman, Harvard University; Nancy Goldstein, Brandeis University; Rachel Gomel, McGill University; Jade Gorman, University of Maryland; Gerald Graff, Northwestern University; Edward Graham, State University of New York, Maritime College; Lila V. Graves, University of Alabama, Birmingham; Elizabeth S. Green, Boston College; Lissa Greenough, Harvard University; Allen Grossman, Brandeis University; John Guillory, Yale University

Dorothy J. Hale, Yale University; Mary Louise Hall, Siena Heights College; Kim Hamilton, Brandeis University; Linda Hardy, Victoria University, New Zealand; Mary Hanson Harrison, Northwestern University; Joan E. Hartman, City University of New York, College of Staten Island; Britton J. Harwood, Miami University; Donald Hedrick, Colgate University; Carolivia Herron, Harvard University; Margaret R. Higonnet, University of Connecticut; David Hillman, Harvard University; David Hirsch, Harvard University; Margaret Homans, Yale University; Susan R. Horton, University of Massachusetts, Boston; Sue E. Houchins, Scripps College; Peter Hughes, University of Zurich; George E. Humphrey, Massachusetts College of Pharmacy and Allied Health Sciences; Lynn Hunt, University of Pennsylvania

Kazuo Iwata, Aichi Gakuin University

Barry Jacobs, Montclair State College; Mary Jacobus, Cornell University; Anne Janowitz, Brandeis University; Barbara Johnson, Harvard University; Stephen Jones, Harvard University, Center for Literary and Cultural Studies; Sally Jordan, Brandeis University; Gerhard Joseph, City University of New York, Graduate School

Andre Kaenel, University of Geneva, Switzerland; Jonathan Z. Kamholtz, University of Cincinnati; Sara E. Kamholtz, University of Cincinnati; Louise M. Kawada; Carol Kay, New York University; William Keach, Brown University; Suzanne Keen, Harvard University; Dion Kempthorne, University of Wisconsin; Christopher Kendrick, Washington University; Maggie Kilgour, McGill University; Arthur F. Kinney, University of Massachusetts, Amherst; Jon Klancher, Boston University; Jeffrey Knapp, Harvard University; Charles A. Knight, University of Massachusetts, Boston; Lisbet Rausing Koerner, Harvard University; Deborah J. Kops, Northeastern University Press; Laura H. Korobkin, Harvard University; Beth Kowaleski-Wallace, Simmons College; Yasuko Koyanagi, Chofu Gakuen Women's Junior College; Joseph E. Kramer, Bryn Mawr College; Leslie Kurke, Harvard University

G. P. Lair, Delbarton School; Rena A. Lamparska, Boston College; Kathleen W. Lampert, Wayland High School; John Lavagnino, Brandeis University; Joshua Leiderman, Harvard University; Sura Levine, Hampshire College; Marjorie B. Levinson, University of Pennsylvania; Alan Levitan, Brandeis University; Barbara Levy, University of Puerto Rico; Jonathan Levy, State University of New York, Stony Brook; Kathryne V. Lindberg, Harvard University; Francoise Lionnet, Northwestern University; Joanna Lipking, Northwestern University; Lawrence Lipking, Northwestern University; Joseph Litvak, Bowdoin College; Rick Livingston, Yale University; Paula Loscocco, Boston College; Joseph P. Lovering, Canisius College; Sister Alice Lubin, College of St. Elizabeth; Sara Lundquist, Boston College

John L. Mahoney, Boston College; Cynthia N. Malone, City University of New York, Baruch College; Bette Mandl, Suffolk University; Leonard H. Manheim, State University of New York, Nassau College; Darrel Mansell, Dartmouth College; Jean I. Marsden, University of Connecticut; David Marshall, Yale University; Mary Pat Martin, Yale University; Wallace Martin, University of Toledo; John Maynard, New York University; Maureen M. McAndrews; Theresa McCarthy, University of Connecticut; Deborah McDowell, University of Virginia; Bruce McIver, Union College; Michael McKeon, Rutgers University; Cathleen T. McLoughlin, City University of New York, Graduate Center; Donald C. Mell, University of Delaware; Anne M. Menke, Harvard University; Helena Michie, Brandeis University; D. A. Miller, University of California, Berkeley; Leland Monk, Boston University; Rebecca A. Monroe, Harvard University; Michael Moon, Duke University; Paul Thomas Murphy, University of Colorado, Boulder

John Raymond Nealis II, Delaware Academy; Elizabeth Neild, Harvard University; John Nesselhof, Wells College; Shirley Neuman, University of Alberta; Karen Newman, Brown University; Brigitte Nicolet, Skidmore College; John Norman, Harvard University; Mary Nyquist, University of Toronto

Charles A. Owen Jr., University of Connecticut

Barbara Packer, University of California, Los Angeles; M. Cristina Paganoni, Universita Degli Studi Di Milano, Italy; Stanley R. Palombo, M.D., George Washington University; Andrew Parker, Amherst College; Patricia Parker, Stanford University; Coleman O. Parsons, City University of New York; Annabel Patterson, Duke University; Cornelia Pearsall, Yale University; Donald Pease, Dartmouth College; Ruth Perry, Massachusetts Institute of Technology; Vincent F. Petronella, University of Massachusetts, Boston; Burton Pike, City University of New York, Graduate School; Allison Pingree, Harvard University; Mary Poovey, The Johns Hopkins University; John Price, Middlesex School; Christopher Pye, Williams College

Maureen Quilligan, University of Pennsylvania; Laura Quinney, Harvard University

Paula Rabinowitz, University of Minnesota; Arnold Rampersad, Columbia University; Margaret Reid, Harvard University; Thomas Reinert, Wellesley College; Linda Reinfeld, State University of New York, Buffalo; Lawrence Rhu, Harvard University; Alan Richardson, Boston College; John Richetti, University of Pennsylvania; Harriet Ritvo, Massachusetts Institute of Technology; Bruce Robbins, Rutgers University; Jeffrey C. Robinson, University of Colorado, Boulder; John Rogers, Yale University; Linda Roman, University of

Delaware; Phyllis Rose, Wesleyan University; Alan Rosen, Boston University; Kenneth Rosen, University of Southern Maine; Laura Rosenthal, Northwestern University; Katherine Rowe, Harvard University; Peter L. Rudnytsky, Columbia University; Richard Russell, Harvard Medical School; Mary Russo, Hampshire College; Nancy Ruttenburg, Harvard University

Elaine B. Safer, University of Delaware; Shirley Samuels, Cornell University; Karen Sanchez-Eppler, Amherst College; Suzanne Schloetelburg, University of Heidelberg; Louis Schwartz, Brandeis University; Regina Schwartz, Duke University; Eve Kosofsky Sedgwick, Duke University; Mark Seltzer, Cornell University; Kalpana Seshadri-Crooks, Tufts University; Sheila Shaw, Wheaton College; Vernon Shetley, Wellesley College; Michiko Shimokobe, Yale University; Lauren Silberman, City University of New York, Baruch College; Patricia L. Skarda, Smith College; Barbara Herrnstein Smith, Duke University; Anita Sokolsky, Williams College; George Soule, Carleton College; Ian Sowton, York University; Patricia Meyer Spacks, Yale University; Libby Spiller, Harvard University; Hortense J. Spillers, Cornell University; Gayatri Chakravorty Spivak, University of Pittsburgh; Robert Sprich, Bentley College; Peter Stallybrass, University of Pennsylvania; Susan Staves, Brandeis University; Margaret Storch, Bentley College; Karen Swann, Williams College; Stephen R. Swords, University of Colorado

Mihoko Takeda, Nagoya Junior College; Yuichi Takeda, Aichi Gakuin University; Glover Taylor, Harvard University; Glynys Thomas, Simmons College; Viola G. Thomas, Tufts University; Stephen Tifft, Williams College; David Tomlinson, U.S. Naval Academy; Claudine Torchin-Kahan, Brandeis University; Marianna Torgovnick, Duke University; Evelyn Tribble, Temple University; Edward Baron Turk, Massachusetts Institute of Technology; Gordon Turnbull, Yale University

Hiroko Uno, Shiga University

Sara van den Berg, University of Washington; Gretchen Van Ness, Boston College; Ann Jessie Van Sant, Tufts University; Helen Vendler, Harvard University; Eric von Zinkernagel, Harvard University

Candace Waid, Yale University; Melissa Walker, Mercer University; Lee Wallace, Southampton University; Lindsay Waters, Harvard University Press;

Nicola J. Watson, Oxford University; Caroline Webb, Wellesley College; Marjorie Wechsler, Lesley College; Saundra Segan Wheeler, Yeshiva University; Sally Whitney, Bryn Mawr College; Jennifer Wicke, Yale University; Carolyn Williams, Rutgers University; Patricia Williams, City University of New York, Law School; Joshua Wilner, City College, City University of New York; Laura Winters, College of St. Elizabeth; Calhoun Winton, University of Maryland; Elizabeth Wolf, University of Southern California; Shira Wolosky, Hebrew University

Patricia S. Yaeger, Harvard University; Kay Young, Harvard University